THE
SUPREME
COURT
AND ITS
GREAT
JUSTICES

THE SUPREME COURT AND ITS GREAT JUSTICES

SIDNEY H. ASCH

New York

Published by Arco Publishing Company, Inc.
219 Park Avenue South, New York, N.Y. 10003

Library of Congress Catalog Number 74–125940

ISBN 0–668–02372–4

Printed in the United States of America

Book designed by Fred Honig

CONTENTS

–IV–

DECADE OF THE NEW DEAL

–V–

INTO THE POLITICAL THICKET

–VI–

THE FORK IN THE ROAD

★

Introduction

"DOES IT NOT SEEM THAT WE HAVE HAD ENOUGH OF THESE UPSIDE-down corkscrew thinkers?" asked Senator Russell Long of Louisiana, as the floor debate began on President Nixon's choice to fill the Supreme Court seat vacated by Abe Fortas. "Would it not appear that it might be well to take a B student or C student who was able to think straight compared to one of those A students who are capable of the kind of thinking that winds up getting 100% increase in crime in this country?" And Senator Roman Hruska continued in the same vein. "There are a lot of mediocre judges and people and lawyers," said the Nebraskan statesman. "They are entitled to a little representation, aren't they? We can't have all Brandeises, Frankfurters and Cardozos." We must admit that legal incompetents have also sat on the Supreme Court. But this apparently was the first time in its history that a seat for mediocrity had been proposed for the Supreme Court.

Acrimony over the nominee to the High Court is an old story. George Washington was bitter over the defeat of his nomination of John Rutledge to be the second Chief Justice. Rutledge sat on the bench for a few months before he was officially rejected by the Senate. He ended up mentally deranged.

President Andrew Jackson was furious when he learned that his nomination of Roger B. Taney as Associate Justice had been defeated by the Senate. In his anger, he refused to admit the clerk from the Senate who came to advise him officially of the rejection, charging that it was after midnight and that he wanted no message from such "damned scoundrels." Subsequently, Jackson submitted Taney's name again, but this time for the post of Chief Justice. The bitter debate that ensued lasted for two and a half months. Daniel Webster and Henry Clay led the fight against the confirmation of Taney, who had served as United States Attorney General and as Secretary of the Treasury. When the Senate finally approved him, 29 to 15, a New York newspaper commented, "the pure ermine of the Supreme Court is sullied by the appointment of that political hack." Years later, after appearing before Chief Justice Taney many times, in an emotional scene Clay expressed his regrets for having sparked the opposition.

President Tyler, in the closing days of his administration, had trouble with the Senate, which was dominated by a Whig majority. The Senate stalled the approval of the two Democrats he had nominated. These tactics were based on the misdirected hope that the Whig candidate for President, Henry Clay, would be elected and that two of their own party could be placed on the Supreme Court. Instead, Democrat James K. Polk was elected. He had his own problems with Senate confirmations. He was forced to withdraw his initial nominees and substituted two others. Only one of them, Samuel Nelson, was approved.

President Grant had to try three times to find a Chief Justice who could run the Senate hurdles successfully. Morrison R. Waite of Ohio was approved but not until two other names had been withdrawn. One of those rejected, Caleb Cushing, was vilified by the press which described him as the "familiar and supercilious" friend of President Grant, possessing a "crafty nature" and an "erratic temperament."

In 1916, when Louis D. Brandeis was named by President Wilson, a distinguished committee, including former presidents of the American Bar Association and William Howard Taft, advised the Senate committee that they were bound by "painful duty" to report that Brandeis was "not fit" for the Court. The Judiciary Committee hearings dragged on for four months and Brandeis was finally approved by a straight party vote on the Senate floor.

President Hoover, too, had plenty of trouble with his nominees. His designation of Charles Evans Hughes to be Chief Justice evoked bitter opposition, led by Senator George W. Norris of Nebraska and his band of liberals. An acrimonious fight ensued, the Senate Judiciary Committee voted against him, but three days later he was confirmed by the entire Senate. In 1930 the Senate rejected the nomination of John J. Parker of North Carolina. As a lower court judge, Parker had gained the enmity of labor by his support of "yellow dog" contracts and labor injunctions.

The controversy over the appointment by President Roosevelt of Justice Hugo L. Black in 1937 flared up after the Senate confirmation, not before. The Judiciary Committee had approved him in less than a week. But then it came to light that Black had been a member of the Ku Klux Klan.

Justice Abe Fortas ended up resigning from the Supreme Court in the wake of charges made when President Johnson tried to name him Chief Justice to succeed Earl Warren. Then-candidate Nixon successfully maintained that lame-duck Lyndon Johnson should not exercise his powers as President to make an appointment. With Nixon in office, however, the Senate rejected, in turn, the names of Clement F. Haynsworth and G. Harrold Carswell, Nixon's candidates for Fortas' seat. It has been argued that the Senate should not deny a presidential appointment unless serious and specific qualifications have been established. However, Supreme Court Justices unlike Cabinet members, ambassadors, and other political subordinates, are not responsible to the President and frequently remain in office long after the President is gone.

Storms of controversy have not only broken out over the appointment of Justices to the Supreme Court of the United States but also over the role of the Court in the American system. At times, the Supreme Court has been the dominant institution in the American political system. At other times, it has stood in the shadows while other agencies of government have been in the forefront. For example, the Court over which Earl Warren presided was bold and confident, unafraid to tackle the issues that agitated America. One need not be a Supreme Court student to realize that Chief Justice Warren Burger sees the job of the Court in a different light.

In the period between 1810 and 1829 when the Chief Justice of the Court was John Marshall, he not only dominated the Court but also dictated the nature of the federal system and the direction it was to take. Following the catastrophic Dred Scott decision, the Court went into a decline. It did not emerge as a powerful American institution until the latter portion of the nineteenth century, the era of an exuberant and unrestrained capitalism. It was a time when Presidents seemed to merge into undistinguished anonymity and the Congresses did no better. The Supreme Court was the principal branch of government, at the zenith of its ability, energy, and drive. It totally dominated America.

Following another period of decline, the Supreme Court became stuffed with outstanding jurists. It exercised great power in the late 1920's and early 1930's. Chief Justice Hughes ran the Court well, and he successfully outmaneuvered President Roosevelt's court-packing plan. The Court and Roosevelt took years to adjust to one another. By 1937 the crisis over the Court was over. Paradoxically, the Court shifted its stand and supported President Roosevelt's programs. However, the "shift in time that saved nine" reflected how emphasis on the protection of individual rights, rather than those of property, was paramount. By 1951 the Court drifted once more into a period of general lassitude, except for querulous contention among the Justices. It was made more marked by the conflicts between Congress and the Presidents.

The appointment of Earl Warren as Chief Justice by President Eisenhower in 1953 marked a resurgence and transfusion of the Court. Its renaissance was stimulated by the Justices added by Presidents Eisenhower and Kennedy. The Warren Court was prepared to tackle some of the most vexing problems that the Court, in prior periods, had avoided and that the other branches of government had ignored. Whether its decisions had the effects intended or whether they were a stretch for authority beyond the reach of the Court is almost beside the point. The Supreme Court of Earl Warren was ready to confront the problems that challenged America and to deal with them in spite of public opinion. Chief Justice Warren E. Burger has committed himself to a more passive role for the Court.

America seems to be in midpassage. We know something of the place from where we have come. But we all must be apprehensive of where we are headed. Surrounding us are confrontations between the affluence that technology pours out so lavishly and the destruction to man that it threatens; between the demands for greater personal freedom and the pressure of a regimented society for conformity with its increasing encroachment on privacy; between the deep-throated demands of the black, the young, and the poor for a more substantial stake in America and those who have vested interests in the established order. America faces an eye-to-eye confrontation between authority and the individual.

⟨Law is the instrumentality through which the government intervenes to make those adjustments necessary to keep the community functioning in accordance with its objectives⟩ Obviously, if there is confusion about goals, the law reflects these conflicts. The cacophony of the opposing forces in

America is not just discord; it is the counterpoint of majority rule and minority rights in an integral theme of democracy. The Supreme Court, in the background, points to the future. The nine men in black robes represent the final arbiter of governmental power in America. These gentlemen—not the members of Congress, not the President, and not the Cabinet—have the last say as to the validity of acts of public officials. The Justices determine how the legislators shall be elected, which child shall sit next to which at school, when and how suspects shall be questioned, and each year it gives hundreds of other directions as to how life in America shall proceed. The voice of the people may ultimately be louder, but until then it is the Supreme Court that commands.

There are only a few formal checks on the Court, and they do not seem too effective. The Senate has the power to refuse to confirm a Justice who has been proposed by the President. But only once before the rejection of Clement F. Haynesworth and G. Harrold Carswell has the Senate exercised this prerogative in the twentieth century. It has, only once in the history of the Court, attempted to impeach a Justice, and then without a conclusion. And there have been only three amendments to the Constitution, adopted by the people, designed to modify the effect of a decision of the Supreme Court. No matter how much the political theorists prattle about "checks and balances," for the most part it remains the Justices of the Supreme Court who have given the last word to the President, to the Congressmen, and to the vast, august world of officialdom.

If we are honest with ourselves, we must acknowledge that while it is a "government of laws, not of men," as pointed out by Chief Justice Charles Evans Hughes, "We are under a constitution, but the constitution is what the judges say it is." And these judges, like all public officials, reflected the entire spectrum. Presidents can leave office in four years, but their appointments to the Supreme Court can linger for decades, affecting the lives of American citizens.

It has been said that many men change after donning the black robes. What is probably more accurate is that a man is freer to express his true self after becoming a Justice. He does not become smarter, or change his political point of view, or shed his prejudices. He usually continues to project the traits that endeared him to the President who appointed him. At times, however, a man may undergo a metamorphosis once he becomes a Justice. McReynolds, Jackson, Holmes, and Frankfurter were not understood by the Presidents who appointed them. But, for the most part, the Justices have continued to mirror the social policies of the pressure group or the lobby, the political party, and the Chief Executive who advanced them, long after their sponsors were no longer on the scene. Therefore, the Supreme Court has been a restraining influence on the government in power. When the Justices have extended the Court's jurisdiction to act affirmatively to deal with the problems in America, they have not always succeeded precisely in the way they expected. Certainly, the problems of the Warren Court in dealing with school segregation, deficiencies in suffrage and representation, and treatment of those accused of crimes suggest that there are substantial difficulties for the Court in dealing with problems that can be handled with greater expedition by the Congress or the President.

For most of its history, the Court has ducked such affirmative responsibilities. It has done so by categorizing a problem as being "political," rather than "legal," and thus refusing to consider it. Another way of avoiding certain decisions has been by ruling on some narrow procedural technicality, rather than dealing with the underlying and overwhelming issue of public policy. The Court, too, has the power to decide which cases it will consider. Obviously, this is almost an express power to avoid unpleasant disputes. When it does not review a ruling of a lower court, in effect the ruling of the inferior court stands as the law of the land.

Whether we agree with the work of the Supreme Court

or not, it would be unwise to undervaluate its power. This power is bolstered by two myths. One is the idea that the Justices, as a collective, "find" the law, rather than make it. The second is that once an active human being enfolds himself in the black robe he becomes an oracle, a disembodied spirit, emancipated from human emotions, prejudices and retribution.

If we are to understand the Supreme Court as it operates and as it affects America, we must look to the men who have played their historic roles as its Justices.

If John Marshall had not been Secretary of State for the outgoing administration, a rabid Federalist serving under a Republican President, the precise ruling in *Marbury v. Madison* might well have been different. It cannot be without significance that Henry Billings Brown, who was responsible for the majority view of *Plessy v. Ferguson,* believed that black people were inherently inferior. Certainly, the fact that Benjamin N. Cardozo's father resigned from the New York State Supreme Court in disgrace had some significant part in molding the Justice into a paragon of civil virtue and dedication.

Early in his career, Hugo L. Black was member of the Ku Klux Klan for a brief period. Therefore it does not seem irrelevant to learn, also, that his first client was a black convict; that he argued civil rights cases in Alabama more than fifty years ago; that he agitated against third-degree police tactics as a young lawyer; that the Klan fought him when he ran for the Senate. It is illuminating to learn that Chief Justice Taft in 1929 was afraid that if he retired President Hoover would use the opportunity to appoint "extreme destroyers of the Constitution," to the Court. "I am older and slower and less acute and more confused," confessed Taft, "however, as long as things continue as they are, and I am able to answer in my place, I must stay on the Court in order to prevent the Bolsheviks from getting control."

Pierce Butler had been a spokesman for big business so

long before he came on the bench that he could never accept
the regulation of business by government. "Are we to go into
a state of socialism," he put to a banker's association, "or are
you men, and men like you, prepared to go out, take off your
coats, and root for old-fashioned Anglo-Saxon individualism?"
As a regent of a state university, he took a special delight in
firing faculty people who held views contrary to his own. It
does not seem surprising, therefore, that Justice Butler consistently decided against those expressing views with which
he disagreed or considered radical, or those regulations that
seemed to threaten business. Butler failed his college course
in "Constitutional Law," but this did not prevent him from
recasting the law of the United States Constitution to conform to his view of it.

Before rejecting G. Harrold Carswell, the Senate learned
that in 1948, as a campaign vow, Carswell pledged to "yield
to no man" in his "firm, vigorous belief in the principles of
white supremacy." Certainly, the espousal of labor's cause by
attorney Louis D. Brandeis, or the hands-off attitude of
Governor Frank Murphy toward the automobile sit-down
strikers, gave significant indications of how these men would
perform on the Court.

It is unfortunate that so little is known or made available
about the nominees to the Supreme Court. There have not
been a hundred Justices who have sat on the High Court.
Only about a third have had real biographies written. Yet
these hundred men have left a permanent mark on their own
America and the America to come. It is true that the Supreme
Court has the perpetuity of corporate existence.

The Court is a composite of the individual judges who
have graced it, and of their interaction. Giants such as Marshall, Taney, Miller, Holmes, and Warren produced their
great decisions not just as solo performers but as part of a
team. The efforts of these masters were shaped by their contemporary associates and by Justices who sat before them.
Many of such Justices are forgotten and virtually unknown.

Who remembers Bushrod Washington, Henry Baldwin, Robert Grier, Mahlon Pitney, Edward Sanford, to name a few? Yet all contributed.

Unlike the executive branch, the membership of the Supreme Court never changes all at one time. Marshall sat for a third of a century and Black has been a Justice for as long. They are an important part of a tapestry that stretches from the earliest days of the republic until today. The almost one hundred men who are part of this history have produced about four hundred legal treatises that constitute the Supreme Court reports. Its pages have shaped the history of the United States. One of today's great Justices, Hugo L. Black, was privileged to know Holmes and to sit with Hughes, Stone, Brandeis, Cardozo, Frankfurter, Douglas, Jackson, and Warren.

Because the Supreme Court has been so close to the throbbing pulse of America, it seems worthwhile to recount its history. Its story may not only shed light on our past but it may illuminate the future as well. The history of the Supreme Court is, above all, intertwined with the men who wore its robes.

I

THE SUPREME COURT UNFOLDS

–1–

John Jay

THE ORGANIZATION MAN

ON A COLD MONDAY AFTERNOON, FEBRUARY 1, 1790, THE Supreme Court of the United States convened for the first time at the lower end of New York City. The chambers in the Royal Exchange Building were jammed with onlookers. Since only three of the six Justices—John Jay, William Cushing, and James Wilson—were in attendance, there was no quorum. The next day, a fourth Justice, John Blair, Jr., the three judges, and John Randolph, the new Attorney General of the United States, were formally inducted. The other two appointees did not bother to attend this ceremony.

Each of the Justices present wore a costume that he deemed appropriate. Jay, the Chief Justice, was attired in a black robe, with salmon-color facing, his garb at Dublin University. Cushing perched a wig on his head, English style, but lost his composure at the last moment and discarded it. When the session ended, the group recessed for libations at a nearby tavern.

If we are to understand the Supreme Court today, it is important to understand its origins. The legal foundation of the Court was described by Article III of the Constitution, which still states that: "The judicial power of the United

States shall be vested in one supreme Court, and in such inferior Courts as the Congress may from time to time ordain and establish." Congress undertook its responsibility by passing into law the Judiciary Act of 1789. The law provided for a federal court system with trial courts and a number of appeal tribunals throughout the United States. The highest court of appeal from these lower federal courts was to be the Supreme Court of the United States. In addition, the Supreme Court could hear appeals from state courts of cases that presented federal problems.

As established by the Judiciary Act of 1789, the Supreme Court was made up of a Chief Justice and five Associate Justices. The Constitution itself did not create the machinery to bring the Supreme Court into actual being; but the Constitution authorized the Congress to do so. At different times, then, Congress has been able to vary the number of Justices from five, six, seven, nine, or ten, and ultimately back to the present number of nine. In addition, Congress controls the function and organization of the Supreme Court, as well as the time and place of its sittings and its procedure.

Studying the Constitution itself or the acts of Congress that relate to the Supreme Court will throw little illumination on the mechanisms by which the Court acquired its exalted position. The authoritative and dominant role of the Court rests essentially upon two concepts. The first is the right of judicial review, the acknowledged authority of the Supreme Court to invalidate any piece of legislation—congressional, state, or local—or any action by a public official acting under such law on the ground that it violates the Constitution of the United States. It is, therefore, the Supreme Court, not the Congress or the President, that has the final word on the legality of governmental action.

The second concept upon which the authority of the Supreme Court rests is its right, indeed responsibility, to explain the meaning of words and phrases in a piece of legislation, and to interpret the applications of such legislation in a particular case or controversy. It is understandable that decisions on any federal or state laws are influenced by the interpretation that each Justice gives to his own political or public policies. Neither the Constitution nor the Judiciary Act of 1789 refers to judicial review or to this authority to interpret, but these accepted procedures are close to the root of the Supreme Court's power.

At the Constitutional Convention, those who favored the power of judicial review happen to be those most solicitous about preserving the status quo and the protection of property rights. Such proponents included Alexander Hamilton and, by a quirk of fate, James Wilson and Oliver Ellsworth, both destined to be members of the Court. They expressed a fear that the members of Congress would be too subjugated to the tyranny of the masses, and might thereupon pass laws giving away the property which these Federalists deemed sacred. Those signers who were against judicial review were, like Ben Franklin, fearful of dictatorial control by a few men. These opponents viewed such power as characteristic of pre-Revolutionary society, and were determined to rid the country of its unjust influence. They believed that the egalitarianism of legislators, who were closer to the people, would be healthy. In any event, the matter of judicial review was never definitely resolved at the Constitutional Convention.

After the Convention concluded its work, a tremendous political wrangle ensued over the ratification of the Constitution by the states. Somehow, the proponents of the Constitution managed to convey the impression that the Supreme Court would be the guardian of the people against rapacious public officials. But these Federalist politicians knew something else. They knew that if they could secure the appointment of sympathetic judges, judges who could serve for life, the establishment would have a powerful ally, and property rights would be protected.

The Constitution was ratified. It can hardly be a surprise that the "father of his country," George Washington, who was at the same time an ardent Federalist, with the advice and consent of a Federalist Senate, filled every spot on the Supreme Court and every other federal judgeship as well, with deserving and loyal Federalists.

With evenhanded impartiality, and with professional political know-how, President Washington designated three Justices from the South and three from the North. What they shared in common was a passion for the Federalist Party, a conservative philosophy, and a bias in favor of property interests.

To fill the post of Chief Justice of the United States, Washington chose John Jay of New York, the patrician scion of aristocratic lineage. Jay had won recognition as a Revolutionary supporter, as a member of the Continental Congress, as chief justice of the New York State Supreme Court, as one of the draftsmen of the Constitution of his home state, as a diplomat representing his country, as a proponent of the new Constitution for the United States, and as a participant in a myriad of other governmental and political projects.

In spite of these most impressive qualifications, Jay was not sensitive or brilliant, nor was he given to deep philosophic speculation. The seat of the Chief Justice simply represented another varied interest to John Jay. Thus, he twice ran for governor of New York without stepping from his post on the bench. And when finally he was elected governor, he casually resigned from the Supreme Court.

Nevertheless, John Jay was a good choice, considering the alternatives. President Washington also thought about James Wilson and John Rutledge, two Southerners. Like Jay, both were zealous about protecting property and in their affinity with the "haves" against the "have-nots." John Rutledge succeeded in having inserted into the Constitution a provision that protected the slave trade for an additional twenty years. And James Wilson, pursuing what he conceived to be his interests as creditor, rather than debtor, managed to have a provision incorporated into the Constitution prohibiting states from enacting statutes that impaired "the obligation of contract." Wilson later fell into bad financial straits, and his own provision bound him to honor his debts.

Of the three, Wilson had the best legal mind but lacked the judicial temperament and the diplomacy required by the job. Washington was personally disposed toward Rutledge but desisted from appointing him Chief Justice because he felt it would give the South too much weight in the fledgling government. For that reason, he tendered Rutledge a seat as Associate Justice. Rutledge accepted Washington's offer, but he never actually sat on the Court. In February 1791 Rutledge resigned to become chief justice of the South Carolina Court of Common Pleas.

The other aspirant to the post of Chief Justice was James Wilson. Wilson was a pre-Revolution pamphleteer, a signer of the Declaration of Independence, a member of the Continental Congress, a moving force at the Constitutional Convention, a successful lawyer, a fantastic promoter and business entrepreneur, a professor of law, and a legal writer. Yet from these great heights he was to plummet to the depths when his financial manipulations failed. Wilson served as an Associate Justice under Jay as his Chief, plodding along with his deep-seated Federalist convictions. By the time that Jay resigned, Wilson's affairs were in total disarray. His reputation was tarnished by his connection with the Yazoo land grabs, which involved the bribing of members of the Georgia legislature. As a result, he was not appointed to the Chief Justiceship for a second time. Disappointed and broken, Wilson ended his days dodging creditors and running to avoid the debtor's jail.

The other Justices appointed by President Washington were less impressive. William Cushing, a former chief justice of the Supreme Court of Massachusetts and a descendant of a distinguished family of lawyers, was totally undistinguished himself. And yet, as luck would have it, he was to spend twenty years on the Supreme Court, double the tenure of any other Justice then sitting on the Court.

John Blair, a second-rater, was inconspicuous both as a

delegate to the Constitutional Convention and as a Virginia judge. He did, however, attain a great financial success by speculating in government bonds. At the Convention, Blair was a staunch supporter of judicial review. Yet the most significant factor in his background leading to the Supreme Court appointment was his intimate friendship with President Washington.

The remaining member of the Court was James Iredell. His sole judicial experience was as a pedestrian lower court judge in North Carolina. Although young, his appointment was a political reward for his successful efforts as head of the North Carolina Federalists, dragging his home state into the new nation.

The three Justices who came from the South did not bother to attend the swearing-in ceremony. The others who did sit, did so for no more than a few days. The only business of the Court was to admit a few lawyers to practice; then the Court adjourned. It is notable that in the first two years of its existence, the Supreme Court heard but a single case, and it was dismissed on a technical point by the brethren of the robe without fuss.

In view of the paucity of judicial business and his chagrin at not having been appointed Chief Justice, it is not surprising that Rutledge resigned his post to assume that of chief justice of the Supreme Court of the State of North Carolina. His vacancy was not easily filled. President Washington offered the position to three lawyers, one of them being Rutledge's nephew, and they all rejected the offer. Finally, a minor judge named Thomas Johnson took the job, but he didn't last long. In two years he quit, and his post was then filled by New Jersey's William Paterson, a true Federalist, well-to-do, and a former delegate to the Constitutional Convention.

The original Justices were obligated by their job to ride circuit in order to sit in inferior federal courts, which convened in different parts of the country. Each circuit was manned by two, and later one, Justice. Today this judicial chore has been largely abolished, but Justices of the Supreme Court occasionally sit in lower courts on certain matters.

In 1792, while on circuit, four of the Justices went so far as to declare a congressional act unconstitutional. The act in question required judges to serve as commissioners in fixing the pensions of wounded veterans of the American Revolutionary forces. They held the law invalid on the ground it thrust upon the judiciary a task which was not truly judicial in nature and thus violated the requirement of separation of powers among the three divisions of government.

The same year, also in circuit courts, the Justices asserted their power to annul laws passed by state legislatures, holding that these acts violated the United States Constitution. They voided a law of Rhode Island which sought to help debtors. Their theory was that the law violated the "obligation of contract" clause of the United States Constitution. Similar statutes enacted by other state legislatures shortly thereafter met the same fate.

Eventually, a small number of cases percolated into the Supreme Court. Most were instituted by creditors who had claims against various states and who were convinced that to try to collect in the courts of these states would be fruitless. Although the Federalists, including some of the sitting Justices of the Supreme Court, had pledged that the federal courts would not be used for this purpose, they promptly forgot their earlier integrity. One of these cases[1] was lodged against Georgia. That state refused to appear. Yet, in the face of this nonappearance and the fact that John Jay pledged himself against such construction, the Court decided against Georgia. Iredell appended the first dissent of the new Court. The outcry throughout the country was enormous. A bill was proposed in the Georgia legislature providing that any federal marshal who attempted to carry out the decision of the Su-

1 Chisholm v. Georgia, 12 Dallas 419 (1792).

preme Court would be hanged "without benefit of clergy." Thus, the decision of the Federalist Supreme Court was never enforced. What followed was the rapid ratification of the Eleventh Amendment to the United States Constitution, which prohibited suits against the states in the federal courts.

The Court also established another important principle. President Washington submitted to the Court a number of international law problems concerning the establishment of special "prize courts," to hear cases involving captured ships, questions relating to the rights of citizens on the high seas, the effect of treaties, and other touchy issues stemming from the war between England and France. The Supreme Court Justices refused to become involved in simply giving advice, even at the request of the President. They would never decide a question of law except in a formal "case or controversy." Finally, when the Court was presented with a case that contained the main issues that Washington wanted answered, it stood behind the sovereignty of the United States.[2] Today the Court does not answer questions in the absence of an actual "case" or "controversy." The manner they insist upon often creates a serious delay, sometimes until long after the issue is dead. Another result of the refusal of the Court to give advisory opinions except through properly presented cases is that it saves for itself the opportunity to have the last word on vexatious political problems.

Jay was Chief Justice for five years, one of which was spent outside the country on a diplomatic mission to Great Britain. He was much criticized for taking this assignment, in much the same manner as Justice Robert Jackson was criticized for serving as war crimes prosecutor at Nuremberg after World War II. It is interesting, though, that Jay was not criticized for having run twice for governor of New York without resigning from the Court.

Rutledge's wife passed away in 1792 and he was alone in Charleston. He had been hit by serious financial losses result-

[2] Glass v. The Sloop Betsey, 3 Dallas 6 (1794).

ing from investments in merchant ships, which had to be sold
at a loss. And then, when John Jay was elected governor of
New York, and even before Jay had resigned, Rutledge wrote
to Washington: "I take the liberty of intimating to you privately that . . . I have no objection to take the place which
he holds . . . my pretensions to the office of Chief Justice
were at least equal to Mr. Jay's in point of law knowledge,
with the additional weight of much longer experience and
much greater practice . . ."

Rutledge was named Chief Justice by Washington and
served for only one term. Because of certain intemperate
remarks, the Senate refused to confirm his appointment. A
suggestion that he was insane spread rapidly. After his rejection he became a recluse, but the actual state of his mental
condition was never resolved.

The job was then offered to and turned down by Patrick
Henry and then William Cushing. It was not offered to
Justice Wilson, who was being beseiged by his creditors.
Finally, it went to Oliver Ellsworth of Connecticut, who had
been successively a lawyer, professor of law, banker, politi-
cian, and very influential at the Constitutional Convention.

Pleasant and self-effacing Justice John Blair resigned, to
be replaced by an opposite type. Tremendous, uncouth, a
behemoth from Maryland, Samuel Chase was dynamic and
volatile. Chase had an unquestioned legal mind, and it dominated the intellectual domain of the Court. He was an un-
abashed Federalist partisan, which required almost a
complete metamorphosis of the young idealist Chase who was
a signer of the Declaration of Independence, a rebel, a son of
liberty, and a civil libertarian. He was a political activist,
both in and out of court. His intemperate diatribes against the
Republican Party caused him to be impeached, the only
Justice ever to be so treated, although he was never convicted
by the Senate.

During the period from 1795 to 1800, the Court was
dominated by Ellsworth, the Chief Justice, and Chase. Wilson

died and was replaced by Bushrod Washington. The latter was an unkempt snuff-user of small build and of smaller ability. He sat on the Court for thirty-one years, espousing the cause of Federalism to the end, which was decades after that party had lost power. Iredell died, and was succeeded by a North Carolinian, Alfred Moore, who retired after four years of ineptitude.

During these years the Court was characterized by devotion to the cause of Federalism. Conflict between the wealthy and aristocratic Federalists, who were pro-British, and the Republicans, influenced by the Jacobins of the French Revolution, became more severe. The Federalists enacted the Alien and Sedition laws. The Alien Act was never enforced, but the Sedition Act made it a crime, punishable by imprisonment and fine, to "write, print, utter or publish any false, scandalous and malicious writing . . . against the government of the United States, or either house of the Congress . . . or the President of the United States, with intent to bring them . . . into contempt or disrepute. . . ." To the entire range of federal judiciary, all loyal Federalists, any and all remarks against their party were "false, scandalous and malicious." This law was viciously enforced against editors of newspapers with Republican leanings. Responsible citizens, including newspapermen and a Congressman, were convicted and sentenced to long prison terms. The sentencing judges simply ignored the First Amendment. Mere friends and supporters of editors also went to jail, including those who tried to raise money to pay the fine of one convicted editor. This act was a merciless weapon. Consider the case of farmer Fries who was convicted twice, once by Iredell and then by Chase, who ordered him hanged on the ground that refusal to pay a federal tax amounted not just to sedition, but to treason. President Adams pardoned Fries. And when "the reign of witches," as Jefferson called those years of terror, were over, those imprisoned were pardoned and the fines refunded.

The Alien and Sedition acts never reached the Supreme

Court on constitutional grounds, but in the lower federal courts the Federalist judges functioned both as prosecutors and judges, until the Alien and Sedition acts were finally erased.

In those formative years, the Supreme Court had time to decide a few cases and establish basic powers. In one of them, they held that a federal tax on carriages was valid under the Constitution.[3] With only Chase, Paterson, and Iredell sitting, the court casually assumed the authority to pass on the validity of an act of Congress. However, even a staunchly Federalist Court; and one dedicated to stretching its reach, was afraid to decide whether a state law violated the constitution of that state.[4] The Justices knew that a strong ruling in those times of strong state loyalties would have resulted in a public reaction, which even they as Federalist judges were not ready to face.

Iredell, Cushing, Paterson, and certainly Chase had been unabashedly outspoken both on the bench and off in spreading the Federalist gospel. This preaching came from strong personal conviction not personal advantage, since the Justices were all appointed for life. Chase did not sit at all during one term of the Court because he was out on the hustings in Maryland doing his best to support the re-election of President Adams. Chief Justice Ellsworth was out of the country on a diplomatic mission for the Federalist President, trying to avoid a war with France. Cushing was unable to sit because of illness.

All these political efforts on behalf of the Federalists did not stop the Republicans from electing Thomas Jefferson as President. But before he took office, the old Federalist administration managed to secure the passage of the Judiciary Act of 1801. That act provided, in part, that on the death of the first sitting Justice, the number of Justices on the Supreme Court would be reduced to five. That would prevent Jefferson

[3] Hytton v. United States, 3 Dallas 171 (1796).
[4] Calder v. Bull, 3 Dallas 386 (1798).

from making his first appointment to the Supreme Court. Another maneuver in the act abolished the requirement that the Supreme Court Justices ride the circuit. It established sixteen federal circuit courts and, of course, sixteen new federal justices. Thus, the act assured that these new judges would all be appointed by President Adams before he vacated office and confirmed by his Federalist Senate.

Of course it was a good idea to relieve the Justices from their duties of "travelling post boy," as Iredell once referred to himself. Riding circuit imposed great physical hardship on the members of the bench, and certainly cut down on the time available to them for their Supreme Court duties. The Federalist plan did work. It attracted little comment in the press. Chief Justice Ellsworth was not well, and, burdened with fatigue, he resigned from the Court before the election that made Jefferson President. John Jay would not accept reappointment to that post. Adams ignored the aspirations of Paterson, who wished the post. Instead, President Adams appointed a new Chief Justice just one month before the Republicans took office. Although the Republicans remained in power for a quarter of a century, the appointee outlasted them all.

The new Chief Justice was a well known and influential politician from Virginia. He was born and brought up in a log cabin. In his prior forty-five years, he had received little formal schooling, legal or otherwise, and had no judicial experience. He was however, a rabid anti-Jeffersonian, and after the election, John Marshall, the new Chief Justice, remarked: "The Republicans are divided into speculative theorists and absolute terrorists. With the latter, I am disposed to class Mr. Jefferson."

–2–

John Marshall

BIG DADDY TO THESE
UNITED STATES

TWO GIANTS OF THE SUPREME COURT SHARE MANY OF THE SAME qualities that brought them to greatness. These two are Earl Warren and John Marshall. Neither was a captive of legal gibberish; both kept sight of the objectives they sought; both saw the Supreme Court as the tool for achieving national purposes that they felt were imperative.

John Marshall utilized the law as an instrument of Federalist policy and his own philosophy. He eschewed the passive role of simply genuflecting to legal history and precedent. He actively pursued the national goals he thought important, with decisiveness and boldness, unfettered by neurotic conflict about making mistakes or overstepping bounds. It was Marshall, more so than the early Presidents or perhaps even the draftsmen of the United States Constitution, who dictated the framework of the federal system and charted the course America was to follow in its political and economic development. By a "broad construction" of the powers delegated to the central government, by a "strict construction" of what was left to the states, Marshall laid down the foundation for a strong federal government. Thus, Marshall built up the power of Congress to create a national bank, or to control navigation, or to set up a bankruptcy system, at the expense of the states or localities.

Marshall's overwhelming conviction that the United States was supreme suffered from temporary lapses when he disagreed with specific policies or acts of the federal government. Another clue to Marshall's work on the Court perhaps can be seen in his abiding dedication to the protection of private property—for his Federalist cronies, for the entrepreneurs of an emerging capitalism, for the creditor-bankers. In Marshall's day, the federal government was the guardian of the sacred rights of property, and the states were the repositories of liberalism, the rights of the masses of people.

By a series of extraordinary personal feats, Marshall came to dictate to the Supreme Court. He then caused this Court to impress its will upon the entire judiciary branch. The judiciary effectively controlled the federal government. The federal government pushed back the states. So, by a series of brilliant steps, Marshall created an institution that dominated America for the thirty-four years of his tenure as Chief Justice and to a large extent ever since.

The social distance which Marshall traveled during his lifetime makes these accomplishments even more impressive. As a self-made man, he had little sympathy with those who could not make it and complete rapport with those of the propertied class, of which he considered himself a member. Marshall lifted himself from the rough childhood on the rugged frontier. His formal schooling was just a "lick and a promise," and his law school education consisted of nothing more than a few short months of instruction at The College of William and Mary. Marshall suffered chilblains and frosted fingers as a soldier in the Revolution while attending General George Washington and the ragged army during that anguished winter at Valley Forge.

His exuberant boldness, the fierceness of his intellectual powers, his pioneer resourcefulness, pushed him straight up in his professional career as a lawyer and as a Federalist politician. His political experience, as a member of the Virginia legislature, as a Congressman, as one of the envoys from whom bribes had been demanded by the French, heightened his mistrust of legislative bodies and his disdain of democratic rhetoric and revolution. Constant monetary pressure plagued Marshall, a fact often overlooked in biographies of him. He belonged to a syndicate that purchased an extensive tract of land in the northern neck of Virginia from an heir of Lord Fairfax. Until 1806, he barely was able to scrounge up enough funds to meet the notes relating to this purchase. He received fair compensation as a result of his work as American minister to France. But he continued to turn down offers of public office, including an appointment to the Supreme Court in 1798. President Adams then tendered him the office of Secretary of State, which he accepted. When Ellsworth resigned from the Court, President Adams had a second chance to name Marshall Chief Justice.

As evidence of the low estate of the Supreme Court may be cited the fact that, at the time John Marshall was inducted as Chief Justice, its home was a borrowed Senate committee hearing room in the basement of the Capitol building. Facilities had not been provided for the Court in the architectural plans for the new Capitol building. The inattention to court affairs exhibited by Ellsworth and the attention spent by Chase to politicking rather than judicial work all contributed to the doldrums in which the Supreme Court found itself.

So, it was in this cramped twenty-four-by-thirty-foot chamber that Chief Justice John Marshall and his five Federalist colleagues began to hear the appeals that were to enshrine the Supreme Court in American history. At first, cases slowly dribbled in, and the Court hacked away at them dutifully. By 1811, ten years after Marshall had taken over, there were seven Justices, five of whom were Republicans. Only Bushrod Washington, who was to last for almost two more decades, came from Marshall's Federalist party. But somehow, still, Marshall managed to mesmerize the Court. Aided by a strong ally, Joseph Story, who was ostensibly Republican, the Chief Justice manipulated almost all the other Republicans: Henry Brockholst Livingston, Robert Trimble, and Gabriel Duval. The loyal opposition was brilliantly represented by William Johnson, whose legal virtuosity has been overlooked chiefly because he was so frequently on the losing side, expressing dissent.

Marshall enveloped the court within the mantle of his powerful convictions, his personal magnetism, and his persuasive logic. The base figures demonstrate his control over the work produced by the Court. During his tenure, the Court decided one thousand one hundred six cases in which it handed down both an opinion and a decision. In nearly half of these, John Marshall authored the opinion. And the Chief Justice only dissented in nine of all the eleven hundred six cases. Johnson, the first Republican appointee, explained Marshall's control to President Jefferson this way: "Cushing is incompetent, Chase could not be got to think or write. Paterson was a slow man and willingly declined the trouble, and the other two judges (Marshall and Bushrod Washington) you know are commonly estimated as one judge."

But how did John Marshall continue his domination even after the tide of Republican political victories had all but erased Federalist judges from the Supreme Court? The answer, at least partly, must be in the way Marshall made use of the club-like atmosphere of the Court. Remember that the Justices, at least while the Court was in session, constituted a working fraternity. They lived and ate at the same boarding house in Washington. They exchanged the same political gossip, interlarded with personal concerns. They spent time together taking walks and having a few drinks. And of course they worked together, reasoned together, and argued together. In the congeniality and warmth of physical proximity, daily discussion, and intimacy of the relationships, the Chief always showed his strength.

It is easy to forget the kind of man Marshall was. He was a thoroughly political person, rough hewn, casual and outgoing, carrying his leadership easily. The iron fist was not apparent; it was rule by charismatic charm. Nor need we describe Marshall as a Machiavellian schemer, full of guile and tricks. He was direct and outspoken in his hatreds whether they were his archenemy President Thomas Jefferson or cheap money. Such manly directness must have drawn admiration from his judicial associates as did his skill in handling the legal skirmishes and hurdling the legal road-blocks with which Jefferson's Republicans sought to embarrass him.

As a first order of business, the newly elected President, Thomas Jefferson, stimulated Congress into repealing the Judiciary Act of 1801 which was the law creating the new judicial circuits. Jefferson knew that the newly created seats were quickly populated by deserving judges of Federalist persuasion by the outgoing administration. In addition, to make sure that Marshall's Court could not declare the repeal invalid, the Congress, using its authority under the Constitution to make "regulations" for the federal courts, shut down the Supreme Court for a year. Marshall knew when not to fight and he accepted this. He bided his time.

His opportunity came. Just before President Adams yielded his office to President Jefferson, Adams designated forty-two new justices of the peace for the District of Columbia. These "midnight appointments" were made so late that Adams could not have the formal commissions prepared. As soon as Jefferson was inaugurated, he precipitately ordered the Secretary of State, James Madison, to hold onto these commissions. Four of the uncommissioned justices of the peace, including William Marbury, sought a writ of mandamus, or order directing Madison to deliver the commissions. The preliminary order issued by Marshall was disregarded by Madison. When Congress closed the Court for a year this was one of the matters still outstanding.

Today, the actual decision in *Marbury v. Madison*[1] is unimportant. Its precise ruling was not even important at the

[1] Marbury v. Madison, 1 Cranch 137 (1803).

time it was decided. Mr. Marbury's tenure as a justice of the peace would have just about ended by the time the Court was ready to consider it. But that did not prevent the Chief Justice from using the case to suit his purposes.

Certainly, Marshall knew very well that if the Supreme Court ordered the delivery of the commissions, Madison would ignore the mandamus as he had the preliminary order. The Court (and Marshall) would then be powerless to do anything and be humiliated. Marshall was also aware of the consequences if Madison had correctly refused to deliver the commission: it would leave the Supreme Court a helpless victim of presidential or congressional whim. He disposed of the problem by a masterly combination of political adroitness and legal astuteness.

First, he chastened Madison and Jefferson for not delivering the commissions. He boldly asserted that Marbury and the other frustrated would-be judges were clearly entitled to their commissions. But then, less loudly, he decided that because of a technical point the Court did not have the mandamus power and could not order the delivery of the commissions. The Court unanimously reached this conclusion by holding that the portion of the Judiciary Act of 1789, which states that the Supreme Court could issue writs of mandamus, violated the Constitution of the United States. The act was void for that reason. So Marshall used a question that was moot—the invalidation of a Federalist law (not Republican), a petty procedural point—to establish for all time the authority of the Supreme Court to declare laws of Congress void when they are contrary to the Constitution.

The patina that history has cast on the decision in *Marbury v. Madison* has covered over some questions Marshall did not answer. For instance, what made the Justices more qualified than Congress or the President to determine the constitutionality of legislation? How was it that attorney Marshall, who argued the validity of an act of Virginia before the Supreme Court itself only seven years before *Marbury v.*

Madison, earlier contended "judicial authority can have no right to question the validity of a law, unless such a jurisdiction is expressly given by the Constitution"? And how was it that Marshall, for all his bold talk, did not attack the power of Congress directly by the decision, but simply held that the United States Supreme Court did not have the power to issue a writ of mandamus?

In the short week after *Marbury v. Madison* was decided, the Marshall Court did have the opportunity to declare unconstitutional the repeal of the Judiciary Act of 1801 by the Republican Congress, but it ducked that challenge. Instead of holding that the repeal act, which among other things required Supreme Court Justices to sit in lower federal courts, was unconstitutional, now Marshall justified the assignment on the ground that the practice was time sanctioned. Yet, he could have used the same historic practice as a basis for issuing a writ of mandamus in the Marbury case. The probable explanation for such an obvious logical discrepancy was that Marshall was an excellent politician, and his political acumen warned him when to stop taunting the Republican President and Congress.

Marshall's unerring political sense was demonstrated by his response to the impeachment of Justice Samuel Chase, the old faithful Federalist. Chase had been indiscreet enough to level a blast at Jefferson's Republican administration. To put the many critical federal judges in their place, the House of Representatives initiated impeachment proceedings against Chase, the old political warhorse. Chase escaped conviction only because a squabble ensued among his Republican inquisitors; it concerned the question of whether a breach of constitutionally required "good behavior" had to be labeled "criminal conduct" before a judge could be impeached. Acquitted, Chase served for seven more years.

Marshall despised the Republican administration at least as much as did Chase. Yet he saw that the threat of judicial impeachment was a sword of Damocles hanging over the bench of the Supreme Court. And testifying as a witness for Chase, he hemmed and hawed, instead of coming forthrightly to the defense of Chase. In his anxiety, he went so far out of his natural character as to indicate during the trial a willingness to surrender judicial review if that were necessary to protect the judges. He wrote to Chase: "A reversal of those legal opinions deemed unsound by the legislature would certainly better comport with the mildness of our character than a removal of the judge who rendered them. . . ." This certainly was a far cry from his position in *Marbury v. Madison*.

Thomas Jefferson never really accepted the dominant position of the Supreme Court and refused to back down on his feud with Marshall. Long after he had left the office of President, Jefferson, in a letter written in 1820, said "An opinion is huddled up in conclave, perhaps by a majority of one, delivered as if unanimous, and with the silent acquiescence of lazy or timid associates, by a crafty chief judge, who sophisticates the law to his own mind, by the turn of his own reasoning." Eventually, the vitriol of Jeffersonian Republicanism toward the Court drifted into acquiescence and acceptance by the administrations of Madison and then Monroe. The position of the United States Supreme Court was secure, and the Marshall Court concentrated its energies and attention on the expansion of the nation, the capitalist imperative, the subjugation of the states and the rights of the people. Over the years, but with less frequency, proposals were made by the Republicans for curtailing judicial tenure, for easier methods of removing judges, and for restraint on the Court's power, but these efforts died aborning.

After *Marbury v. Madison,* the three most significant cases of the Marshall Court were decided during the period between 1819 and 1824. These cases had much in common. Each declared laws passed by a state legislature void because they violated the United States Constitution. Each strengthened burgeoning free enterprise in the United States. Each was a milestone in the socioeconomic development of America and still stands as current legal doctrine.

The Dartmouth College case[2] evokes nostalgia and sentiment in the hearts of all who have ever read the emotional appeal of Daniel Webster to the United States Supreme Court: "It is . . . a small college—and yet there are those who love it." Dartmouth College had been organized under a charter granted by George III of England. It was run—lock, stock, and barrel—by a board of trustees which perpetuated itself and in its own image. Thus, it was a private institution, answerable only to itself. It may sound familiar, but the people controlling the board, and hence the affairs of the college, were hidebound traditional Federalists, even long after the country, as well as the state of New Hampshire, had switched over to the liberal Republicans. Stimulated by a Republican grumbling on the campus and responding to popular pressures, the state legislature enacted a statute which was designed to open Dartmouth to the people of New Hampshire by ventilating the board with politically designated trustees. The Federalist board recoiled and retained the great advocate, Daniel Webster, to plead their cause in the Supreme Court.

Marshall decided in favor of the old-line Federalist trustees. He invented a legal doctrine categorizing the charter from King George III as a contract. He also enunciated the new idea that the obligations under the King's charter were still in force, in spite of the intervening American Revolution, and in spite of the creation of the State of New Hampshire. Marshall then reached the conclusion that the act of New Hampshire was void because it "impaired the obligation of contract" in contravention of the United States Constitution. This decision protected the oligarchic trustees of Dartmouth. But it had far more important consequences. It left the control of higher education and intellectual life in America in the hands of private corporations. The principle of the Dart-

[2] Dartmouth College v. Woodward, 14 Wheaton 518 (1819).

mouth College case was extended to enshrine the charters of all sorts of business corporations especially as they related to transportation for toll roads, bridges, canals, turnpikes, and so on. It gave hope and security to the investors of America, and preserved economic monopolies.

The case of *McCulloch v. Maryland*[3] carried the same message. Congress had established the Bank of the United States after the War of 1812. The Bank had been extending credit with a lavish hand to its friends. Then, under the pressure of hard times, the Bank put a squeeze on its smaller debtors. Aroused by this discriminating conduct, a number of states tried to lash back at the Bank within their jurisdictions by passing onerous taxes. Obviously, these impositions were intended to drive these branches out of business.

The branch of the Bank of the United States in Baltimore, Maryland, did not pay the state tax. The state sued to collect the tax, naming McCulloch, the Bank's cashier, as defendant. McCulloch is remembered in legal history as the named defendant in this great case. What is not recalled is that McCulloch was convicted in subsequent years for feloniously converting more than three million dollars of the Bank's funds.

Daniel Webster, who had not lost a single case in the Supreme Court for many years, had represented the Bank of the United States. Predictably, Marshall and the Justices decided in favor of the Bank. The Court ruled that the tax imposed by Maryland was unconstitutional, as were the analogous imposts by the other states. To reach this result, Marshall was constrained to find that the Constitution authorized Congress to establish banks. Of course, no such power was expressly granted by the Constitution, so Marshall found it through other means. He used the explicit power of Congress to control currency and other provisions of the Constitution as a jumping-off place to infer the power of Congress to create a national bank. By invoking the broad construction,

[3] McCulloch v. Maryland, 4 Wheaton 316 (1819).

he devised a system by which Congress could use its limited express powers to exercise an extensive and unregimented authority.

Having established that Congress could create a national bank, Marshall then turned his attention to the validity of taxation of the federal bank branches by the states. He reasoned that, since both the federal and state governments were recognized as sovereign under the Constitution, each entity had to respect the lawful activities and institutions of the other. Thus, an unwritten rule stated that a tax imposed by a state on a legitimate activity of the national government was illegal because "the power to tax involves the power to destroy." Of course, the great legal maestro might have reasoned that some taxes do destroy, others do not, and thereby reach a different result. For reasons best known to him, the Chief Justice chose not to do so.

Five years later, the Marshall Court again expanded the powers of the national government by diminishing those of the states. In *McCulloch v. Maryland* Marshall wrote of dual sovereignty, and implied equal status for the states with the federal government. In the case of *Gibbons v. Ogden*[4] he came out squarely in favor of supremacy of the national government in those areas in which it had authority to function. Curiously, this decision evoked favorable public response, although it was another victory for the established rich who had a stake in a strong national system.

A man named Ogden bought an interest in a steamboat company once owned by Robert Fulton. That company, some time before, had managed to get the New York Legislature to give it a monopoly to ply the waters of New York with their steamboats. Gibbons ignored this monopoly granted by the legislature and operated a rival steamboat business. Ogden sued to stop Gibbons' operation. If Marshall were consistent with his reasoning in the Dartmouth College case, he would have ruled that the monopoly given to Ogden was a contract

[4] Gibbons v. Ogden, 9 Wheaton 1 (1824).

and therefore could not be upset. But this would not have satisfied the commercial needs of the financial community that favored more efficient and competitive steamboat service around New York City. The restricted and inadequate service offered by the Ogden monopoly did not meet the needs of the expanding business community, or even those of the general public.

Marshall held that the provision of the United States Constitution that gave Congress the authority to "regulate commerce . . . among the states," meant that the states could not interfere with "interstate commerce," even though Congress had not passed any law regulating such commerce. While Gibbons' steamboats did stop at several New Jersey ports, the language of the Constitution hardly seems to be directed at this sort of traffic. But Marshall plunged ahead in his opinion, wrote that New York State could not interfere with the prerogative of the federal government by granting a steamboat monopoly, and branded the action by the state legislature as violative of the Constitution. Gibbons' right to run a steamship line was secure. And any other operator could start a similar navigation enterprise. More important, a rule was enunciated which said that if Congress had a specific power under the Constitution, the states could not exercise such power, even if there was no express prohibition against such state activity in the Constitution. This rule, with some modifications, has persisted until today.

In addition to these landmark cases in the triumphant ascendancy of the federal government, the Marshall Court sanctioned a few deals that were not very fragrant and had more to do with crooked interests rather than national expansion. Among them were the claims to the Yazoo land, the deal in which Justice James Wilson was involved and which prevented him from becoming Chief Justice. The claims were predicated on a sale by the Georgia legislature of millions of acres at an unconscionably low price. The legislature undeniably was bribed to sell the land at insignificant amounts.

Later, with a newly elected complement of honorable members, the legislature repudiated the transaction. In the interim, the land claims had been sold to a number of speculators who counted on political maneuvering to make a fast profit from the deal. The Supreme Court held[5] that it had to close its eyes to the dishonest conduct of the Georgia legislature. The claims were to be enforced. As a result the speculators ultimately received almost five million dollars. This decision encouraged enterprising scoundrels to buy legislators and subvert public officials to grant monopolies, land grants, franchises, and other benefactions. The risk was minimal since the Supreme Court had uttered the principle that it would not look behind legislative financial acts even if they were lined by fraud. Marshall's decision in Yazoo supplied the legal doctrine for the railroad land-grabbers who appeared on the scene toward the end of the nineteenth century.

The Marshall Court also upheld a number of questionable and fake claims[6] to lands in Florida or Louisiana. The claims were based upon forged copies of claims granted by Spanish officials just prior to the time that the United States secured the territory. The most lucrative of these claims seemed to wind up in the hands of New England speculators who often were able to hire Daniel Webster to represent them. (Webster was usually successful in the Supreme Court.) Marshall upheld the claims on the theory that the Court could not look behind, in spite of patent fraud. There were more than ninety such cases.

Marshall's record with respect to the Indians and blacks is not exactly inspiring. When gold was found on Cherokee land in Georgia, unscrupulous white traders sought a land grab, mostly by dishonest means. The Marshall Court became so involved that President Jackson, in disgust, suggested that

---

[5] Fletcher v. Peck, 6 Cranch 87 (1810).
[6] For example, The Cherokee Nation v. The State of Georgia, 5 Pet. 1 (1831).

Marshall enforce the decision himself. The deal that the Cherokees received at Marshall's hands was so underhanded that even Justice Story, the "stooge" of Marshall, referred to it in a letter in a most passionate disclaimer: "Depend upon it, there is a depth of degradation in our national conduct . . . There will be, in God's Providence, a retribution for unholy deeds, first or last."

Marshall countenanced the exploitation of the black population in the South. For once he did not support strong national interests. When Southern states enacted legislation prohibiting Northern blacks from coming into their jurisdictions, Marshall did not argue that these laws violated federal control over interstate commerce. And Marshall, the owner of slaves, used all sorts of legal technicalities to water down the effective operation of the congressional legislation limiting the trading of slaves.

Yet, Marshall was concerned with federal supremacy in dealing with state bankruptcy laws. These were laws that helped debtors at the expense of creditors. He wrote the unanimous opinion, but in order to get the support of his doughty band he finally ended up with a turgid, narrowly technical, and complicated opinion.[7] As a consequence, the Court was later to decide over his dissent, in a four-to-three decision, that the state bankruptcy laws were not totally unconstitutional. It was a bitter pill for Marshall to swallow.

This occurrence presaged a new attitude on the Court. In 1828, a year after the decision, Andrew Jackson was elected President. His election was a popular reaction to President John Adams' conservative views and Marshall's stand on the national banks and state bankruptcy laws. When Justice Johnson wrote for the majority: "It is among the duties of society to enforce the rights of humanity," Marshall dissented as much from this philosophy as from the precise decision of the case itself. It is unfair to the other Justices of the Marshall Court that they sat in his shadow. The loyal opposition was William Johnson. Johnson was a member of the Court from

[7] Sturges v. Crowninshield, 4 Wheaton 122 (1819).

1804 to 1834. Of the seventy-four dissents written during this period, six were those of Marshall and thirty-four were written by the capable Republican, Johnson. Only thirty-two years old when nominated, he possessed the integrity and inner convictions that would protect him from being seduced by Marshall.

Joseph Story, who had come to the Court at age thirty-two, was seduced by Marshall. A gentleman and Harvard scholar, he was also an amateur politician, a banker, and a lawyer. Ostensibly a Republican, he simply could not escape from the Federalist milieu in which he moved. Like so many other Presidents before and after him, James Madison made a mistake in judging his judicial appointments. President Jefferson had warned his successor Madison not to appoint Story. But Madison had been unsuccessful with his first three attempts to fill the vacancy, and he was quite impressed—as indeed he should have been—with Story's background and academic excellence. Joseph Story, hailed in legal circles for his law-teaching at Harvard and his treatises on legal subjects, has often been regarded as one of the great men of the Supreme Court. Yet, he was little more than an appendage to his mentor, John Marshall (except in cases involving the rights of Negroes). It is ironic that it was Johnson from South Carolina who had the intestinal fortitude to forfeit membership in the Marshall club because of his belief that human values were more important than property values.

After the Marshall Court declared an act of Congress unconstitutional in *Marbury v. Madison*, it did not invalidate a single piece of legislation thereafter.

A spirit of humanism blew across the land by the time Marshall passed away. This was evidenced by the election of Andrew Jackson as President and then by his reelection. John Marshall for thirty-four years on the Court stood for the Federalist political and an economic point of view. Finally, in 1835, a new Chief Justice was appointed by President Jackson. He was Roger Brooke Taney of Maryland.

–3–

Roger B. Taney

AMBASSADOR FROM THE OLD SOUTH

ALTHOUGH THE NAME OF TANEY HAS BEEN "HOOTED DOWN THE pages of history," this melancholy and dour-visaged Chief Justice, with all his conflicts and his morbid sensibilities, was neither understood as a person nor has his work on the bench been completely appreciated.

John Marshall forged the Supreme Court into a powerful tool of national power, as opposed to the assertions of the states. Its role as the final arbiter of constitutional controversies seemed anchored in acquiescence. All this was not so clear to Marshall, however, as his long reign on the Court was drawing to a close. The Court was dominated by Jacksonian Democrats who espoused the philosophy that was anathema to Marshall. Referring to the appointment of Roger Taney, Daniel Webster wrote, "Judge Story thinks the Supreme Court is gone, and I think so too."

But such concern was quite excessive. Marshall himself had been willing to see Taney as a colleague on the Supreme Court, at an earlier date, and although a Whig paper complained that "The pure ermine of the Supreme Court is sullied by the appointment of that political hack," Taney's ability was recognized by some. Henry Clay, one of those who had opposed Taney's approval by the Senate, was gracious enough to tell Taney, just a few years later, "no man in the United States could have been selected, more abundantly able to wear the ermine which Chief Justice Marshall honored."

Roger B. Taney was a man who seemed twisted by inner torments, describing himself in an incomplete and sporadic sketch as "this morbid sensibility." He was also a man of delicate health. Taney was Catholic, and this viewpoint never abandoned him. As he wrote to his son-in-law in 1845, "I do not exactly understand why Friday has become the fashionable day for dinners here." The new Chief Justice, in deference to the Jackson style, handed down decisions in trousers rather than knee breeches, the latter being traditional. He reflected the Jacksonian philosophy underscoring personal rights, in contrast to the concern of the Federalists and Whigs for property rights. He was to write in an early opinion, "while the rights of property are sacredly guarded, we must not forget that the community also have rights, and that the happiness and well being of every citizen depends upon their faithful preservation." Yet, paradoxical as it may seem, Taney reinforced the property values that Marshall limned before him. Marshall, in evaluating Taney, apparently understood the real man and what he stood for. In contrast to his deep-seated commitment to agrarian property rights, he distrusted the merchant and banking interests. While he believed in the gradual freeing of the slaves, he believed that the black man was inferior and not entitled to specified rights under the Constitution. Nor was he willing to accept universal emancipation of the slaves by dint of Northern coercion. And finally, while he believed in the union, he was emotionally committed to his home state, Maryland, and to states rights.

He was a product of his time and his heritage. His father, Michael Taney, was the fifth member of his family to bear the same name in southern Maryland. Michael Taney always lived on the same plantation, amid his slaves and material comforts. Since the plantation was to be inherited by the eldest son, Michael Taney selected law as the calling for his second son, Roger. After he became a lawyer, Roger served in the Maryland legislature for several terms. His stature as a legislator grew, and he finally became leader of the Federalist party in Maryland.

During the War of 1812 with England, the Federalist party became severely split. The New England faction sought an early end to the war because its shipping and other mercantile interests were suffering. Taney, as a representative of the agricultural interests in Maryland, was bitterly against ending the war. "My family on both the father's and mother's side have been for so many generations Maryland, that I have always felt strong Maryland attachments." The Federalist organization fell apart, and in the 1820's he joined forces with Andrew Jackson, who was a landowner and a slaveowner in Tennessee. Taney was attorney general of Maryland, and in 1831 he was rewarded politically by an appointment as Attorney General of the United States. Although the job paid only four thousand dollars a year, he hoped to augment it by practicing in Maryland and by private practice before the Supreme Court of the United States.

While Attorney General, Taney sharpened his arguments in defense of states rights and the fostering of property rights. Having lived through that period of hostility toward freed slaves and terror of the revolutionary blacks made real by the Nat Turner insurrection, Taney tried to adopt a practical view of the slavery question. As Attorney General he was asked to give an opinion on the validity of a South Carolina statute that required free blacks on foreign ships to be imprisoned while the ships were in port. The blacks were released when the ship left port if the costs of imprisonment were paid. Taney decided that this statute did not violate a treaty with Great Britain, which specified that permission to enter the country was expressly subject to the laws of this country, including the laws of South Carolina. As a slaveowner, Taney was protecting Southern whites who feared the free black man. Yet, to a Northern problem Taney gave a different answer. Taney supported a Pennsylvania statute that decreed slaves entering the port cities will become free on entry. There was no treaty in this case. Taney was moderate in his relations with his own slaves; he had freed several and he had helped one black buy his freedom.

By the time Marshall's tenure had come to an end in 1835, the political picture had completely changed. The Federalist party was all but forgotten. The Republicans were split into two factions vying for power, the Democrats and Whigs. A wave of democratic feeling and bitterness between different sections of the country had resulted in the collapse of the traditional parties. In fact, the election of 1824 saw four Republican candidates for President—Henry Clay, John C. Calhoun, John Quincy Adams, and William Crawford—each representing different sectional interests. The fifth was a military hero and a Democrat, Andrew Jackson. The election was thrown into the House of Representatives because no candidate could achieve an electoral majority. Jackson won the popular vote, but John Quincy Adams, by political maneuvering, was able to win in the House of Representatives. But he was President only one term. In 1828 Andrew Jackson and the Democratic Party were swept into office.

With the election of Jackson, the American frontier had come into its own. The farmers and artisans found a champion against the Eastern money establishment. The Democrats sought a restriction of federal power under the Constitution and freer money, so as to help debtors pay off debts. A specific goal of President Jackson was to close the United States Bank. Taney, who was then serving as Secretary of State, pulled the federal money out of the Bank when Jackson refused to renew its charter.

Roger Taney's distrust of the financial and banking interests is evidenced by his battle against the Bank of the United States. Taney dictated the critical points of President Jackson's veto message in 1832 concerning the proposal to renew the Bank of the United States. He implemented Jackson's proposal to withdraw government funds from the Bank. President Jackson's veto message criticized the existence of judicial review, urging that the decisions of the Supreme Court "must not . . . be permitted to control the Congress or the Executive." Of course, when Taney finally became Chief Justice, supported by judicial cohorts, he became more sympathetic to the exercise of power by the Court. But he continued to believe in local control rather than tremendous aggregates of power supported by government.

He emphasized this predisposition in *Charles River Bridge v. Warren*,[1] which was decided during the very first term of his tenure as Chief Justice. The majority, speaking through Taney, ruled that the charter of a bridge company should not be interpreted so broadly as to give it a monopoly over the Charles River in Boston. They rejected the arguments of Daniel Webster, deciding that charters granted by a state should be narrowly construed so as to promote the interests of the members of the local community. Although the decision seemed to strike down economic rights, by refusing to enforce monopoly it encouraged corporate competitive enterprise. While in the Dartmouth College case the court had decided that charters by the state were contracts and hence could not be impaired, such a precedent applied strictly in this case would have thwarted the burgeoning capitalist enterprises in America.

Taney followed up this approach with *Bank of Augusta v. Earle*,[2] by ruling that a corporation chartered in one state might act in other states, like individuals. This decision encouraged national economic enterprise. Taney actually was pursuing the same goals as Marshall. The great nationalist Daniel Webster could state after the decision, "the Supreme Court is yet sound; and much as we cherish Whig victories,

---

[1] Charles River Bridge v. Warren Bridge, 11 Pet. 420 (1837).
[2] Bank of Augusta v. Earle, 13 Pet. 519 (1839).

yet we cherish this conservative victory more; it is a triumph of the Constitution and Union again."

In the License cases of 1847[3] Taney expressed the same concern for the rights of local communities in a broad sense as had been expressed in the Charles River Bridge case. In it, the Supreme Court assumed the responsibility to strike a balance between individual rights and state police power. Taney defined the state "police power" to mean "nothing more or less than the powers of government inherent in every sovereignty." And, by means of this power the state is allowed, "for the safety or convenience of trade, or in the protection of the health of its citizens," to control the rights of individuals and property.

In the maintenance of a solid balance between the nation and the states, Marshall pushed for the extension of national power. Taney was not prepared to extend the commerce clause so as to destroy the power of the state to regulate. He relied rather on the idea of a concurrent power residing in the state to control commerce. In 1851, in *Cooley v. Board of Port Wardens*,[4] the Court resolved the issue of whether a certain governmental power is exclusively in the federal government or whether there is a concurrent power in the state. The ruling declared that it depended on the subject matter of the power and whether said subject matter was of the type to require exclusive legislation by Congress. The states have the power to regulate unless the subject matter requires exclusive regulation in a national and uniform manner. If regulation is not required by a uniform and national system, each of the states may act on the matter in accordance with local needs.

While the Taney Court was able to come to a resolution of the conflict between the nation and states in the regulation of commerce, it could not effect such a reconciliation on the more basic conflicts between state and federal supremacy. The Constitution itself did not specify the balance but only

[3] License Cases, 5 How. 504 (1847).
[4] Cooley v. Board of Port Wardens, 12 How. 298 (1851).

that the federal power is supreme in the areas assigned to it by the Constitution.

Despite the concern of the Taney Court for states rights, it was ready to preserve the supremacy of the nation. A good illustration is the case of *Abelman v. Booth*.[5] Although it was finally decided in 1859, for a number of years before the controversy it aroused agitated public opinion. The case was based on the federal conviction of Booth, a crusading Milwaukee newspaper editor. As an abolitionist, he procured the release of a runaway slave from federal custody. Convicted for violating the Fugitive Slave Law, Booth was freed through a writ of habeas corpus in the courts of Wisconsin on the ground that the statute violated the United States Constitution. The Wisconsin court then refused to recognize an appeal to the United States Supreme Court on the theory that the state ruling was final. The Taney Court upheld the right to appeal to the Supreme Court. It aroused as much bitter attack as had the Dred Scott decision and the Justices were accused of a bias in favor of slavery.

Both the Dartmouth College and the Charles River Bridge cases emphasized the radical economic changes that had taken place from the early days of the republic up until the Civil War. During this time, these changes were reflected in the changing American politics and in the composition of the Court. President Andrew Jackson named no less than seven new Justices during his two terms. However, the new spirit of America was not reflected as rapidly in the Supreme Court as in the other two branches of government. Thus, although the Federalists were out of power by 1812, the Supreme Court was still dominated by their ideology until Marshall's death in 1835. And under Chief Justice Roger B. Taney, the Court was under the domination of the Democrats until the Civil War, out of step with the party in control of the country.

Taney actually tried to achieve a new equilibrium of

[5] Abelman v. Booth, 21 How. 506 (1859).

power between the federal government and the states. However, he did not follow the Jacksonian doctrine of limiting the power of the Supreme Court, although this was Democratic dogma. The Court attained great status under Marshall. During his tenure, Taney enhanced rather than diminished the importance of the Court. Both Taney and the Court would have maintained this high standing if it had not been for the issue of slavery and the decision in the Dred Scott case. As a result of that ruling, the Supreme Court came under a dark shadow until the end of the nineteenth century. It is only in recent years that Taney's reputation is being restored. While there were a number of fundamental causes of the Civil War, one of the events that actually triggered the fighting was Dred Scott.

The seeds of this momentous case had been planted years before when Dred Scott had been brought by his master, Dr. Emerson, through Illinois, a free state, into part of the Northwest Territory where slavery had been abolished under the Missouri Compromise. Then, taken back to the slave state of Missouri, Dred Scott was persuaded to try to establish his status as a free man by going to court. The courts in Missouri ruled that once Dred Scott was returned to Missouri he resumed his original slave condition. Some ardent abolitionists refused to let the matter rest there. To shoehorn the case into the federal courts and up to the Supreme Court, it was necessary to satisfy the jurisdictional requirement of diversity of citizenship. Thus, Scott was "sold" to John F. A. Sandford of New York (who promised to free Scott and his family regardless of the outcome of the case, and did so). The only issue actually before the Court was the status of Scott. The Court could have decided (as was its initial reaction) that Dred Scott's freedom was a concern of Missouri, where he was situated, not the legal concern of the federal government. This would have ended the case of *Scott v. Sandford*[6] but politics would not let the issue die so easily.

[6] Dred Scott v. Sandford, 19 How. 393 (1857).

In 1856 the Court had nine members, two having been added to cover newly established western and southwestern circuits, a short time after Taney became Chief Justice. Taney, Campbell, Catron, Daniel, and Wayne were from the South. McLean, Curtis, Nelson, and Grier were geographically and ideologically from the North. Justice McLean, who wanted desperately to be President of the United States, indicated that he was going to use his dissent as an extensive attack against slavery. Justice Wayne of Georgia promised a counter-blasting dissent in support of slavery. Abolitionist Curtis of Massachusetts came to support McLean by threatening an exegesis affirming the Missouri Compromise. Ironically, the Missouri Compromise had already been repealed by Congress several years earlier. What was to be anticipated therefore was a Donnybrook revolving around the broadest issues of slavery. The Justices decided to hear and reconsider the case once more.

Just a few days before the Supreme Court handed down its opinion in the Dred Scott case, President Buchanan, as part of his inauguration speech, had stated that the issue of slavery "is a judicial question, which legitimately belongs to the Supreme Court of the United States before whom it is now pending, and will, it is understood, be speedily and firmly settled."

President Buchanan, a Pennsylvanian with some Southern sympathies, was less than candid when he asked the country to accept the Court's decision in Dred Scott. The President knew that the Court had already decided, knew who voted for what, and knew that the decision would not be made public until two days after his inauguration. As a matter of fact, at the request of Justice Catron, Buchanan wrote to Justice Grier from his home state, Pennsylvania, asking him to vote with the majority. He wished to avoid a five-to-four vote, with only Southerners voting for slavery. Grier complied so that when the Court ruled that the Missouri Compromise (already repealed) was unconstitutional, it

was a six-to-three vote, and Grier joined with the five Southerners to make this total.

There were nine separate opinions, and eight were political platforms. The only exception was the opinion of Justice
Nelson who refused to extend his remarks beyond the basic
analysis first proposed by the Court. Of all these political
tracts, the most patently partisan was the majority opinion of
Chief Justice Taney, even surpassing the polemic delivered
by McLean.

The Chief Justice was not content to rest simply on the
ground that the Missouri Compromise violated the Constitution. He also added that no black could be a citizen of the
United States, and therefore did not have the right to institute
a suit in the federal courts. Either one of these grounds would
have been enough under ordinary circumstances to end the
case. But Taney and his five colleagues were not content to
stop there. In language reminiscent of the contemporary
contretemps over race relations, the majority twisted the
sanctimonious sentiments expressed in the North, a place
"where the labors of the Negro race was found to be unsuited
to the climate and unprofitable to the master." It scorned the
New England shipowners who became wealthy "in the slave
trade, procuring cargoes on the coast of Africa and transporting them for sale" to Southern buyers. While Taney's
attack on the abolitionists' hypocrisy might have been justified, it only infuriated the North and destroyed the position of
Taney as an impartial jurist.

Before the decision, Abraham Lincoln of Illinois had
counseled moderation and patience, although he had pointed
out insightfully that "our judges are as honest as other men
and not more so. They have, with others, the same passions
for party, for power, and the privilege of their corps . . .
Their power is the more dangerous as they are in office for
life, and not responsible, as the other functionaries are, to the
elective control."

But Lincoln lost his patience after the decision. "Familiarize yourselves with the chains of bondage and you prepare your own limbs to wear them. Accustomed to trample on the rights of others, you have lost the genius of your own independence. . . . And let me tell you, that all these things are prepared for you by the teachings of history, if the elections shall promise that the next Dred Scott decision and all future decisions will be quietly acquiesced in by the people."

In spite of the strong feelings educed in the North by Dred Scott, the Supreme Court persisted in its proslavery stance. In the case of the Wisconsin abolitionist,[7] involving a clear violation of the act of Congress aimed at the cessation of assistance to runaway slaves, the Court approved the law, although it undoubtedly violated the first ten amendments (the Bill of Rights). In language reminiscent of Marshall, Taney supported the national government over the states and judicial power over the whole system. Said Taney: "If such an arbiter had not been provided for in our complicated system of government, internal tranquility could not have been preserved and if such controversies were left to the arbitrament of physical force, our Government, state and national, should fail to be a government of laws, and resolution by force of arms would take the place of courts of justice and judicial decisions."

The decision initiated a call for resistance to the federal act on the ground that Taney's decision involved states rights. Ironically, it was the South which then urged supremacy of the national government. Lincoln was elected. Soon Southern and Northern men and boys were bleeding and dying for the national government or for their states (but in a complete reversal of their position of a year before).

Taney and his court lingered as ghost-like apparitions of a dead order. Taney, unlike Marshall, could not checkmate a hostile President. He was more than eighty years of age. The country was at war. President Lincoln, in the attempt to keep Maryland out of action and out of the Confederacy, had sus-

[7] Abelman v. Booth, 21 How. 506 (1859).

pended the writ of habeas corpus (under which those wrong-fully detained can demand to be heard before a civil judge). Merryman had been thrown into jail by the local military commander and was obviously set up for conviction by a military tribunal. An application for a writ of habeas corpus was presented to Taney, sitting in circuit, and he obliged. The writ was ignored by the commander, and Taney then ordered him held in contempt of court.[8]

Taney stated that only Congress, with the President, could suspend the right of habeas corpus. If the civil courts could have its powers "usurped by the military power at its discretion, the people of the United States are no longer living under a government of laws but every citizen holds life, liberty and property at the will and pleasure of the army officer in whose military district he may happen to be found." Both Lincoln and the commander ignored the Taney writ of habeas corpus, Merryman languished in jail, and the war went on. Whatever Taney's motivations were, the old gentle-man had courage.

During the next two years, Taney lost three Justices either through death or resignation. Lincoln appointed as his first replacement Noah Swayne of Ohio, the candidate of important commercial interests supporting the Northern cause. David Davis of Illinois, who was appointed because he was a close friend of Lincoln, turned out to be a felicitous choice. The third was Samuel Miller of Iowa, one of the unsung bright lights in the history of the Supreme Court. Their mettle was soon to be tested.

The Prize cases[9] in 1863 presented the only significant decision of the Supreme Court during the war. It decided the validity of the proclamation in 1861 by President Lincoln of a blockade of the Southern ports. Union ships had seized four vessels and had claimed them as prizes. The owners of these ships claimed that the proclamation was unlawful in the

[8] *Ex Parte* Merryman, Fed. Cas. No. 9, 487 (1861).
[9] Prize Cases, 2 Black 635 (1863).

absence of a state of war declared by Congress. The Court conceded that the proclamation of an embargo by Lincoln marked the beginning of the Civil War. But could the President initiate a war without violating the requirement that war can be declared only by Congress?

The Supreme Court sidestepped a direct answer to the question. But, it reasoned, on the assertion of a challenge, the President could take emergency action even in the absence of a declaration of war by Congress. The narrow holding of the Prize cases was that after the firing on Fort Sumter the President could act as if a state of war existed without waiting for Congress, and he could take such steps as he considered necessary. The broader implications of the Prize cases were that the President could legally recognize a crisis as constituting a war and take action he deems appropriate even before Congress acts.

The vote was five to four, the three new appointees being in the majority. Obviously without them the result would have been different. It is probable that Lincoln would have treated a contrary ruling with the same disregard as he treated the Court's decision in the Merryman case. The Justices saved themselves some grief by deciding to uphold the action of the President. Taney, as a last feeble gesture, joined the dissenters. He had met defeat. Six months before Lincoln was assassinated Taney died. The principles he espoused did not die with him, although the slaveowning civilization of the southern planter was gone. Some of his ideas were to be expressed by many who came later and some were even adopted by later Courts.

II

RECONSTRUCTION
AND
PROPERTY RIGHTS

–4–

Samuel Miller

REBELLION AND RECONSTRUCTION

DURING THE WAR BETWEEN THE STATES, THE SUPREME COURT did very little more than ratify the measures used by the government in power to suppress the rebellious states. The single outstanding decision of the Supreme Court during the Civil War was the one made in the Prize cases of 1863.[1] It seems even more significant today in the wake of the argument that the war in Vietnam is not a legal undertaking for the United States. The implication of these cases seems to be that there are times when the President can recognize a *de facto* state of war, and initiate certain military steps that would ordinarily only be valid after Congress had declared a state of war.

The Court was also faced with a number of questions as a result of the suspension of the writ of habeas corpus during the war; it was generally felt that this suspension attacked the protection of personal freedom as guaranteed under the Constitution. Are laws that safeguard human liberty to be silent during war? It seems significant that the Supreme Court did not tackle this thorny question while passions and battles raged. Here, too, as in the past, the Court avoided a direct confrontation. Congress passed a statute in 1863 that pur-

[1] Prize Cases, 2 Black 635 (1863).

[55]

ported to give the President the authority to suspend the writ of habeas corpus when "in his judgment, the public safety may require it." And Congress enacted other measures during the Civil War authorizing the President to take other necessary steps. The Court avoided a decision on the President's authority to take such action of his own by ruling that the laws passed by Congress duly ratified the suspension of the writ of habeas corpus and the other measures taken by Lincoln.[2]

Samuel Miller was appointed to the Supreme Court in 1862 and sat as an Associate Justice for twenty-eight years. As a jurist, Miller saw the United States torn by the fire and bloodshed of rebellion. He sat during the entire painful period of imperfect reconciliation and abortive reconstruction. Sam Miller judged in an era that saw America transformed into an industrial colossus. And in 1890, the year Miller died, the American frontier officially closed, and an important period of national history ended.

Miller was born on April 5, 1816, in the heart of bluegrass Kentucky. The oldest of eight children, he gave up his casual schooling to serve as apprentice in a relative's pharmacy. Taken under the wing of a local physician, he went on to earn a medical degree from Transylvania University, and for more than a decade he practiced medicine in a hamlet located in the Cumberland Mountains of Kentucky. He was overcome by the burdens of tending the sick and bored by the lack of intellectual challenge. He was fascinated by the public issues of the day and became immersed in the law books of the lawyer with whom he shared offices.

When he was thirty-one, in 1847, Miller became a lawyer. He was a supporter of Cassius Clay, and like his mentor believed in the emancipation of the slaves. By the time Kentucky adopted its new constitution in 1850, Miller realized that it was not a favorable climate for his new career. Miller and his family moved to Keokuk, Iowa, where he was quite successful in developing a law practice. He was a man of

2 *Ex Parte* McCardle, 6 Wallace 318 (1867); 7 Wallace 506 (1868).

warm and humanitarian impulses. All during his life, he opposed capital punishment. He also supported public education, federal assistance to local government, unfettered immigration, liberalized suffrage, liberal construction of the provisions of the Constitution, and an expansion of democratic institutions. While he distrusted the financial interests, he could not totally accept Jacksonian politics. He freed his slaves and became a Republican. By 1860 Miller was an influential leader of the Republican Party in Iowa and an important Lincoln backer. And when the Civil War broke out, he put his money to work for his beliefs by giving personal notes to support the Union cause.

There were three vacant seats on the Supreme Court after Daniel and McLean died and Campbell resigned. In 1862 Lincoln also was confronted with the demand to reorganize the judicial circuits so as to satisfy certain of the states which were now part of the Union. He complied and Miller was urged upon Lincoln from many quarters as the right man to be the first appointment from a state west of Mississippi. His home-town newspaper argued that Miller's "strong common sense and clear comprehension of the spirit and marrow of the matter, prevents his being overwhelmed by the dust of antiquated precedents or entangled by the cobweb filaments of more modern technicalities." The *Keokuk Weekly City Gate* also described him as "the beau ideal of a Western lawyer and Western judge." Sam Miller was a fitting representative of the Old West, a rugged man standing over six feet and weighing over two hundred pounds, with piercing eyes in a large head with finely molded features. He exuded confidence, exuberance, and unbridled physical energy, whether he was riding, dancing or singing, working, or just laughing. Yet he was not only the athlete, but also the philosopher, for he displayed the same directness and intellectual capacities in facing intellectual problems as he did those involving the physical. He would lunge toward a problem, seize it firmly, and wring hard until the problem was disposed of.

He would not put up with pomposity or sham. Once in

St. Louis, while presiding over the circuit court, he exploded at a lawyer who was pontificating at length: "Damn it," roared Miller, "come to the point." The lawyer, taken aback, asked, "What point, your Honor?" The judge shouted, in exasperation, "I don't know, any point, some point!" His directness and scorn of pompous talk sometimes involved him in disputes, but few could long resist his outgoing warmth, his humor, his friendship, and his courage.

As a Justice of the Supreme Court at the outset of the Civil War, he was committed to preserving the Union. And he was realistic enough to recognize that the national government required the ability to tax if it were going to meet its needs. While Miller believed in the maintenance of state and local government, he understood that the national government was the most viable instrumentality for coping with the emerging American problems. He also believed strongly in human liberty and in the ideals of postwar Reconstruction, but he was ready to accept what was within the realm of possibility. Thus, he stood behind President Lincoln and his war effort in cases that brought into question the Union blockade of Southern ports, the issuance of greenbacks, the status of military trials, and the right of habeas corpus.

The Civil War, by force of arms, settled one central issue. It forever laid to rest the assertion that the union was based on an agreement among the states which could be repudiated by any one of them. This proposition, established by blood and gunshot, was legally confirmed by the Supreme Court in *Texas v. White*,[3] which was handed down a short time after the end of the war. The issue presented was whether Texas, which had sought to secede, was still a member state of the United States, and therefore able to institute suit as a state. The defendants claimed that since Texas had, in fact, left the union, and still was not represented in Congress, it could not institute a lawsuit. The decision was that since the attempt by

[3] Texas v. White, 7 Wallace 700 (1868).

Texas to secede was without effect, it continued to be one of the United States. Hence, as any other state, it had the right to bring suit. The majority in *Texas v. White* wrote that these United States was "an indestructible union, composed of indestructible states." One must wonder what the Court would have ruled had the Southerners been successful in their rebellion.

While the Supreme Court indulged in the myth that the state of the union remained unaltered during the Civil War, the conduct of national affairs was hardly consistent with this philosophy. During the postwar period of Reconstruction, the Bill of Rights and other basic provisions of the Constitution were overlooked while the areas of the South were largely left to military control and treated as "conquered provinces." The Supreme Court was never given a chance to decide on the validity of the Reconstruction Act or the actions which were taken under its authority. A former Justice, Curtis, described this period in the history of the Supreme Court by saying, "Congress, with the acquiesence of the country, has subdued the Supreme Court. . . ."

Although the Court was sympathetic to the South, it avoided the chance to declare the acts of Reconstruction, passed over the veto of President Johnson, unconstitutional. This prompted a cabinet member to remark: "The Judges of the Supreme Court have caved in, fallen through. . . ."

So the Supreme Court slipped from the decade of the Dred Scott decision, into its Civil War impotency, down into its doldrums of the early Reconstruction period. Sensing this institutional vulnerability, Congress proceeded to emasculate the Court by authorizing the change in the number of Justices to ten, then reducing it to seven, and then bringing it back to nine (where it is today). All this was maneuvered within seven years, without public outcry, and for blatant political reasons. It is only a student of the Supreme Court who will remember the three Chief Justices who served following the Civil War: Salmon P. Chase, Morrison R. Waite, and Melville

W. Fuller. They were a far cry from the fecund and long-tenured Marshall and Taney.

In his first term, Lincoln filled five seats on the Court. Although Justice Daniel died in 1860, before Lincoln came into office, Buchanan left the vacancy for his successor. By the winter term of 1861, two additional openings existed because McLean died and Campbell left the Court. Justice Campbell resigned because he felt that his first loyalty was not to the union but to his home state of Alabama. Early in 1862, President Lincoln named Noah Swayne of Ohio to fill the Daniel vacancy, Samuel Miller of Iowa to replace McLean, and David Davis of Illinois to succeed Campbell. The following year, Lincoln appointed Stephen J. Field to the new opening created for the Tenth District of California and Oregon.

The seat of the Chief Justice, after Taney's demise at age eighty-seven in 1864, was taken over by Salmon P. Chase of Ohio. He presided over the Court for nine years, but accomplished little to raise it from the obloquy into which it had fallen. In appointing Chase, President Lincoln observed, "we wish for a Chief Justice who will sustain what has been done. . . . We cannot ask a man what he will do, and if we should, and he should answer us, we should despise him for it. Therefore we must take a man whose opinions are known." If Lincoln had survived, he would have experienced, as have so many other Presidents, the transformation that overcomes men once they become clothed in the Court's black robes. Chase, who had been a strong abolitionist, was plucked from the Senate of the United States by Abraham Lincoln, to become a member of the Cabinet. The fact that he was a "sculptor's ideal of a President" enhanced his standing with President Lincoln, who certainly was not insensitive to political factors. Lincoln should have anticipated the unpredictability of Chase since, while brilliant as Secretary of the Treasury, he was as changeable as quicksilver. His most consistent motivation was to secure a nomination to run for

President. It drove him to pursue the Republicans, the Democrats, and the liberal Republicans. Perhaps Lincoln considered this in shunting Chase from the mainstream of political life to the bench.

There were a few notable cases decided under the aegis of the Chase Court. For one thing, by a close vote of five to four, the Court declared unconstitutional a law that imposed a loyalty oath upon lawyers.[4] With the pressures and passions remaining after the Civil War, this was a significant legal decision. Chase's tenure was also marked by the legal controversies engendered by the attempt of the legislature of Iowa to encourage the railroads to expand through that state. It was in several cases involved in this litigation that Justice Samuel Miller expressed the fervor and logic in his dissents that finally forced his prorailroad brethren to retreat. Miller's statement that he doubted that the majority ruling of the Court would "induce the Supreme Court of Iowa to conform its rulings to suit our dictation,"[5] encouraged that court to ignore the ruling of the United States Supreme Court in three cases, until the Iowa court finally capitulated. Samuel Miller was described by Chief Justice Chase as "beyond question the dominant personality . . . upon the bench."

The Chase Court expressed its views on civil liberties in a case entitled *Ex Parte* Milligan.[6] Although the unanimous court bravely wrote, "The Constitution of the United States is a law for rulers and people, equally in war and peace. . . ," it waited until after the Civil War to utter these sentiments. Ironically, during the Civil War, in the Merryman case and in other situations, although the habeas corpus was approved, its use had been denied and the Justices chose not to demonstrate their courage by speaking out. By 1866, the vindication of Taney's position gave him no satisfaction, for he was dead.

The origin of the dispute was the problem facing Lincoln

---

[4] *Ex Parte* Garland, 4 Wallace 333 (1867).
[5] Gelpeke v. Dubuque, 1 Wallace 175 (1864).
[6] *Ex Parte* Milligan, 4 Wallace 2 (1866).

because of the activities of the Copperheads, Confederate sympathizers in the Midwest consisting of persons who felt the Southern position was correct and others who were simply disenchanted Democrats wanting the Civil War to end at any cost. While they did not represent the views of most Westerners, they created a serious enough problem to cause Lincoln to act. On the theory that disloyal people were not entitled to the benefits of the Constitution, he suspended the writ of habeas corpus in Indiana, although it was not even in the area of fighting. Those who aided the enemy or engaged in disloyal activities were to be arrested and court-martialed.

Milligan was a civilian arrested on order of the commanding general of the District of Indiana. The military tribunal that tried him found Milligan guilty of conspiracy against the government, assisting the rebels, starting insurrection, and violating the rules of war. About a week before he was scheduled to be hung, he sought the federal court in Indiana for a writ of habeas corpus. Unable to find an answer, the United States circuit court submitted the problem to the Supreme Court as a question of law. The Supreme Court decided unanimously that the military commission had been unlawful and, further, that such military tribunals could not be established either by the President or Congress, except where the civilian courts were suspended in actual theaters of war. The decision was vociferously condemned in Congress by the radicals who were the majority. The Court paid for its courage. Congress chastised the Supreme Court by reducing its membership from ten to seven. And soon the Court fell into line.

Ignoring the Milligan decision, Congress still provided for rule and trial by the military in the South (the same procedure that had been ruled illegal in Milligan). A petition to prevent the enforcement of the Reconstruction Act of 1867 was presented on the ground that it was clearly violative of the Constitution. The proceedings for injunction brought against the President and Secretary of State were thrown out by the Supreme Court as not being within the authority of the judiciary to decide. The issue of the validity of the Reconstruction acts was submitted to the Court in the McCardle case.[7] A Mississippi newspaper editor was held for trial by a military comission. He sought a writ of habeas corpus and attacked the provision of the Reconstruction Act which allowed military detention and trial of civilians. After being turned down by the circuit court, McCardle then appealed to the Supreme Court under a statute that permitted such appeals from circuit court rulings. The High Court unanimously decided that it had the authority to hear this appeal. It was extensively argued before the Justices and they reserved decision.

The Supreme Court, just two years before, prohibited the trial of civilians by a military commission in the Milligan case. It certainly appeared that the Supreme Court would use this precedent to dictate the result in the McCardle case. To prevent this result, Congress quickly passed a law taking away the jurisdiction of the Court to hear appeals in habeas corpus cases. President Johnson, who was himself under fire in an impeachment trial that had been instituted against him, met the attack by Congress on the Supreme Court with an emphatic veto. Congress passed the bill again, over the President's veto.

The Court then heard new arguments in McCardle on whether Congress could take away its authority over a case in which it had already heard arguments and thus convened. Now the Court backed away from the case. It ruled that Congress had effectively legislated to take away its jurisdiction over the appeal. The action by Congress, in the words of a reporter, "put a knife to the throat of the McCardle case." This is the only time that Congress has taken away the authority of the Supreme Court to prevent a decision on the constitutionality of a specific legislative act.

Congress had been forced by the tremendous costs of the

[7] *Ex Parte* McCardle, 6 Wallace 318 (1867); 7 Wallace 506 (1868).

Civil War to make certain changes in the currency system. In three Legal Tender acts, it provided for the issuance of about a half million dollars in United States notes not backed by gold or silver. It provided that such greenbacks, as they were known, were to be deemed legal tender at face value in payment of all debts. The constitutionality dispute related to whether Congress could make paper money legal tender by its act. During the conduct of the Civil War, the Supreme Court was careful not to decide a case questioning the constitutionality of the Legal Tender laws. Once the Civil War was ended, the issue could no longer be dodged.

President Lincoln made Chase the Chief Justice. When Chase was Secretary of the Treasury he issued paper money of dubious legality to meet the enormous costs of the Civil War. In addition to Chase, the other sitting Justices who were also appointed by Lincoln were Swayne, Davis, Miller, and Field. The latter, Stephen J. Field, was appointed in 1863 as a tenth member of the Court. He was from California, a newly created tenth circuit. Field was the friend and received the political backing of Leland Stanford, the financial tycoon with interests in the Central Pacific Railroad. Field sat on the august court for thirty-four years, zealously employing his substantial legal ability to protect and promote the nascent American capitalism.

The fight to uphold the validity of the cheap money that was issued to pay off Civil War obligations of the Union was in the interests of the poor, the debtors, and the railroads. The railroads largely financed their expansion on funds borrowed on the strength of bonds bearing fixed interest and therefore supported "cheap" money.

The controversy among the Justices was bitter and angry. In spite of his connection with the issuance of the easy money, Chase saw that his best interest lay in changing his position. Field was ultraconservative and supported the creditor class rather than the railroads. When Justice Grier vacillated, his associates unanimously asked Justice Field to suggest to the enfeebled seventy-six-year-old Grier that he retire. Grier did retire and in 1870 the Legal Tender acts were declared unconstitutional. It is ironic that twenty-seven years after Field sought the resignation of Grier, he himself received a similar message. He was then reminded of his part in the Grier incident, and he mumbled, "Yes—and a dirtier piece of work I never did in my life."

In a four-to-three decision,[8] Chase, for the majority, said it was not proper to issue paper money. Miller dissented, and wrote that the law authorizing the greenbacks was a "necessary and proper" concomitant of the power of Congress to wage war. However, Congress and the new President, Ulysses S. Grant, would not accept this decision, which involved about a half billion dollars in greenbacks, without further fight. Congress had just passed legislation increasing the membership of the Court from seven to nine. On the very day that the Court's decision in *Hepburn v. Griswold* was issued, President Grant appointed two new Justices. They were William Strong of Pennsylvania, and Joseph P. Bradley of New Jersey, who was the attorney for the United Railway Company of New Jersey. No time was wasted: the two were confirmed in short order. The Legal Tender acts were once more directed to the attention of the Court and by the next year, through legal legerdemain, Chief Justice Chase was now leading the dissent. The majority, composed of the earlier dissenters, plus the new Justices, Strong and Bradley, overruled the earlier decision and piously ruled that Congress had the legal authority to issue paper currency.[9]

The Legal Tender cases are perhaps less important today for the actual holding than for the light they throw on the way the Court functions. Some historians do not concede that President Grant packed the Supreme Court in order to guarantee the reversal of *Hepburn v. Griswold*. But certainly the coincidence was quite remarkable. The contemporary

[8] Hepburn v. Griswold, 8 Wallace 603 (1869).
[9] Legal Tender Cases, 12 Wallace 457 (1870).

press reported that the switch by the Court in its Legal Tender rulings "will greatly aggravate the growing contempt for what had long been the most respected . . . department of our government, the judiciary."

From this low plateau, the Court could only rise up again, and it followed the Marshall Court and Taney Court tradition: it served the establishment, the burgeoning system of free enterprise. Immediately following the Civil War, the Court entered a period of passivity. This was soon to give way to a bristling and exuberant adolescence, which matched the growth of American capitalism. America expanded along the track of the fire-eating, smoke-belching railroads, to the clamor of the new exuberant industrial growth, and with the buccaneering raucous banking and commercial empire-building. The Supreme Court was the handmaiden of this new America.

It was not strange therefore that most of the lawyers appointed to the Court during this period represented the protection of business interests, including two Chief Justices, Waite and Fuller. It was irritation with this blinding prejudice that moved Justice Miller to tell his colleagues: "It is vain to contend with judges who have been, at the bar, the advocates of railroad companies, and all the forms of associated capital, then they are called upon to decide cases, where such interests are in contest. All their training, all their feelings are from the start in favor of those who need no such influence."

But the Court was the champion of big business, and the basis of its renaissance was the "due process of law" clause of the Fourteenth Amendment, which was directed to bring about several results. One was to eliminate the impact of the decision in the Dred Scott case, which ostensibly banned citizenship for the blacks. For this reason, the Fourteenth Amendment read: "All persons born or naturalized in the United States are citizens." It further sought to prevent the states from denying these new citizens their equal rights by the added proviso that no state "shall deprive any person of life, liberty or property, without due process of law," or "deny to any person within its jurisdiction the equal protection of the laws."

The due process clause clearly was derived from the Fifth Amendment, the heart of the Bill of Rights. The Fifth Amendment prohibits the *federal* government from depriving "any person of life, liberty or property without due process of law." As one of the first ten amendments, it was included to make sure that no person could be clapped into jail or fined or executed without some kind of regular trial procedure. But the due process clause in the Fourteenth Amendment, and the Fifth as well, came to mean a good deal more than just the protection of Negro rights. First, the language was general, rather than specific, in its coverage so that it could be used to protect all individuals, white or black, and their civil rights and liberties.

But the clause has come to mean, in addition, something extremely different from what its language seems to say. To lawyers, the concept of due process of law is the heart of the constitutional guarantees. Perhaps as many as fifteen hundred cases in the Supreme Court have involved due process. Only some of them have concerned the civil rights of blacks or those charged with criminal conduct. These cases have often decided whether the due process clause of the Fourteenth Amendment prohibited a law passed by a state legislature limiting the activities of a business concern.

For such application of the Fourteenth Amendment, two giant steps had to be taken. The first was for the Court to include corporations within the category of "persons" protected by the Fourteenth Amendment. The second was for the Supreme Court to expand the Fourteenth Amendment from simply checking the procedure by which government went about its business to limiting the substance of what it tried to do.

The Court, which had such a strong pro-business bias,

was quite prepared to make the first giant leap. Whether the Fourteenth Amendment was designed originally to protect corporations or not, the Supreme Court held that corporations came within the group of "persons" protected by the amendment. The issue of whether corporations were "persons" for this purpose was raised in *Santa Clara County v. Southern Pacific Railroad*[10] in 1886. Chief Justice Waite, the ex-railroad attorney, cut off oral argument on this point by curtly declaiming: "The Court does not wish to hear argument on the question of whether the provision in the Fourteenth Amendment to the Constitution which forbids a State to deny to any person within its jurisdiction the equal protection of laws, applies to these corporations. We are all of the opinion that it does." Although the Court did not discuss this question in its opinion, that ended debate over the matter. Today, the law is well settled that the Fourteenth Amendment affords both corporations, as well as individuals, due process of law and equal protection of law.

The recognition by the Supreme Court of the corporation as a "person" within the Fourteenth Amendment was but the first step. The Fourteenth Amendment became the citadel of big business only when the Court was willing to recognize that the Constitution restricted the state regulation of business activities and supervised the way in which the regulation was carried out by governmental agencies.

The metamorphosis of the due process clause as a substantive restraint on government activity against business did not take place right away. In the first case involving the application of the due process clause, the Supreme Court seemed reluctant to impute more than procedural safeguards to due process of law. It was only after business began to flex its muscles, with a Supreme Court dominated by the Republican railroad lawyers from the North, that the idea of "substantive" due process, with its tremendous potential for protecting free enterprise, gradually took over.

[10] Santa Clara County v. Southern Pacific Railroad, 118 U.S. 394 (1886).

The Court considered this notion as early as 1872, in the Slaughterhouse cases,[11] which first examined the Fourteenth Amendment. The legislature of Louisiana gave one concern an exclusive monopoly of all the slaughterhouse business in New Orleans for a period of twenty-five years. Ostensibly, and certainly partially in fact, this was required as a health measure. Other slaughterhouse operators, threatened with economic extinction, retained Campbell, a former Justice of the Supreme Court, to plead their case. Among his arguments was his contention that his clients' business concerns had been "deprived of property without due process of law." The Court rejected his contention, and adopted the narrow view that the Fourteenth Amendment was directed only to protect the rights of black people. However, the entire Court did not favor this restricted view. Four of the Justices vigorously dissented from the casual dismissal of the due process argument. Justice Field strongly dissented, urging that due process prohibited the Louisiana law from granting the monopoly to a single firm. His views did not win that day but they constituted the opening wedge.

It was Justice Miller, writing for the majority, who won that day. It was his shining hour of all the twenty-eight years during which he occupied a seat on the High Court. In language employed with the precision of a surgeon's scalpel (he had been a physician before he became a lawyer) he excised the fatuous legal surplusage and met the precise issues. And he was not a Federalist apologist for the interests of private property. He wrote from the depth of his conviction for human rights rather than those of business.

Miller examined the historic sources of the three amendments adopted after the Civil War, and stated: "no one can fail to be impressed with the one pervading purpose found in them all, lying at the foundation of each, and without which none of them would have been even suggested; we mean the freedom of the slave race, the security and firm establishment

[11] Slaughterhouse Cases, 16 Wallace 36 (1872).

of that freedom, and the protection of the newly made free-
man and citizen. . . ." He cautioned his brethren that the
acceptance of the broader interpretation of the due process
clause "would constitute this court a perpetual censor upon
all legislation of the states. . . ."

In spite of his trenchant analysis, four of his colleagues
dissented, including Chief Justice Chase. A few weeks after
the Slaughterhouse Cases were decided, Chase died. It is
ironic that Chase, who had been so unsuccessful while he was
on the bench ultimately was supported by the Court in his
position. And Miller, in the year that he died, saw the majority opinion that he wrote for the Slaughterhouse cases repudiated by a Court which now was the champion of business
against the states and local governments.

In the famous granger cases of 1877 and in *Munn v.
Illinois,*[12] the Court supported the power of the states to
regulate the rates of railroads and other businesses affected
with a public interest. But in 1890 it ruled that the state
power to regulate even railroads was subject to judicial scrutiny to insure due process of law and it set aside a state law
establishing railroad rates it deemed unreasonable. And
finally, in 1897, in *Allgeyer v. Louisiana,*[13] a state statute that
prohibited an individual from contracting with a marine
insurance company from outside the state to issue insurance
within the state, was held subject to Supreme Court scrutiny
to determine if business had been unduly harassed.

12 Munn v. Illinois, 94 U.S. 113 (1876).
13 Allgeyer v. Louisiana, 165 U.S. 578 (1897).

–5–

John Marshall Harlan

"RIGHT RATHER THAN CONSISTENT"

ALTHOUGH PRESIDENT GRANT HAD CONGRESS UNDER HIS THUMB, he couldn't quite inveigle its members to go along with either of the first two men he proposed as replacements for Chief Justice Chase. One, shortly before, had been subjected to public calumny as a member of Grant's Cabinet. The other was thought to be a Copperhead, and was old and decrepit. The President, under the duress of these complaints, was finally compelled to recall the nominations. He did not search among the pool of great legal ability available to him across the country. He bypassed Justice Miller who was thought, even by those who vehemently opposed his philosophy, to be the possessor of the country's outstanding judicial talent. When the President finally came up with the name of a relatively obscure and mediocre lawyer from Ohio, counsel to a railroad, the Senate rushed to confirm him, relieved that the choice had not been worse.

With Morrison R. Waite as the Chief Justice in title only, the Court slipped from its narrow and humanist approach to the Fourteenth Amendment. Under the persistent pressures of big business and the advocates of the railroad interests, as well as Justices with vested interests, the Supreme Court as a body was powerless.

The railroads, pushing west across the prairies, had, in a paroxysm of rapacious greed, corrupted state legislators and other officeholders, and piled excessive discriminatory rates on captive shippers. Then their lawyers pulled out the legal doctrine first enunciated by Marshall in the Dartmouth College case to the effect that the rights granted by state legislatures created inviolate "obligations of contract." The railroad lawyers refused to look behind the bribery and chicanery upon which these rights rested. As a defensive reaction to the railroads as a group, the farm belt organized a group agitating against the stranglehold of big business on the country.

Through political action, these grangers soon captured a number of states in the Midwest. They secured the passage of laws regulating the rates of railroads, as well as farm storage facilities. The operators of the grain elevators and warehouses went to the courts,[1] their theory being that even a slight limitation of their substantial profits was a deprivation of their property under the due process clause of the Fourteenth Amendment. This time the Court failed big business.

Chief Justice Waite, writing for the majority, wrote that the business of grain storage was like that of ferries, stagecoaches, bakers, and millers under the English common law and hence, "clothed with a public interest." They could be regulated as an appropriate exercise of the police power of the state. Wrote he, "for the protection against the abuses by legislatures, the people must resort to the polls, not to the courts." Only Field, the loyal champion of unfettered free enterprise, dissented.

In less than five years, four of the majority Justices in the granger decisions were no longer on the Court because of death or resignation. Three undistinguished Presidents filled the openings with three undistinguished and safe jurists. A judge from Georgia named William B. Woods, who started as a carpetbagger from the North, was one. A persistent railroad lawyer from Ohio, Stanley Matthews, was finally confirmed

---

[1] Munn v. Illinois, 94 U.S. 113 (1876).

by the Senate by one vote on the second time his nomination was presented. The third was Samuel Blatchford, a judge from New York, who had been a staunch railroad solon before he went into the Court.

The last of the quartet was not undistinguished, but was quite safe. Horace Gray, chief justice of the supreme court of the Commonwealth of Massachusetts, was famous for his financial backing and for his careful tradition-bound decisions on the New England bench. For twenty years on the United States Supreme Court he labored mightily but produced only one memorable opinion in which he affirmed the right of the federal government to deport any alien it wished.[2] Even that archconservative, Justice Field, dissented.

During these years, the Supreme Court was busy protecting business from government. It was also emasculating the Fourteenth and Fifteenth amendments in a flagrant way. To make these post-Civil War amendments effective instruments for insuring the rights of the black people, Congress passed the Civil Rights acts. These laws established criminal penalties to be invoked against those who took away either personal or political rights of Negroes or deprived them of "equal protection of laws." These Civil Rights acts were frustrated in the 1870's and 1880's either by the way they were interpreted or by being declared unconstitutional. The Fifteenth Amendment prohibits the states from preventing people from voting "on account of race, color, or previous condition of servitude." Yet the Court declared that an act of Congress that made it a crime for a state official to prevent people from voting was too broad to be constitutional.

In another case,[3] the Supreme Court, under the protection of federal law, stopped the punishment of Louisiana state officials for their extreme mistreatment of blacks who had the temerity to try to vote. The indictment did not mention the color of those intimidated. The Court used the following

[2] U.S. v. Wong Kim Ark, 169 U.S. 649 (1898).
[3] United States v. Cruikshank, 92 U.S. 542 (1875).

pretext: "We may suspect that race was the cause of the hostility, but it is not so averred." The High Court encouraged the lawlessness and blitzkreig tactics of the Ku Klux Klan by setting aside an act of Congress that was designed to handcuff the Klan. It reasoned that the Fourteenth Amendment could not be used as a weapon against private persons who sought to deprive the civil rights of blacks, only against state officials.[4] The Court did decide that Negroes could not be kept off juries because of their race.[5] Even this decision was not given effect by the Court for more than half a century.

The most disastrous decision of this period was rendered in 1898 in *Plessy v. Ferguson.*[6] The question presented was whether or not an act of the Louisiana legislature that ordered separate railroad accommodations for black and white passengers violated the provision of the Fourteenth Amendment requiring equal protection of laws. The Supreme Court rejected the contention that "the enforced separation of the two races stamps the colored race with a badge of inferiority." It decided that the mere separation of the races did not violate the requirement of the equal protection of laws. So long as the facilities for the blacks were "equal," the Fourteenth Amendment was not violated. The ruling rested upon the position that segregation as such is not equivalent to discrimination against the Negro. Said the majority opinion, it did not spring "by reason of anything found in the act, but solely because the colored race chooses to put that construction on it." Using the separate-but-equal doctrine of the Plessy case, the Supreme Court created a legal foundation for the continuance of a segregated America.

In his dissent, Justice John Marshall Harlan stated this idea most movingly: "Our Constitution is color blind, and neither knows nor tolerates classes among citizens." Who was

4 Civil Rights Cases, 109 U.S. 3 (1883).
5 Strauder v. West Virginia, 100 U.S. 303 (1880).
6 Plessy v. Ferguson, 163 U.S. 537 (1896).

this John Harlan who sounded as if he were sitting in the Court a full century after his time? There was little in Harlan's boyhood that reflected such a point of view. Growing up in the Southern manorial tradition among the Clays, Crittendens, and Breckinridges as family friends—and with household slaves—he reflected the Whig philosophy of his father who was successively, Secretary of State, Attorney General of Kentucky, and Congressman from his Kentucky district. After an early allegiance to Presbyterian fundamentals, devout Sabbath observance, Bible study, and temperance, Harlan left to study law at Transylvania University, absorbing the usual Coke, Blackstone, Williston, as well as Story and Kent. Above all, he imbibed the belief that property was sacred and that the nation and the Constitution were supreme.

In 1853, Harlan was admitted to the bar, a bright-eyed dynamo with a thatch of red hair. He traveled on horseback, living out of his saddlebags, during the course of a debating career. Often, Harlan would debate Democrats twice his age before huge and enthralled audiences. His advance notices described him as the "young giant," and he developed a reputation promoting "orthodox . . . Know-Nothing scripture," an amalgam of anti-Catholic, proslavery, and antiforeign propaganda. Although Harlan abhorred the institution of slavery and wished to see the slaves free, he believed that to free the slaves at their level of education would be catastrophic. Furthermore, he felt that there was a property right in slaves, which the national government was obligated to protect in the territories, and which the states had to recognize. For that reason, John Harlan thought the Dred Scott decision was correct.

Yet, once Fort Sumter was attacked, Harlan immediately sought to keep Kentucky out of the Confederacy. By the fall of 1861, he was a colonel in the Union forces and thereafter saw much action. The war made a deep impression upon the young soldier, and his boyhood ideas began to change. It was his contact with German immigrant boys and the Kentucky mountaineers in his regiment, under fire, that led him to point out: "When war menaced this country, it was the poor and the sons of the poor who sprang to its defense." And his antagonisms to Catholics dissipated as a result of his baptism of fire. "I see now with great distinctness old Father Mash pushing on foot with the boys."

For the next several decades, Kentucky politics was an incredible melange of alliances, reorganizations, and eruptions of new parties. Harlan was elected as state attorney general in 1863, as a Kentucky unionist attacking Lincoln's doctrine of emancipation and his suspension of the writ of habeas corpus. Yet, he freed his slaves. In 1865, when the issues in Kentucky were the Thirteenth Amendment and Reconstruction, Harlan challenged the Thirteenth Amendment as "a flagrant invasion of the right of self government" and he predicted chaos as a result of the operation of the Freedman's Bureau. In 1867, he became immersed in a fight within the Kentucky Presbyterian Church and moved from Frankfort to Louisville. As a result of these experiences and friends, he gravitated to the Republican party. By 1868, it was clear that a two-party system would emerge in Kentucky, Republican and Democrat. So, in 1868 he was compaigning for General Ulysses S. Grant as the Republican candidate for the Presidency. By this time, he had accepted the war amendments and defended the Republican Party for having sponsored the Thirteenth Amendment and the Fourteenth Amendment. Grant was elected.

By 1871 the Republican party was established in Kentucky. Harlan inveighed against the Democrats for throttling the Kentucky economic growth by their refusal to look forward and end race hatred. He lashed out at the monopoly of the Louisville and Nashville Railroad, supported by the Democrats. When he attacked the Democrats for refusing to help German immigrants, his opponents brought out his speeches of years before attacking foreigners and reading aloud his Know-Nothing scriptures.

Harlan felt that the future belonged to the strong Kentucky mountaineers and espoused the granger and Populist sentiments in Kentucky. He consistently urged an income tax, arguing that "the rich owed it to the poor to contribute to the education of the latter." The overriding issue of the day was Negro rights. Harlan felt that the war amendments, now part of the Constitution, were, like the Bible, entitled to unquestioned compliance. He saw "no safety in the land of ours except in rigid adherence to the law." This was his answer to the assaults, the whippings, the lynchings, and the robberies that swept through Kentucky like a plague. The Democratic state administration could not cope with this virtual anarchy. By the campaign of 1872, it was a brainwashed Harlan who mounted the stump on the issue of Negro rights. He urged that law and order could result only from recognizing the rights of the freed black men and that violence had to be suppressed even if it required federal intervention. Attacked on his past record, Harlan answered: "Let it be said that I am right rather than consistent."

For the next few years Harlan threw himself into running for public office and with the campaigns of the Republicans. When Rutherford B. Hayes was elected President in 1876, there was no question but that the leader of the Republican party in Kentucky had been a potent factor in the delivery of the important votes. In the spring of 1877, President Hayes had to find a replacement for Justice David Davis who resigned from the Court to become a United States Senator. By the fall, Hayes, who was looking for a Southern replacement, wrote to one of his friends: "Confidentially, and on the whole, is not Harlan the man? Of the right age, able, of noble character, industrious, fine manners, temper and appearance. Who beats him?" Since there seemed to be no answer to those questions, on October 17, 1877, the President submitted the name of John Marshall Harlan to the Senate for confirmation. But before Harlan was confirmed he faced the bitter charges that he was not a "real Republican." After heartbreaking

controversy and cloakroom maneuvering, the Senate confirmed him and he took office on November 29, 1877.

Harlan sat on the Supreme Court for thirty-four years.
When he first became a member of that bench, it reflected
faith in a strong union, the conception of the Reconstruction
amendments as being geared to securing the rights of the
former slaves, and of the nation's obligation to protect free
enterprise. Harlan has usually been seen as a "New Deal"
liberal who was before his time in fighting reaction and
financial oligarchy. Actually, he was an anachronism in his
court. He saw the issues of freedom, of individual liberty, and
the rights of private property, as being one and the same. He
followed the philosophical tradition of John Locke and John
Stuart Mill, who saw the rights of the individual and his
property as inseparable.

Harlan died at the beginning of the twentieth century,
while still on the job. The Court lost a man who started as a
slaveowner and an antagonist of the Civil War amendments
and ultimately shifted to become the only consistent and
ardent advocate of black civil rights on his Court. He was an
individualist who fought for the equality under law for black
and white and for unionists and capitalists. His faith was
grounded in the tenets of Protestantism and the Constitution.

In 1888, when Chief Justice Waite died, President Cleveland replaced him with a lawyer who was virtually an unknown in America at the time his name was referred to the
Senate, as it is today even though he served for twenty years
as Chief. That man was Melville W. Fuller. Due to a fortunate combination of events—the politics of geography, the
fact that he was a Democrat from the right place—Fuller was
very suitable for the seat on the bench. Having been counsel
to the interests of Marshall Field, Phillip Armour, and the
Chicago, Burlington, and Quincy Railroad, his views were
those of a Chicago corporation lawyer. It followed that his
views on the bench were supportive of business and unre-
markable save for his hatchet job on the Sherman Anti-Trust

Act in the Knight case[7] and his bungling of the income tax law in the Pollock case.[8]

Fuller came from Kansas and was the nephew and protégé of Justice Field. He followed the views of his uncle slavishly during Field's life and even after his uncle's death. A greater influence on that bench than Chief Justice Fuller was David Brewer. The Fuller Court was dominated by political "twins," Brewer and Rufus Peckham of New York. While they were still sitting in lower courts, both Brewer and Peckham refused to follow the decision of the Supreme Court in *Munn v. Illinois*,[9] which authorized the states to regulate railroads and other businesses affected with a "public interest." It wasn't long before the Supreme Court knocked out the granger case decision.[10]

The net result was that the Court assumed the role of examining state laws to make sure that they did not violate the Fourteenth Amendment. The principle was established by a case[11] in which a railroad complained about the regulation of its rates by a commission established by the Minnesota legislature. The majority opinion ruled that such regulation could be reviewed by the state courts to insure that they were "reasonable." Rates deemed unreasonable would be held to violate the due process clause that was guaranteed to railroads and other business concerns by the Fourteenth Amendment. As Justice Bradley pointed out, and he was not anti-business by any means, the decision in this case virtually rescinded the decision in the granger cases. "The governing principle of those cases was that the regulation and settlement of the fares of railroads and other public accommoda-

---

[7] U.S. v. E. C. Knight Co., 560 U.S. 1 (1895).

[8] Pollock v. Farmer's Loan & Trust Co., 158 U.S. 601 (1895).

[9] Munn v. Illinois, 94 U.S. 113 (1876).

[10] Wabash, St. Louis and Pacific Railway Co. v. Illinois, 118 U.S. 557 (1886).

[11] Chicago, Milwaukee & St. Paul Railway v. Minnesota, 134 U.S. 418 (1890).

tions is a legislative prerogative and not a judicial one. This is a principle which I regard as of great importance. . . . All human institutions are imperfect—courts as well as commissions and legislatures." For the next three decades about seven hundred cases came up to the High Court from its invitation to have that honorable body check to see whether a particular state act violated the amendments that originally were designed to protect the rights of the black people.

The year 1895 saw decisions in three cases which shaped the destiny of America. The first involved Eugene V. Debs, President of the Railway Union, and once a locomotive fireman.[12] The railroads, now plagued by their unionized workers over wages and incensed over rates, found a federal district judge in Chicago who was willing to order Debs to call off a Pullman strike under the penalty of jail. A strike ensued, however, but there was no violence. Over Illinois' Governor Altgeld's strenuous objections, federal troops were called in and the strike was broken.

Debs was precipitously thrown into jail. He sought relief from the Supreme Court on the ground that he had not been afforded a jury trial by the judge, and also that there did not seem to be any act of Congress to justify the action taken. Justice Brewer rejected a requirement for congressional authorization or a trial by jury and said there was a basic obligation to protect interstate commerce from even peaceful interference. As a result, the injunction became an extremely popular instrument to be used against labor unions until the Norris-LaGuardia Act, some thirty years later, put a halt to the abuse of the injunctive power.

Although unions could be enjoined, even when authorized by an act of Congress, the public could not secure appropriate redress from the monopolistic power of big business. In the Knight case,[13] Chief Justice Fuller rendered one of his few memorable opinions. Five years before, Congress

12 *In Re* Debs, 158 U.S. 564 (1895).
13 U.S. v. E. C. Knight Co., 560 U.S. 1 (1895).

had passed the Sherman Anti-Trust Act with the hope that it would break up the increasing number of trusts and monopolies that were threatening to engulf major segments of American industry. The Knight case, which put the new law to its first test, concerned the acquisition of the capital stock of four other companies by the American Sugar Refining Company. It had "acquired nearly complete control of the manufacture of refined sugar within the United States." But, said Fuller, making a distinction that persisted for half a century, there is significant legal difference between "commerce" and "manufacture." The sugar-refining industry was engaged in "manufacturing," and the Sherman Act could only affect "interstate commerce" under the powers given to Congress by the Constitution. Therefore, the sugar trust could not be interdicted by the Sherman act. Fuller's uncle (Justice Field) must have smiled from his grave.

The last of this trio of big business decisions was the Pollock case.[14] The Court held that the income tax law of 1894 was invalid, although a similar law had been sustained before. The advocate against the tax, the great barrister Rufus Choate, warned the bench that the "communist march" must be halted, and it must be battled "now or never." It was also argued that the income tax was based on a doctrine worthy of "a Jacobin Club—new doctrine of this army of 60,000,000— this triumphant and tyrannical majority—who want to punish men who are rich and confiscate their property." In writing for the majority, Justice Fuller snidely referred to the "speculative views of political economists or revenue reformers." "The present assault upon capital," stated Justice Field, "is but the beginning." He saw income tax as incident to "a war of the poor against the rich; a war constantly growing in intensity and bitterness."

Four of the Justices dissented. Among the comments were: "a judicial amendment of the Constitution"; "dislocates . . . principally for reasons of an economic nature—a sover-

14 Pollock v. Farmer's Loan & Trust Co., 158 U.S. 601 (1895).

eign power expressly granted the general government"; "decision involves nothing less than a surrender of the taxing power to the moneyed class. . . . Even the spectre of socialism is conjured up to frighten Congress from laying taxes upon the people in proportion to their ability to pay them." Justice Howell Jackson from Tennessee, who had just been appointed to the Supreme Court (and who died shortly thereafter), fumed: "This decision is, in my judgment, the most disastrous blow ever struck at the constitutional powers of Congress." But the press, speaking for the vested property interests, supported the decision. "The work of socialist revolution has gone far," opined the *New York Sun*, "but it breaks at the foot of the ultimate bulwark set up for the protection of our liberties." And then, with unintended wit, "Five to four, the Court stands like a rock."

The decision was finally vitiated by the Sixteenth Amendment, but it took eighteen years of unremitting work and agitation in order to formally amend the Constitution.

As the nineteenth century drew to a close, the Court which had flourished and waned in importance was at the height of its power. And then, just after the twentieth century unfolded, President Theodore Roosevelt replaced the plodding and unimaginative Justice Horace Gray with a judge who also bore a distinguished name: Oliver Wendell Holmes, Jr. The Boston jurist was sixty-one years of age, already sagacious and experienced from his work as the chief justice of the highest court of Massachusetts. He became the greatest of all American jurists. Yet, except in quality of mind and work product, he never became the leader of the Court, for he otherwise would not have been labeled "the great dissenter."

–6–

Oliver Wendell Holmes, Jr.

DOWN FROM OLYMPUS

HOLMES BROUGHT TO THE SUPREME COURT A FAITH IN AMERICA that only John Marshall before him exhibited. He also brought a twinkling personality, an agnostic philosophy of life, and a fierce skeptical intelligence. He epitomized the fruition of the New England tradition, stretching back to his physician father, Oliver Wendell Holmes, Sr., "autocrat of the breakfast table." To his dying day, Holmes carried within his nostrils the stench of dead young soldiers, the whine of flying shells, the exhilaration of battle and trickle of cold sweat, and the pain of wounds he had suffered after he exchanged the Harvard crimson to don the Union gray.

His life was a busy one, all years of constant activity until his death at age ninety-four. Once mustered out of the Union ranks as a lieutenant-colonel on July 17, 1864, he turned his talent and energies to law, practicing in Boston for more than a decade, culminating this experience with the publication of his book *The Common Law* in 1881. In spite of the importuning of President Eliot of Harvard, he left the cloistered Harvard Law School and his role as scholar and teacher to become a judge of the supreme court of the Commonwealth of Massachusetts. After two decades as an associate justice on that bench, the last three years as its chief justice, President Theodore Roosevelt appointed him to the Supreme Court of the United States. There he served as its brightest talent for thirty years, and when he was ninety-one in 1932 he resigned. Said Holmes, "I am on the side of the unregenerate who affirms the worth of life as an end in itself as against the saints who deny it."

Holmes was a "liberal" but in the pristine meaning of that much abused word. He was a stalwart Republican from conservative back-bay Boston. His politics were those of a New England Brahmin, a conservative who denounced left-wing propaganda as "drivel," who had little confidence in the Democrats. In presidential elections, Holmes favored Hughes, Harding, Coolidge, Hoover, and Hoover again (over Franklin D. Roosevelt). But in spite of his political predilections, he was an *intellectual* liberal, ready to listen to views other than his own and to respect those of others. This liberalism shines with a luminosity through all his work on the Supreme Court.

When Holmes first ascended the bench as Associate Justice there were: the ineffectual Chief Justice Fuller; independent John Harlan, becoming more cautious with advancing years; those opportunity twins Brewer and Peckham, with their business orientation; capable and rococo-tongued Edward D. White, former sugar magnate and United States Senator from Louisiana, destined to become Chief Justice; and the three other spokesmen for the railroads (in addition to Fuller), Henry Brown from Michigan, George Shiras from Pennsylvania, and Joseph McKenna from California.

Shiras never broke from his pedestrian role or his prorailroad predispositions. Under the stimulus of Holmes' inspiration, McKenna from time to time forgot his psychological ties to the business community. And Brown had one temporary severance from his traditional orientation when he appended his searing, charitable, dissenting opinion in the income tax case. By the time Holmes resigned, thirty years later, his associates were Chief Justice Hughes and the mercurial Owen

Roberts. The conservatives were Van Devanter, McReynolds, Sutherland, and Butler. Holmes' companions in dissent were Brandeis and Stone. Holmes managed to survive seven of his brethren, including one who reached the bench after him, Chief Justice William Howard Taft. All of these jurists, at one time or another, were subjected to the rapier mind, the warm humanism, and the healthy skepticism of Oliver Wendell Holmes. Yet, on the critical questions, he had difficulty getting more than two or three of them to vote for his position.

In the thirty years between 1902 and 1932, America went through a complete change of life style. The Court retained its character as patron saint of big business, marred only by a single aberrational decision which held that the due process clause did not forbid a state law limiting the hours of factory work for women.[1] In 1910 Fuller's place was taken by White, who to that date was the only member of the Court ever to be promoted to Chief Justice. The period from his appointment to World War I was an era of benign liberalism. This was less the influence of the pompously verbose Chief Justice than that of Charles Evans Hughes, then serving his first term of two rendered by him. It seems noteworthy that during this interlude there was a significant decline in the number of Holmes' dissents.

Even before World War I ended, the Court reverted to conservatism or downright reactionalism. When Chief Justice White died in 1921, President Harding, true to form, made safe and sound William Howard Taft the new Chief Justice. Taft, originally from Ohio and later Connecticut, had the distinct honor of serving his country first as President and then as Chief Justice. Genial Taft was immense in girth but less impressive in his record on the High Court. Apparently, however, Taft enjoyed judicial work. While President, he once confessed, "I love judges and I love courts. They are my ideals on earth of what we shall meet afterward in Heaven under a

[1] West Coast Hotel Co. v. Parrish, 300 U.S. 379 (1937).

Just God." During Taft's tenure Holmes saw fit to step up the tempo of his dissents.

Then in 1930 the President reintroduced the distinguished Charles Evans Hughes as Chief Justice after an absence from the Court. Hughes, more set in his ways than during his first tenure, was older, scarred by the claws of Borah, LaFollette, Norris, and the band of twenty-six Senators who fought against his confirmation. Holmes drew his rapier in defense of causes he thought important. But now Hughes' time was running out. After a few rear-guard dissents, in 1932 he finally yielded in the fight, and resigned.

In addition to Taft and Hughes (on his first stint as Justice) there were other Justices who should be noted. William Rufus Day had been a crony of President McKinley and an outstanding railroad attorney. During the Spanish-American War, the President had named his close friend as Secretary of State. Day was responsible for the purchase of the Philippines by the United States for twenty million dollars, rather than a simple annexation through force of arms, as was more usual. President McKinley, apparently in disgust at such a move, designated him a federal judge. Later Theodore Roosevelt elevated him to join the substantial group of former railroad lawyers who graced the Supreme Court bench. For two decades Day served in a solid and unobtrusive way, his big business predispositions forming his ideological orientation, and his decent impulses occasionally shining through in sporadic dissents.

Associate Justice Mahlon Pitney was a more frequent dissenter, in even greater quantity than Holmes. The trade-union movement vigorously opposed his appointment and with good cause. He was a rigid technician who employed his skills as a lower court judge in New Jersey to do battle with labor. And his antiunion views were ratified by his colleagues of the High Court. Another colleague of Holmes during his long years on the bench was Edward Sanford of Tennessee, whose sweet and compliant personality made him a satellite of the affable Chief Justice Taft, just as in earlier days other

Justices had been dominated by their Chiefs. Taft and Sanford died almost at the same time, as if to demonstrate their empathy. And then there was John H. Clarke of Ohio, a generous and moral man who left the Court after a short time to devote himself to the cause of world peace. It is noteworthy that fifteen years after his retirement he surfaced from relative obscurity as the only former Justice alive to publicly fight the scheme of President Franklin D. Roosevelt to pack the Supreme Court.

Viewing the nature of Holmes' influence on the Court during the three decades of his tenure requires more than a chronological rundown. His philosophy is revealed most clearly by studying his handling of certain problems.

The first group of problems attacked by Holmes were those in which the Supreme Court invalidated laws passed by Congress. The most striking of these cases involved the attempt by Congress to ameliorate the lot of working people or children. An example was a law that required compensation by a railroad in situations where a worker was maimed or killed as a result of its negligence. The law was not particularly innovative since many states had already passed legislation similar to the Federal Employers' Liability Act. Yet a majority of five, in 1908, held the entire act unconstitutional on the ground that it did not specify that workers of *interstate* railroads were covered, and consequently it encroached on the rights of the states.[2] Four Justices, Holmes included, dissented. In the time that it took Congress to pass another law including the magic word "interstate," and the Court to uphold it four years later, many injuries occurred to railroad employees, lives were lost, and millions of dollars were thus saved by the railroads.

In the same year it threw out the Federal Employers' Liability Act, the Court dealt another blow to the railroad workers in another case.[3] An act of Congress made it a crime for a railroad to fire a worker for joining a union. This legisla-

[2] The Employers' Liability Cases, 207 U.S. 463 (1908).
[3] Adair v. U.S., 208 U.S. 161 (1908).

tion also rejected "yellow dog" contracts, by which workers agreed not to join unions as a condition of being given a railroad job. A majority of seven Justices invalidated the act, arguing that it violated the interstate commerce clause because it poached on a subject reserved to the states. The Court also reasoned that, by interfering with a contract between a railroad and its workers, the act violated the due process clause as guaranteed by the Fifth Amendment. Ironically, the majority opinion was written by John Harlan. Near the end of a long and productive life that stretched back to the time of Andrew Jackson, Harlan confused the freedom of agrarian or frontier freedom with the often illusory freedom of a workingman in the industrial society.

Although Holmes was only eight years younger than Harlan, he understood such a distinction. Said he: "I quite agree that the question what and how much good labor unions do is one on which intelligent people may differ . . . but I could not pronounce it unwarranted if Congress should decide that to foster a strong union was for the best interests, not only of the men, but of the railroads and the country at large." He sarcastically pointed out that it was just as much a matter of interstate commerce to permit Congress to pass a law protecting railroad unions as it was to allow a law requiring the installation of couplings for safety on railroad cars (which the Court had upheld).

Again, a few years later, the majority struck down an act of Congress that established minimum wages for employed women on the ground that it violated freedom of contract protected by due process of law.[4] It had been urged before the Court, as it had before the Congress, that this measure was necessary for the health and morals of women. But the five old men thought otherwise: "the ancient inequality of the sexes . . . has continued 'with diminishing intensity.'" And, like the men of the world, the Court philosophized: "The relation between earnings and morals is not capable of stan-

---

[4] Adkins v. Children's Hospital, 261 U.S. 525 (1923).

dardization. It cannot be shown that well paid women safe-guard their morals more carefully than those who are poorly paid." Holmes, in his dissent, remonstrated that the Justices were overstepping their judicial roles: "The end, to remove conditions leading to ill health, immorality and the deterioration of race, no one would deny to be within the scope of constitutional legislation. . . . When so many intelligent persons, who have studied the matter more than any of us can, have thought that the means are effective and are worth the price, it seems to be impossible to deny that the belief *reasonably* may be held by *reasonable* men."

The attempts by Congress to abolish child labor were also destroyed by the otherwise loving fathers and grandfathers on the Supreme Court. The first act passed by Congress simply forbade shipment from one state to another of products made in a plant that employed children. The Court, by a five-to-four vote, held that the right of Congress to regulate interstate commerce did not give it the authority to legislate on a matter so within the province of the state as the manufacture of merchandise.[5] Holmes, in declaring against the moral posture of the Court and the usurpation of legislative prerogative, dissented: "But if there be any matter upon which civilized countries have agreed . . . it is the evil of premature and excessive child labor. I should have thought that if we were to introduce our own moral conceptions where in my opinion they do not belong, this was preeminently a case for upholding the exercise of all its powers by the United States. But I had thought that . . . this Court always had disavowed the right to intrude its judgment upon questions of policy or morals. It is not for this Court to pronounce when prohibition is necessary to regulation . . . as against the product of ruined lives."

Thus thwarted by the Supreme Court in its use of the commerce clause, Congress invoked its power to impose taxes as a device to end child labor. It simply imposed a federal tax

[5] Hammer v. Dagenhart, 247 U.S. 251 (1918).

on products made by children at such a high rate that it would be uneconomical to employ minors, even at the meager wages they were usually paid. The trick of using the power to tax in order to discourage activities that Congress did not like, rather than simply to produce revenue, was approved by the Court before. Congress successfully imposed taxes on the narcotics trade to discourage the use of drugs. It successfully imposed taxes on oleomargarine to help dairymen and discourage homemakers from using the butter substitute. Yet, when it came to the humane attempt to curb child labor, suddenly the Court held that the invocation of the power to tax for achieving desirable social ends was illegal.[6] It was not until the New Deal Court, almost a score of years later, that child labor was dealt an effective end through the Fair Labor Standards Act.

In a number of other cases the Supreme Court restricted the powers of Congress to tax the wealthy, even where the purpose actually was to raise revenue. They defeated the attempt by Congress to plug loopholes in the federal gift and estate tax laws.[7] They permitted avoidance of taxes when corporate profits went to stockholders as new stock rather than in money.[8] They ruled, in a self-serving decision, that under the Constitution Congress could not tax the salaries of federal judges.[9] In all these cases Holmes dissented. It is significant that Justice Holmes and his colleague Brandeis continued to pay their income taxes, in spite of the Court's ruling. A long time later, this decision was overruled by an objective and selfless Court.[10]

During Holmes' long tenure, the Supreme Court declared laws of Congress unconstitutional to make the law conform to their idea of public policy; and in many cases they achieved

[6] Bailey v. Drexel Furniture Co., 259 U.S. 20 (1922).

[7] Nichols v. Coolidge, 274 U.S. 531 (1927).

[8] Towne v. Eisner, 245 U.S. 418 (1918); Eisner v. Macomber, 252 U.S. 189 (1920).

[9] Evans v. Gore, 253 U.S. 245 (1920).

[10] O'Malley v. Woodrough, 307 U.S. 277 (1939).

the same result by interpretation. The Supreme Court applied the Sherman Anti-Trust Act to halt the merger of the Northern Pacific and Great Northern railroads.[11] It ostensibly broke up the monopolies by American Tobacco and Standard Oil.[12] But it refused to invoke the criminal penalties of the act. And it used the "rule of reason" in applying the Sherman Act so that only such "restraints of trade" as the Supreme Court deemed itself to be "unreasonable" were prohibited. The Court was quite polite to big business in the application of the Sherman Act, but labor unions were quickly stopped when the Justices thought their activities were in "restraint of trade."

The Clayton Act was passed by Congress in the administration of Woodrow Wilson to create the Federal Trade Commission. It was designed to stop price-fixing by fake competitors; to halt the cutting of prices until small competitors were forced out of business; to prevent the designed deception of consumers with dishonest branding or deceptive advertising. But the majority soon whittled the Clayton Act down to the size of the Sherman Act in its efficacy. The Court became the arbiter of "fair" conpetition. As the majority said in the decision,[13] which reversed a ruling of the Federal Trade Commission, the Court laid down the law to the Commission: "The words 'unfair competition' are not defined by the statute, and their exact meaning is in dispute. It is for the courts, not the commission, ultimately to determine as a matter of law what they include . . . The Act was certainly not intended to fetter free and fair competition as commonly understood and practiced by honorable opponents in trade." But the Supreme Court hacked away at the purposes of the Clayton Act so that little was left of the original intention of Congress to protect the consumer.

[11] Northern Securities Co. v. U.S., 193 U.S. 197 (1904).
[12] Standard Oil Co. v. U.S., 221 U.S. 1 (1911); U.S. v. American Tobacco Co., 221 U.S. 106 (1911).
[13] Federal Trade Commission v. Gratz, 253 U.S. 421 (1924).

In the Raladam case,[14] the Federal Trade Commission directed a pharmaceutical firm to desist from deceiving overweight persons with fraudulent advertising claims of weight-loss panaceas. The Supreme Court set aside the order of the Commission. Its reason was that, since all drugs for losing weight were sold through false claims in their advertising, none of the competitors of the firm was unfairly affected. So the Justices of the Supreme Court were quite ready to disregard the Federal Trade Commission, or the Interstate Commerce Commission, or any regulatory agency, when the expert opinions of the administrators came into conflict with the economic or social predilections of the business-oriented judges. And Holmes dissented from these assertions of judicial superiority over acts of Congress and determinations of federal administrative agencies.

The second group of problems that mark Holmes' individuality included the Court's application of the Fourteenth Amendment so as to invalidate state laws. These cases stimulated his most persistent dissents, as in the numerous cases in which the Supreme Court invalidated state statutes on the ground that legislation deprived some person of property without due process of law. There was a period from about the end of Chief Justice Fuller's tenure to the conclusion of World War I during which the Court relaxed its tight rein on state laws. Oregon legislation fixing the maximum hours of work for men and women was sustained,[15] although there were strong reactionary dissents. The majority, with Holmes expressing their view, upheld a Connecticut statute that permitted the sterilization of congenital idiots.[16] Wrote he: "Three generations of imbeciles are enough." It is noteworthy that the case did not deal with business.

In a case involving the right of the state legislature to protect a worker's right to unionize, the Court set the law

---

14 Federal Trade Commission v. Raladam Co., 283, U.S. 643 (1931).
15 Bunting v. Oregon, 243 U.S. 426 (1917).
16 Buck v. Bell, 274 U.S. 200 (1927).

aside,[17] just as it had set aside the congressional law that sought to protect railroad unions. Holmes complained in his dissent: "In present conditions a workman may not unnaturally believe that only by belonging to a union can he secure a contract that shall be fair to him. . . . If that belief, whether right or wrong, may be held by a reasonable man, it seems to me that it may be enforced by law in order to establish the equality of position . . . in which liberty of contract begins. Whether in the long run it is wise for the working men to enact legislation of this sort is not my concern, but I am strongly of the opinion that there is nothing in the Constitution of the United States to prevent it. . . ."

The increasing power of labor unions led to the enactment of state statutes that curbed the issuance of injunctions by courts in labor disputes. In the test case of such statutes, which deemed them illegal,[18] Holmes said in dissent: "Legislation may begin where an evil begins. If, as many intelligent people believe, there is more danger that the injunction will be abused in labor cases than elsewhere, I can feel no doubt of the power of the legislature to deny it. . . ."

The respect which Holmes had for the legislative work product came into conflict with his passion for human rights in a leading case.[19] During World War I, the country was inundated with anti-German passion, and several states in the Midwest passed laws prohibiting the teaching of German in grade schools maintained in the communities of recently emigrated Germans. The majority, through McReynolds, upheld the statute. Holmes dissented.

The third group of problems that point up Holmes' philosophy appeared in the field of individual rights. Holmes dissented in many cases. He disagreed when his colleagues refused to issue a writ of habeas corpus to save Leo Frank, a Northern Jew who had been convicted of a trumped-up

17 Coppage v. State of Kansas, 236 U.S. 1 (1915).
18 Truax v. Corrigan, 257 U.S. 312 (1921).
19 Meyer v. Nebraska, 262 U.S. 390 (1923).

murder charge by a hanging jury in a Southern town.[20] When the majority affirmed a federal district court judge who held a Toledo newspaper in contempt because it dared to complain of his decisions,[21] Holmes responded: "A judge of the United States is expected to be a man of ordinary firmness of character. . . . I confess that I cannot find . . . in the case anything which would have affected a mind of reasonable fortitude."

A narrow majority denied United States citizenship to several persons: to Rose Schwimmer,[22] a recognized pacifist; to a minister who had served as a chaplain in time of war; and to a religious lady who had been a nurse in World War I. The Court's denial was on the ground that none of these persons was willing to swear unqualifiedly that he would bear arms in future wars. Holmes sarcastically replied to his colleagues: "I would suggest that the Quakers have done their share to make the country what it is, that many citizens agree with the applicant's belief, and that I had not supposed hitherto that we regretted our inability to expel them because they believe more than some of us do in the teachings of the Sermon on the Mount."

And when, in 1928, the conviction of a bootlegger on evidence secured by wire-tapping was upheld by a majority of five,[23] Holmes disagreed. "It is desirable that criminals should be detected, and to that end all available evidence should be used. . . . We have to choose, and for my part, I think it less evil that some criminals should escape than that the government should play an ignoble part." The tapping of wires was underhanded in Holmes' view.

During the Bolshevik scare that came in the wake of World War I, a Communist named Gitlow was convicted of breaking the Criminal Anarchy Act passed by the New York

20 Frank v. Mangum, 237 U.S. 309 (1915).
21 Toledo Newspaper Co. v. U.S., 247 U.S. 402 (1918).
22 U.S. v. Schwimmer, 279 U.S. 644 (1929).
23 Olmstead v. U.S., 277 U.S. 438 (1928).

State legislature.[24] Gitlow published a pamphlet that urged writers to cast off their shackles, and it contained the usual diatribes against the existing system. In dissenting, Holmes said: "If in the long run the beliefs expressed in the proletarian dictatorship are destined to be accepted by the dominant forces in the community, the only meaning of free speech is that they be given their chance and have their way."

Holmes enunciated a test that permitted free speech to be curtailed when a "clear and present danger" exists. He expressed this concept in a case involving an antiwar agitator who had been sent to jail for advocating that men eligible for the military draft try to evade it.[25] This time, Justice Holmes wrote the opinion for the majority. He proposed a limitation that those who drafted the First Amendment had not expressed: "The question in every case is whether the words used are used in such circumstances and are of such a nature as to create a clear and present danger that they will bring about the substantive evils that Congress has a right to prevent. It is a question of proximity and degree." Holmes went on, "When a nation is at war, many things that might be said in times of peace are such a hindrance to its effort that their utterance will not be endured so long as men fight and that no court could regard them as protected by any constitutional right."

It was the application of his own clear-and-present-danger test that Holmes dissented against just one year later. Shortly before the conclusion of World War I, four uneducated men and a young lady had been busy scattering leaflets couched in the cliches of Marxian polemics. These five pacifists, born in Russia, were convicted and sentenced under the Espionage Act, which Congress had passed.[26]

Holmes found it necessary to protest.

24 People v. Gitlow, 268 U.S. 652 (1925).
25 Schenck v. U.S., 249 U.S. 47 (1919).
26 Abrams v. U.S., 250 U.S. 616 (1919).

In this case sentences of twenty years imprisonment have been imposed for the publishing of two leaflets that I believe the defendants had as much right to publish as the government to publish the Constitution of the United States now vainly invoked by them. . . . I think that we should be eternally vigilant against attempts to check the expression of opinions that we loathe and believe to be fraught with death, unless they so imminently threaten interference with the lawful and pressing purposes of the law that an immediate check is required to save the country.

The decisions of Justice Holmes provide vivid examples of how misleading it is to tag someone as a "liberal" or a "conservative." Contrary to a commonly accepted view, the less strict interpretation of the Constitution has been made by "conservative" judges in the defense of private property. There were many, many cases up to 1937 that safeguarded the rights of property without any specific mention of such language in the Constitution. In 1905, shortly after Holmes came to the Court, it was presented with a New York statute that limited the work week of bakers to sixty hours. The Court by a five-to-four vote held the law to be contrary to the Fourteenth Amendment, which provides that no state may "deprive any person of life, liberty or property without due process of law."[27] As the majority saw it, "liberty" included the so-called liberty of control, the freedom of a worker to sell and the employer to buy human labor as any other commodity. Their reasoning ran that any state restriction on hours of work unfairly took away the liberty of contract from workers and their bosses.

Justice Peckham wrote for the majority in *Lockner v. New York*, "Statutes of the nature of those under consideration limiting the hours in which grown and intelligent men labor to earn their living, are mere meddlesome interferences with the rights of the individual."

While Holmes believed as did the majority in the efficacy

[27] Lochner v. New York, 198 U.S. 45 (1909).

of the free enterprise system, he did not impute his own economic predilections into his reading of the Constitution. He wrote in his Lockner dissent:

> The 14th Amendment does not enact Mr. Herbert Spencer's "Social Statics," . . . A constitution is not intended to embody a particular economic theory, whether of paternalism and the organic relation of the citizen to the state or of laissez-faire. It is made for people of fundamentally differing views, and the accident of our finding certain opinions natural and familiar, or novel and even shocking, ought not to conclude our judgment upon the question whether statutes embodying them conflict with the Constitution of the United States.

For three decades Holmes shared a bench with judges determined to hold back the federal and state governments from interfering with free competition or the effects of free competition. A memorable case[28] tested a law passed by Congress prohibiting the shipment of goods that were produced by children across state lines. Up until the passage of this law, a state could take no action against child-labor employers because in those jurisdictions where minors were most profitably exploited (factories, mills, and mines), the pressure against reform was greatest; where it did not matter, regulation was possible. So, using its power to regulate interstate commerce, Congress intervened and passed the antichild-labor law.

There is explicit language in the Constitution giving Congress the authority to regulate interstate commerce. Since the days of John Marshall, the power of Congress was said to be absolute. Yet, in 1918, the majority of the Court held that Congress could not forbid the shipment of articles manufactured by children, or traffic in anything else, unless the object itself was "evil." Holmes was quick to point out that just a short time before his brethen did sustain limitations on com-

---

[28] Hammer v. Dagenhart, 247 U.S. 251 (1918).

merce involving intoxicating beverages. Wrote Holmes: "It is not for this Court to say that it is permissible as against strong drink, and not as against the product of ruined lives."

But the conservatives or strict constructionists on the Court read the due process provision of the Fourteenth Amendment in order to shackle the state legislatures, which thought it important to promulgate safety regulations or laws lessening the rigors of the unrestrained economic system. Examples may be cited by the dozens. For instance, in 1925 the Court threw out a Pennsylvania statute that forbade the use of shredded rags in mattresses.[29] A few years later, a law passed in New York fixing the profits of ticket brokers "scalpers" was likewise declared unconstitutional.[30]

Advancing years did not make Holmes myopic with respect to seeing legal reality. At age 89, in 1930, Holmes dissented from a decision that hampered the states who wished to tax holders of bonds:[31] "As the decisions now stand, I see hardly any limits but the sky to the invalidating of those state rights if they happen to strike a majority of this court as for any reason undesirable. I cannot believe that the amendment was intended to give us carte blanche to embody our economic or moral beliefs in its prohibitions."

It seems noteworthy that today Holmes' dissents have become the law, and that the views of the majorities in these cases have simply vanished. The significant point is that Holmes himself employed a double standard in reading the Constitution. He chastized his colleagues for construing the Constitution in the light of their economic predispositions; Holmes would not follow their approach in the economic sphere. At the same time, when he was faced with a problem of freedom of expression, Holmes read the Constitution in the light of his own view of what the Constitution means.

The Abrams case[32] of 1919 serves to illustrate his stand-

29 Weaver v. Palmer Brothers Co., 270 U.S. 402 (1926).
30 Tyson and Brother v. Barton, 273 U.S. 418 (1927).
31 Baldwin v. Missouri, 281 U.S. 586 (1930).
32 Abrams v. U.S., 250 U.S. 616 (1919).

ards. Five rather ineffectual Socialists had been found guilty during World War I of violating the Espionage Act. Their crime consisted of publishing two antiwar handbills. The majority of the Court rejected the claim of the defendants to protection of free speech afforded by the First Amendment. Holmes dissented, joined by Justice Brandeis. Said Holmes:

> Persecution for the expression of opinions . . . seems to me to be perfectly logical. If you have no doubt of your premises of your power and want a certain result with all your heart, you naturally express your wishes in law and keep away all opposition. . . .
>
> But when men have realized that time has upset many fighting faults, they may come to believe even more that the ultimate good desired is better reached by free trade in ideas —that the best test of truth is the power of the thought to get itself accepted in the competition of the market, and that truth is the only ground upon which their wishes safely can be carried out. That at any rate is the theory of our Constitution. It is an experiment, as all life is an experiment. . . .
>
> I think that we should be eternally vigilant against attempts to check the expression of opinions that we loathe and believe to be fraught with death.

Certainly, there is no word or phrase or clause in the Constitution that expressly authorizes this philosophy. This distinction between the sanctity of free speech and the vulnerability of free trade to government controls was not specifically found in the Constitution but rather in the thoughts and mind of Oliver Wendell Holmes, Jr.

By the time Holmes stepped down from his seat, the country was in the throes of a deep economic crisis. Oliver Wendell Holmes was respected by his judicial colleagues, although they did not often follow his lead. To the new generation of "New Dealers" who came to Washington on the coattails of President Franklin Delano Roosevelt, Holmes was the "great dissenter." His words and his vision of America endured.

III

INDUSTRIAL AMERICA AND THE GREAT DEPRESSION

Louis D. Brandeis

SOCIAL REFORMER WITH A BALANCE SHEET

JUSTICES HOLMES AND BRANDEIS, STARTING FROM DISSIMILAR milieus and with different temperaments, somehow had legal philosophies that were quite compatible. Together they represented a judicial point of view different from that held by the majority on the Court in the early part of this century. Their jurisprudence, ultimately triumphant, rejected the severe limitations that the Court laid down on the authority of government to deal with the new social and economic problems of America. In their classic dissents, Holmes and Brandeis challenged the majority with their conviction that the Supreme Court lacked the authority to dictate the laws passed by Congress or state legislatures. The Justices, said Brandeis, did not have the right to declare "a law unconstitutional simply because they considered a law unwise." The business of the Court, "is not to decide whether the view taken by the legislature is a wise view, but whether a body of men could reasonably hold such a view." The question is whether the legislation as applied is so clearly arbitrary that reasonable members of the legislature could not have believed the law to be needed or appropriate for the well-being of the public.

To Justices Holmes and Brandeis, the majority views in

the cases that denied the legislatures the right to forbid child labor or to regulate working conditions froze economic laissez-faire into a matter of constitutional right. Brandeis complained that his judicial colleagues were "largely deaf and blind to the ameliorations which industrial America made necessary." They complacently applied eighteenth century concepts of liberty of the individual and sacredness of private property. Early nineteenth century scientific half-truths like "the survival of the fittest," which translated into practice meant "the devil take the hindmost," were fixed by judicial sanction into a moral law.

Just as Justice McReynolds had strong economic convictions, so, too, Brandeis had pronounced economic views. From his experience in the world of business, he had come to espouse a philosophy of economic democracy, a fear of the coercive power of concentrated business—the "curse of bigness," as he called it. It is not surprising, therefore, that he joined with his brethren to declare the National Recovery Act unconstitutional.[1] He saw tinkering by government with the machinery of the economic system valid, "if it did not create a corporate political system." Thus, in his dissent when the Court set aside a statute of Oklahoma regulating the ice business,[2] he said: "It is one of the happy incidents of the federal system that a single courageous state may, if its citizens choose, serve as a laboratory, and try novel social and economic experiments without risk to the role of the country."

The life of Brandeis is one of paradox. During his life he complained of poor health and bad eyesight. Yet apparently there was nothing organically wrong with his eyes. And in spite of his complaints about bad health he was athletic, working at a pace that would have destroyed a lesser mortal. He continued to pursue his physical and mental labors with only slight restriction until he died, in his middle eighties. He was not poor. Although he never lived on more than ten

[1] Schecter Poultry Corp. v. United States, 295 U.S. 495 (1935).
[2] New State Ice Company v. Liebmann, 285 U.S. 262 (1932).

thousand dollars a year, his earnings were very substantial and his estate consisted of approximately three million dollars.

His parents were immigrants who were of substantial means both in their European home and in Louisville, Kentucky, where they settled. Brandeis himself was on social terms with the most influential people in Louisville, later in Boston, and then in the entire country. "Cultivate the society of men, particularly men of affairs. Lose no opportunity of being acquainted with them." He never was part of hoipolloi. Brandeis was far from being the radical he is pictured as. Although he fought the evils of big business he did very well financially himself. He wished to preserve the economic system rather than destroy it. While he was at different times a Democrat, a Populist, and a Republican, he was much attuned politically and knew how to use politics.

Probably the most widely held mystique about Brandeis relates to his Jewishness. Popularly, he has always been closely identified as a Jew. Yet one of his classmates at Harvard Law School, William B. Cushing, wrote of him in a letter home in 1878, ". . . hails from Louisville, is not a college graduate, but has spent some years in Europe, has a rather foreign look and is currently believed to have some Jewish blood in him, although you would not suppose it from his appearance—tall, well-made, dark, beardless, and with the brightest eyes I ever saw."

Neither parent professed formal religion. They held no membership in either church or synogogue. Fredricka, his mother, said ". . . I do not believe that sins can be expiated by going to divine service and observing this or that formula. . . . Love, virtue and truth are the foundation upon which the education of a child must be based. . . . And this is my justification for bringing up my children without any definite religious beliefs."

Brandeis' ancestral background included no formal religious observances, no nationalist leanings, no cultural interests, such as knowledge of Hebrew or the Talmud. Several members of his family, on both sides, married gentiles. His private law practice and social life were never identified with any one race or sect or interest. His friends were indiscriminately Jews and gentiles. He never attended synagogue services or other religious services. He was married by Felix Adler, the founder of the Ethical Culture Society. Yet, at the height of his career, Brandeis came to Zionism with a conviction and dedication that did not leave him until his death. He became converted to the underlying ideals of Judaism. In speaking before the Menorah Society of Columbia University, Brandeis stressed the Jewish stern sense of duty, as in the Puritans of old, inspired by the prophets; their high intellectual achievements; their submission to leadership, as distinguished from authority; and especially their developed community sense. He became one of the leaders of the world Zionist movement. Despite all trials and throughout lagging years, Zionism for him was no dream but a beautiful reality.

The life of Louis Dembitz Brandeis was indeed fascinating. If Brandeis knew how to use freedom, it was because his parents, Adolph Brandeis and Fredricka Dembitz Brandeis, knew how to find it. His parents fled from Bohemia during the ravages of the revolution of 1848. They both were of middle-class, cultured families, but they came to America motivated by the knowledge that in Europe they could only look backward. Adolph came alone to America to pave the way for his family, as was the pattern for the hundreds of thousands of immigrant families. Immigrants took to the country enthusiastically after the repressions of Germany. Adolph tried farming, unsuccessfully, and then tried manufacturing in Indiana, also unsuccessfully. Later, with his family in the United States, Adolph moved to Louisville, Kentucky, where the family prospered in business. Louis Brandeis, one of four children, was born in 1856. His early life was spent in surroundings of comfort provided by his father's financial success. This success was given a boost by the Civil War. In

1872, some financial setbacks did not prevent Adolph from taking his family on a trip to Europe. Louis spent three years studying in Germany, demonstrating there the superb scholarship that he was to show the rest of his life. This stay also convinced him that freedom was a priceless heritage. "I was a terrible little individualist in those days, and the German paternalism got on my nerves."

On his return to America, he entered Harvard Law School and achieved a brilliant scholastic record. Upon graduation he had an opportunity to teach and did, but he wanted the challenge and excitement of practice. He went back to Louisville to practice, although he had many other fine offers. Later, he came back to Boston to enter a law practice there. From the time he enrolled at Harvard and during his practice, Brandeis met the "right people" socially, politically, and financially. He had only successes. At this young age he desired financial independence, and he systematically was able to amass a fortune through practice and investments. In 1890 he married Alice Goldmark, the daughter of R. Joseph Goldmark, a distinguished scientist and outstanding participant in the Austrian revolution of 1848. He, like the Dembitz and Brandeis families, had fled to America. The Goldmarks were well-off financially and lived comfortably in an elegant area of New York City. The marriage united two very compatible people. They had two children, Elizabeth and Susan. Alice and Louis together widened the circle of friends that the bachelor had formed among the Boston elite.

The Brandeises lived simply but well. They had ample financial resources. They took care of their health and enjoyed vacation spots. Brandeis' practice flourished. He dealt with the heads of large corporations, since his forte was financial organization. In addition to his academic, lawyer, and business friends, his circle of political acquaintances was enormous; the governor and the mayor were easily accessible to him. Although he did not participate in politics in the traditional way, he managed to place his candidates in responsible positions and, frequently, his policies with the right officeholders.

In the 1880's he became involved in various civic movements in Boston. His attack on corruption in the Massachusetts legislature and the undue influence of liquor lobbyists furnishes a good lesson for today: "You can remove liquor dealers from politics by a very simple device—make the liquor laws reasonable." Next he turned to the care of paupers in Boston, and fought to have them treated humanely instead of as obsolescent objects. Brandeis as the lawyer for the people was concerned only with the possible, not the ultimate, utopia. He was no wild-eyed agitator. Financially secure, he organized his law practice so that he could be free to work for feasible reforms, an interest that never abated until his death. Brandeis took on the great corporate giants and beat them at their own game. He understood how the economic system operated—always relying on solid facts and figures—and he worked to strengthen rather than tear down. He fought, successfully, the grants to transportation companies, and to their cousins in the fuel utilities, the gas and electric groups, and the insurance interests, whose assets ran into millions. He fought and beat J. P. Morgan, Sr., who used the vast resources of the New Haven Railroad in the days when it was a colossus, as a powerful financial weapon.

As his activities were making him known as a public benefactor, his enemies were seeking to ruin his reputation and prestige. They could not say that he was not able; the facts refuted that. They therefore sought to make him out as being unethical. The leading episodes that they singled out were the United Shoe Machinery conflict, the fight of the New York and New England Railroad, and several others. The anti-Brandeis feeling charged that in three cases the lawyer maintained a private position that was different from his public position. He was accused of using his inside information for personal profit. Of course, he was later vindicated. Brandeis was not made more popular by his aloofness, by his refusal to back away from a fight, or by the prejudice created in others by the fact of his being Jewish. One of his supporters later tried to explain the hostility to him by putting it this way: "By way of explanation, I must say that we have what I may call an aristocracy of the Boston Bar. I do not use the word at all offensively; on the contrary, they are high minded, able, distinguished men. But they can not, I think, consider with equanimity, the selection of someone for a position on the great court of the country from that community who is not typical, hereditary Bostonian."

Gradually, the sphere of his activities shifted from Boston to Washington, since the tentacles of industry, transportation, and finance extended across state lines and interstate commerce was the concern of the federal government. There, in 1897, the glare of the national spotlight was turned on him when he argued for consumers amid the jeers of tariff-supporting legislators. The next time he spoke up, the entire legal community applauded his skill. This occurred in 1908, when he presented to the United States Supreme Court his brief in *Muller v. Oregon,* a case involving a state statute restricting the working hours of women. For the first time, a case was based on real facts of how industry operates in America, rather than on dull legal precedents. Brandeis brought law and life together. His brief documented the working conditions of women, and the effect that such work had on the physical and emotional well-being of the female. Brandeis revolutionized the art of advocacy, and in doing so changed the role of the attorney. Said he, "the lawyer who had not studied economics and sociology is very apt to become a public enemy."

The Muller case brought Brandeis to the center of the national stage. The Ballinger-Pinchot controversy kept him there. In this imbroglio, Brandeis sought to protect national resources. In 1909 William Howard Taft succeeded Teddy Roosevelt as President. He pledged to continue Roosevelt's conservation policies. Taft appointed Richard A. Ballinger as

Secretary of the Interior. As a lawyer in private practice, Ballinger represented corporations in suits involving public lands. Because of Ballinger's pro-business background, Pinchot, Chief of Forests and the United States Department of Agriculture, was afraid that Roosevelt's conservation policies would be overthrown. A fight developed in Congress relating to the sale of certain public land in Alaska. Brandeis took on the Secretary of the Interior, the Attorney General, and, finally, the President himself. In the hearings that ensued, he showed that they were all lying or at least concealing the facts relating to the transaction. Brandeis handled the arguments dramatically and, needless to say, effectively. Ballinger was cleared, in a manner of speaking, but he finally resigned anyway. The fact that his successor was a friend of Brandeis demonstrated the increasing influence of the man.

After this crusade, Brandeis took up the job of establishing a system of regulation of conditions in the garment industry to New York. For the first time, Brandeis actually came face to face with the immigrants who populated the teeming Jewish ghetto. Brandeis was moved. He proposed the "preferential union shop" as a temporary solution to labor conditions in the garment industry.

From 1910 to 1916 the railroads asked the Interstate Commerce Commission to grant increases in freight rates east of the Mississippi. This measure increased costs by the millions to those shipping goods. A committee was set up to fight these raises, and Brandeis became counsel. He dug into the facts, and was able to show that the railroads did not know how to compute rates. He then demonstrated how, by applying principles of scientific management, the railroad could save millions of dollars without an increase. He won, and as a result made new friends throughout the country; but he also made new and powerful enemies.

From then on, Brandeis battled the trusts. Congress began a series of committee investigations directed toward the pernicious power of big business. It seemed now that the federal government was finally realizing that something was wrong with American industry. Something was at the root of the widespread labor unrest. Congress wanted answers, and it wanted viable remedies to the problems. Congress turned to Brandeis. By now, according to one observer, "Brandeis was the most liked and most hated man at the Bar in America." He had exposed the steel trust. He had examined and demonstrated how, by manipulation of the money system, the financial interests actually owned America. His analysis, *Other People's Money and How the Bankers Use It,* was published in 1914.

During 1910 and 1911 there was considerable political agitation as a result of strikes. The status of President Taft was badly shaken by the Ballinger investigation. Brandeis was convinced that to avoid socialism the federal government had to intervene to curb excesses of business and labor. He decided to support Robert LaFollette for the Presidency. Friends, with similar ideas, they had met before. Brandeis threw himself into the fight for the nomination but LaFollette lost. Brandeis did not feel he could follow Taft again (although he had voted for him before), nor could he identify with what he saw as the pseudo-progressivism of Teddy Roosevelt. The Democrats nominated Wilson. Brandeis urged that all progressives support Wilson. Wilson called him in, and Brandeis threw himself into the campaign on the stump and pulling together issues.

Upon Wilson's election the rumor spread that Brandeis was going to be appointed Attorney General. He began to receive congratulatory letters. There is no question but that Wilson was seriously considering him for that position before Brandeis' old enemies began attacking him for his fees, his ethics and, in addition, his religion. The opposition was very vocal. An example of the type of bigotry in the minds of important Americans at that time is illustrated in a statement made by one enemy: "Brandeis is Gompers, Goldman and Gyp the Blood, rolled into one, and given a degree from Harvard.

. . . Brandeis does not represent America." Yielding to this pressure, Wilson appointed James C. McReynolds as Attorney General. Yet, for the next few years, Brandeis was a vital part of the Wilson administration. He advised the President and helped him when the Federal Reserve Act was drafted. He headed the President's drive against the financial trusts by planning the role of the Federal Trade Commission. He was instrumental in the appointment of outstanding political officials.

How did Brandeis manage to do all this? He strictly managed his time, budgeted few enough hours for his recreation and his family so that he had time for business. Parenthetically, it is amusing to note that, in 1912, Brandeis gave some interesting advice on the rising cost of living:

> More families are ruined through the faults and extravagances of the woman of the household than through the husband's failure to increase his earning capacity. . . . The woman who spends the bulk of her time running to this or that club or card meeting will soon bankrupt her husband, unless he is a Croesus, if indeed she doesn't kill him with indigestion beforehand. . . . The little struggling clerk must bedeck his wife with bizarre clothes so that he can take her out and impress upon those who behold her in all her magnificence that he is making big money, that this excursion is nothing out of the ordinary in his life, and that he is a "big spender"! That is the rock upon which domesticity so often founders.

Sometime in 1912 he became attracted to Zionism. He joined the Federation of American Zionism and rapidly became a world leader in the movement. He was certainly influential in the formulation of the Balfour Declaration by which the British pledged a home state for the Jews. His role was far from passive or honorific. He plunged into the maelstrom of the internal politics of the Zionist movement. He feuded with Weizmann and others. In short, Brandeis, as always, was totally committed. Zionism remained an abiding interest with him.

On Friday, January 28, 1916, President Wilson dropped a bombshell by announcing his appointment of Louis Brandeis to the Supreme Court. The press was livid. It became apparent that the Senate would not confirm without a vigorous fight. A petition from fifty-five Bostonians, including the President of Harvard, said that Brandeis did not have the judicial temperament and capacity, the reputation, or the confidence of the people. The American Bar Association launched an all-out attack against him. After a bitter struggle, he was confirmed because of President Wilson's firm stand and the many leaders who flocked to his defense.

Brandeis sat on the High Court for almost a quarter of a century, from 1916 to 1939. For most of that period, Chief Justice Taft presided as the guardian of the rights of property. The majority of the Justices employed a double standard. They were fierce in their determination to prevent the states from interfering with business, but they were quite prepared to permit the states to limit the freedoms of expression. Brandeis was his own man in each of these two areas.

He was not afraid to permit legislatures to experiment with the regulation of business activities. *Truax v. Corrigan,*[3] decided on the validity of an Arizona law that forbade its courts from issuing labor injunctions except in special cases. The owners of a restaurant in Bisbee, Arizona, sought an injunction to prohibit workers from boycotting and picketing their establishment. The Arizona court denied the injunction on the ground that the law deprived the workers of property without due process of law and the equal protection of laws as granted under the Fourteenth Amendment. The Supreme Court of the United States affirmed this decision by a five-to-four vote. Justice Brandeis dissented, warning his brethren not to "close the door to experiment within the law."

He believed that the legislature should be allowed latitude in its regulation of business, and thus supported a law that fixed the commissions to be paid to fire insurance

[3] Truax v. Corrigan, 257 U.S. 312 (1921).

agents.[4] Brandeis was ready to permit legislatures to delegate authority to administrative experts to make the difficult judgments that complex regulatory systems required. He believed that the Court should respect such expertise.[5]

While Brandeis approved of the economic philosophy of the Sherman Act, he did not reject private arrangements among businessmen that would stimulate reasonable competition. In 1921 the Court was presented with a case involving an association of about four hundred lumbermen who produced about thirty percent of all the hardwood lumber annually produced in America. These association members were required to submit information about their sales, production, and inventory to the assocition statistician. On the basis of this information, members were directed to control their production. This helped raise or maintain prices. The Court held that this action violated the antitrust laws.[6] Brandeis dissented. "The evidence in this case, far from establishing an illegal restraint of trade, prevents, in my opinion, an instance of commendable effort by concerns engaged in chaotic industry to make possible its intelligent conduct under competitive conditions."

He saw that giant business corporations could compete with the state itself, and had the capacity to stamp out small competitors, cooperatives, and other forms of self-help. His enthusiasm for small business was illustrated by his dissent in the Quaker City Cab case.[7] There, the cab corporation objected to a tax, imposed on them by Pennsylvania, which was relatively larger than that imposed on competitors operating as sole proprietorships or partnerships. Justice Butler, for the majority of six, declared the statute constitutional, under the equal protection of laws clause of the Fourteenth Amendment.

Brandeis deserved to be saved from his friends as well as

[4] O'Gorman v. Young & Hartford Fire Ins. Co., 282 U.S. 251 (1931).

[5] Federal Trade Commission v. Gratz, 253 U.S. 421 (1920); St. Joseph Stock Yards Co. v. United States, 298 U.S. 38 (1936).

[6] American Column and Lumber Co. v. United States, 257 U.S. 377 (1921).

[7] Quaker City Cab Co. v. Pennsylvania, 277 U.S. 389 (1928).

his foes. The most impressive quality in his career was restless curiosity, or thirst for knowledge. He sought knowledge to put it to use, not to store it away. He studied the past to understand the present. His expert handling of widely dispersed and distorted facts is well known. What is not so well known is his capacity for indignation and his compassion for the underdog.

He did not write easily or brilliantly like Holmes, but, when he wrote of freedom of speech, his words were vivid and emotional. Brandeis' temperament and his mind were adventurous. This same daring permeated his social ideas and actions. He believed in social experimentation. He believed in freedom for the individual and that its attainment was the responsibility of the community. To him each person was sacred, but he understood the shortcomings of people. He did not envisage utopia for all, but he did see a better life possible for every citizen. Once, when his daughter Susan complained of society, a visitor heard him say, "My dear, if you will just start with the idea that this is a hard world, it will all be much simpler." While his particular talent was facts and figures and finance, this was sublimated by a fertile mind, which made him a social innovator.

While Brandeis respected the right of legislative bodies, whether federal or state, to regulate economic areas of concern, he was less amenable to permitting governmental agencies to interfere with the free expression of ideas or individual liberty. He was ready to protect war protestors.[8] When federal law enforcers tapped the telephone wires of persons suspected of conspiracy to violate the Volstead Act, the majority, speaking through Chief Justice Taft, rejected the claims of the defendants that such procedure involved an illegal search and seizure and violated the protection against self-incrimination. Since these wires were not tapped in their homes or offices, explained Taft, there was neither search nor seizure. Brandeis vehemently disagreed. "The greatest

[8] Schaefer v. United States, 251 U.S. 466 (1920); Pierce v. United States, 252 U.S. 239 (1929); cf. Whitney v. California, 274 U.S. 357 (1927).

dangers to liberty lurk in insidious encroachment by men of zeal, well-meaning, but without understanding."[9]

Brandeis and Holmes, two great dissenters, were linked together by friendship, judicial restraint toward legislative action, and a warm humanism. But in the last analysis, Brandeis acted on a factual foundation where Holmes operated from moral absolutes. "I hate facts," Holmes once declared. Yet, starting from such separate premises, the two jurists generally stood together in conclusion. Brandeis did not pull together his philosophy in a unified statement as did Holmes or Cardozo. To evaluate Brandeis, one must make a case-by-case study, for his beliefs were largely expresssed by his decisions.

Less than twenty percent of his opinions were written in dissent; the remainder were in support of the majority views. He is remembered for his dissents because they so strikingly stated views inconsistent with his time, although many of these advanced views came to be law later in the jurist's lifetime. As he grew old, his deep set brooding eyes, his strong Lincolnesque features, his unruly eyebrows and hair made him a model for a prophet of the Old Testament. President Roosevelt referred to him as "my dear Isaiah," and this was echoed by the clerks. Brandeis died at age eighty-five.

Brandeis' thought is a great legacy for today. In one of the great opinions[10] of the Supreme Court dealing with free speech, Louis D. Brandeis wrote that those American revolutionaries in 1776 believed that "the deliberative forces should prevail over the arbitrary" in this land. They incorporated into the Constitution what they conceived to be the "path of safety" for the American republic. "The opportunity to discuss freely supposed grievances and proposed remedies." Our forebears were committed to "the power of reason as applied through public discussion."

[9] Olmstead v. United States, 277 U.S. 438 (1928).
[10] Whitney v. California, 274 U.S. 357 (1927).

–8–

Charles Evans Hughes

DEFENDER OF THE FAITH

IN 1930 WHEN CHIEF JUSTICE TAFT DIED, THE SUPREME COURT was torn into two factions. One group believed it had the job of stopping legislative attempts that met the needs of the depressed economy and the growing complex society. Taft, Butler, McReynolds, Van Devanter, Sutherland, and Sanford were in this group. The minority group, including Holmes, Brandeis, and Stone, urged that judicial review be more restricted, permitting the legislatures to experiment in an attempt to meet the pressing problems of the day.

In the face of public discontent with the big-business orientation of the Court's majority, President Herbert Hoover chose Charles Evans Hughes to fill the Chief Justice opening. The choice appeared excellent. The *Literary Digest*, in its issue of February 15, 1930, chortled: "The chorus of approval is as emphatic as it is unanimous." Hughes had been an Associate Justice of the Supreme Court from 1910 to 1916, before he resigned to seek the Presidency. In his earlier tenure as an appointee of President Taft he established his fine qualities of character and judicial diplomacy. In view of these admirable characteristics, Hughes advised Hoover: "I don't want a fight over the nomination. . . . If you are convinced that the nomination will be confirmed by the Senate without a scrap, I will accept it. But I don't want any trouble about it." The President and George Norris, Chairman of the Senate Judiciary Committee and maverick Republican from Nebraska, were reassuring. Yet, within a matter of days, Norris himself reversed his stand. Norris and others threw the nomination into a "flaming controversy" by challenging the propriety of Hughes' having resigned from the Supreme Court in 1916 to try to run for President. Norris charged that "no man in public life so exemplifies the influence of powerful combinations in the political and financial world as does Mr. Hughes." Nevertheless, Hughes was confirmed by a Senate vote of fifty-two to twenty-six.

The very next day, mavericks in the Senate attacked the power of the Court. They proposed denuding it of its power to decide whether laws violated the Constitution and also providing that the Justices be elected by the people. The diatribes became increasingly shrill when President Hoover then submitted the name of John J. Parker, a Republican from North Carolina, a sitting federal district court judge, to fill the vacancy caused by the death of Justice Sanford. The Senate rejected Parker. President Hoover then nominated the lawyer who had served as prosecutor in the Teapot Dome scandal, Owen J. Roberts, and he was confirmed by the Senate.

Early in the year 1933, the basic elements of President Roosevelt's national legislative program were beginning to emerge. The legality of many of the measures was yet to be tested. Those problems were dumped into the lap of Chief Justice Charles Evans Hughes. In spite of the great controversy over the confirmation of Hughes, surprisingly little attention was given to his actual views or to the essential nature of the man.

Charles Evans Hughes was born on April 11, 1862, in Glens Falls, New York, to a Baptist minister and a former school teacher. He was the object of his parents' almost constant attention; their admonitions and instruction and preaching became internalized in him as character traits. The little boy's play time was devoted to instruction and moral uplifting. His story book was the Bible and his fairy tales were the miracles described in the holy scriptures. Charles learned group participation by reading in the family circle from the New Testament and Psalms (starting at age five). When Charles was only eight years old, his father gave him a Greek New Testament.

Since he was an only child, his parents thought that it could be beneficial if they adopted a child to provide a companion. When young Hughes got wind of this, he "marched into the room" and said that he thought it would be a "mistake." Having a companion, said he, was less important to him than learning.

Thoroughly immersed in his religious training by 1881, he entered Brown University. Although he wrote home that "I try to follow your injunctions in regard to everything," he was aware of the wicked and tempting world that called him. But his father advised against young Hughes' desire to find a roommate because it would discourage the boy from throwing "yourself on your knees frequently and whenever you were inclined to do so. . . ." The parents' efforts to encourage "pious submission to their counsel" succeeded. Their offspring was erudite, polished, urbane, disciplined, organized, and painstakingly thorough.

But Charles Evans Hughes was much more. He became an outstanding teacher of law and lawyer. He was a superb investigator and outstanding governor. His careers would have been outstanding for any six men: Associate Justice of the United States Supreme Court; candidate for President on the Republican ticket; Secretary of State under Harding; governor of New York State; judge of the World Court; Chief Justice of the United States Supreme Court.

In 1905, appointed counsel to a New York State legislative committee investigating utility rates and then to a committee investigating insurance companies, he was dedicated to unearthing the facts. And under his governorship, New York State led the nation in its concern for social amelioration. This record was compatible with his masterful presentation of the views of five socialist members of the New York State Assembly who had been thrown out in 1920 because of their political ideas. Yet, just a few years later, as Secretary of State under President Harding, he represented an unyielding, limited, and cold imperialism in defense of the American oil interests abroad in dealings with Russia and Mexico.

It is as Chief Justice, however, that Hughes left his deepest mark on American history. Perhaps this term was so significant because it occurred at the critical point when the role of the Court was being reevaluated, both in relation to the legislative and executive branches and in relation to the entire American system.

In 1934 the Court was faced with the issue of the validity of a law passed by the Minnesota legislature giving its courts the power to stay mortgage foreclosure proceedings.[1] It was deep in the Depression, and farmers in debt sought to invoke the provisions of the act. Bankers and other creditors challenged the law on grounds cited in the Constitution—that is, that no state shall pass a law "impairing the obligation of contract." Chief Justice Hughes, writing for the five-man majority, upheld the law on the theory that the moratorium statute did not impair the obligation of the mortgages in Minnesota, it only delayed the remedy. Justice Sutherland in his dissent countered by arguing: "If the provisions of the Constitution be not upheld when they pinch as well as when they comfort, they may as well be abandoned."

The cutthroat competition that was spawned by the national economic Depression brought about other legislation similar in philosophy to the Minnesota moratorium. In New York, the legislature passed a law that established a milk control board with authority to fix prices. Then, an unknown grocer in Rochester, Leo Nebbia, sold two quarts of milk and

[1] Home Building & Loan Ass'n v. Blaisdell, 290 U.S. 398 (1934).

one loaf of bread, all for eighteen cents. The price of a quart of milk alone was set by the board at eight cents. Nebbia was convicted for violating the milk price control law, and the case ultimately reached the Supreme Court.[2] Just as in the mortgage moratorium case, a cleavage of five to four manifested itself. Chief Justice Hughes and Justice Roberts teamed up with Stone, Brandeis, and Cardozo to uphold the law.

And on May 27, 1936, the keystone of Roosevelt's program to combat the Depression, the National Industrial Recovery Act, was declared unconstitutional by a unanimous Court in the "sick chicken" case.[3] The National Industrial Recovery Act marked an attempt to promote industry-wide agreements on wages, hours, and trade practices in an effort to prevent cutthroat competition and restore economic stability. These agreements took the form of codes, proposed by trade associations and approved by the President. The only standards were that the associations be representative, that membership should not be unfairly restricted, and that they should not promote monopolies. A New York poultry dealer challenged his conviction for violating the "Live Poultry Code" for New York City. The decision was predicated on the grounds that Congress had gone beyond its authority to regulate interstate commerce by delegating legislative power to an outside agency.

Just a year later the Court set aside the Bituminous Coal Conservation Act, which was passed by Congress to stabilize the coal industry. The law established two sets of provisions: one was designed to regularize conditions of work; the other had the object of supporting prices. The draftsmen of the act, anticipating challenge, took the trouble to recite in the statute that these objectives were separable, so that one could stand alone if the other set of provisions was held illegal. Yet, the majority of five, through Sutherland, decided in *Carter v.*

[2] Nebbia v. New York, 291 U.S. 502 (1934).
[3] Schecter Poultry Corp. v. U.S., 295 U.S. 495 (1935).

Carter Coal Company[4] that the entire act was inseparable as a single scheme, and invalid. Hughes agreed in a concurring opinion, which rested on the idea that the act was directed at the regulation of industry inside the state, rather than the protection of interstate commerce. Thus, it was by a six-to-three vote that the Agricultural Adjustment Act was invalidated.

It has been reported that Chief Justice Hughes was prepared to vote either way in this case. Attorney General Homer Cummings informed the other members of the Cabinet that "if Justice Roberts had been in favor of sustaining the act, the Chief Justice would have cast his vote that way also." Hughes' theory was that he would vote in such a way as to reassure the public of the Court's stability by making the vote six to three regardless of what the decision was. But if that was his intention, he erred grievously. Public confidence in the Court did not increase and the uncertainty was only aggravated.

Finally, in what was described by Justice Stone as "the most disastrous term of its history," the Court invalidated a law passed by the State of New York fixing a minimum wage for women.[5] Hughes dissented from the majority opinion on the solitary ground that he found "material difference" between the New York case now before the Court and a 1923 case invalidating a similar law, covering the District of Columbia, decided by Justice Sutherland. As a result, both lines of precedent stood intact, and fictitious "stability" was achieved.

These narrowly decided cases, reflecting the economic despair, political contention, and the public frustration that threatened to rend America asunder, in the words of President Roosevelt, "fairly completely undermined," his programs. The battle lines were drawn. Former President Hoover praised "almighty God for the Constitution and the Supreme

[4] Carter v. Carter Coal Co., 298 U.S. 238 (1936).
[5] Morehead v. New York *ex rel.* Tipaldo, 298 U.S. 587 (1936).

Court." Chief Justice Hughes, proud of his role in preserving what he saw as judicial stability, bragged to the American Law Institute, "the Supreme Court is still functioning."

The President, his Cabinet, and a wave of public clamor arose against "judicial usurpation." Roosevelt spoke out, criticizing Hughes and charging that, "the Supreme Court is in politics, with particular reference to the political activities of the Chief Justice, himself." Finally, in January of 1937 President Roosevelt proposed direct confrontation: "The time for action with respect to the Supreme Court really cannot be postponed, and unpleasant as it is, I think we have to have it." Instead of resorting to formal amendment of the Constitution so as to control the Court, the President decided to ask Congress to increase the size of the Court and then to appoint Justices more sympathetic with his goals.

Paradoxically, President Roosevelt's legislative scheme to reorganize the Supreme Court somehow evoked an entirely new public reaction and an unanticipated one. The members of Congress, the officials, the newspapers, and civic associations that had been attacking the Court now sprang to its defense. Senator Burton K. Wheeler headed up the opposition to Roosevelt's "court-packing" plan. Chief Justice Hughes prepared a careful analysis and well-reasoned statement refuting the ostensible reasons for the proposal. He cited the figures to demonstrate that the Court was not running behind in its work and argued persuasively that more Justices "would not promote the efficiency of the Court." In making his statement, the Chief Justice said that he was "confident that it is in accord with the views of the Justices," although "on account of the shortness of time, I have not been able to consult with the members of the Court generally." Although, in fact, Hughes had only the approval of Brandeis and Van Devanter, the impression was given that all of the Justices were behind the statement. The Roosevelt court-packing plan was defeated, but the demand for a new attitude by the Court still existed. And, rather naturally it seemed, the Court adopted a new philosophy, one that was accepting of the New Deal legislation.

President Roosevelt was overwhelmingly reelected while the fight was still in progress. And, just one year from the time that the Court invalidated the New York minimum wage law, it switched its opinion. Hughes led the parade. The Chief Justice himself wrote the majority opinion in *West Coast Hotel v. Parrish*,[6] sustaining the validity of the minimum wage law and on the grounds urged by Stone. *Morehead v. New York* ex rel. Tipaldo,[7] decided just a year before, had been rejected.

The next critical question before the Court was the validity of the Wagner Labor Relations Act. On April 12, 1937, the answer was furnished by *National Labor Relations Board v. Jones and Laughlin Steel Corporation.*[8] The Supreme Court upheld the act, now rejecting contentions that had been so persuasive the other way in the Schecter and Carter cases. Chief Justice Hughes blithely dismissed these contentions and cases by ruling that they "are not controlling here."

Although Hughes pretended that the Court's new position was consistent with its older decisions, his colleagues would not let him off so easily. Dissenting in *National Labor Relations Board v. Jones and Laughlin Steel Corporation,* McReynolds pointed out: "Every consideration brought forward to uphold the Act before us was applicable to support the Acts held unconstitutional in cases decided within two years." Sutherland wrote that the power of the Court, "does not include the power of amendment under the guise of interpretation" and, understandably, President Roosevelt's reaction to Hughes' insistence that the Court had not changed its views was: "It would be a little naive, to refuse to rec-

6 West Coast Hotel v. Parrish, 300 U.S. 379 (1937).

7 Morehead v. New York *ex rel.* Tipaldo, 298 U.S. 587 (1936).

8 National Labor Relations Board v. Jones and Laughlin Steel Corp., 301 U.S. 1 (1937).

ognize some connection between these 1937 decisions and the Supreme Court fight."

It seems clear that Hughes shifted his position, but it is not so clear whether he understood that he was changing his position. Criticizing Hughes, Stone said: "I can hardly see the use of writing judicial opinions unless they are to embody methods of analysis and of exposition which will serve the profession as a guide to the decision of future cases. If they are not better than excursion tickets, good for this day and trip only, they do not serve even as protective coloration for the writer of the opinions and would much better be left unsaid." By 1940 the Chief Justice was forced to confront the issue directly. The Supreme Court then sustained the Fair Labor Standards Act.[9] It held that even an elevator operator in a fur manufacturer's plant fell within the category of interstate commerce, subject to regulation by Congress. Writing for the majority, Justice Stone spoke out loud and clear: "Our conclusion is unaffected by the Tenth Amendment. There is nothing in the history of its adoption to suggest that it was more than declaratory of the relationship between the national and state governments as it had been established by the Constitution before the amendment or that its purpose was other than to allay fears that the new national government might seek to exercise powers not granted. . . ." The position that the Tenth Amendment guaranteed any sovereign subject matter to the states could no longer be flatly stated.

Charles Evans Hughes had a morbid determination to maintain a myth of judicial stability. But the net result of his deception hurt the prestige of the very institution he was trying to protect. The struggle for control of the judiciary, the unwillingness of the majority Justices to understand what Congress and the President were trying to achieve, and the demands of the people all played into the hands of those who preached destruction of the federal system and tried to overturn the American republic, the Constitution, and the Su-

[9] U.S. v. Darby, 312 U.S. 100 (1941).

preme Court. Hughes came to appreciate what he himself
had once pointed out, that proper judicial function rested
more upon "a correct appreciation of social conditions and a
true appraisal of the actual effect of conduct" than on ritual
and formulas. And Roberts, too, saw the light: "Looking back,
it is difficult to see how the Court could have resisted the
popular urge for uniform standards throughout the country—
for what in effect was a unified economy."

An important area to which Hughes directed his attention was civil rights, where his views were more progressive.
In 1931 he spoke for the majority in voiding a state statute
that made the display of a red flag a criminal offense because
it served as a symbol of orderly opposition to the government.[10] The same year he dissented against the majority
decision to deny citizenship to a person who would not
commit himself to bear arms in the future.[11] Shortly thereafter, in *Near v. Minnesota,*[12] he wrote for the majority in
voiding a statute that permitted the banning of "malicious,
scandalous and defamatory" newspapers. The act had been
applied to a newspaper that had published a series of articles
charging a certain gangster with controlling all the crime in
Minneapolis and alleging that the local police officials cooper-
ated with him.

In two cases affecting Communists, he protected the
defendants. In De Jonge[13] he annulled a statute that made it
a crime to assist in the conduct of a meeting called by any
organization advocating criminal syndicalism or sabotage. In
the Herndon case[14] he joined the majority to set aside a
Georgia law that applied to a black Communist charged with
attempting to incite insurrection on the basis of his possession
of a pamphlet and his attempt to enlist members. Generally,

[10] U.S. v. Mackintosh, 283 U.S. 605 (1931); U.S. v. Bland, 283 U.S. 636
(1931).
[11] Stromberg v. California, 283 U.S. 359 (1931).
[12] Near v. Minnesota, 283 U.S. 697 (1931).
[13] De Jonge v. Oregon, 299 U.S. 353 (1937).
[14] Herndon v. Lowry, 301 U.S. 242 (1937).

he voted to uphold the right of picketing in labor disputes.[15] In *Missouri* ex rel. *Gaines v. Canada*[16] he wrote for the Court in requiring a state to provide equal law school facilities within its state for blacks as for whites.

In evaluating the skills of Charles Evans Hughes, it should be recognized that his strategic withdrawal for the Court, in order for the institution to persist, was designed and executed brilliantly by him. Perhaps the closest parallel is the brilliant comparable maneuver carried out by John Marshall, long before in *Marbury v. Madison.* Hughes managed to accomplish what few were able to do; he outflanked one of the greatest politicians of this century, Franklin Delano Roosevelt.

Staid and careful, Charles Evans Hughes, in effect, carried out a bloodless revolution. It is ironic that Hughes and his accomplice Roberts, who sought to create at least the illusion of judicial stability, were the agencies for a constitutional overturn of gigantic proportions. But the price was also enormous; it was the recognition by the public that what had taken place was, in Professor Corwin's phrase, "Constitutional Revolution, Ltd." and that "the Constitution is what the judges say it is."

[15] Senn v. Tile Layers Union, 301 U.S. 468; Hogue v. CIO, 310 U.S. 496 (1939); Thronhill v. Alabama, 310 U.S. 88; Carlson v. California, 310 U.S. 106 (1940).

[16] Missouri *ex rel.* Gaines v. Canada, 305 U.S. 337 (1938).

–9–

Harlan Fiske Stone

DESTROYER OF THE MYTH

FOR A QUARTER OF A CENTURY, HARLAN FISKE STONE, BORN INTO a New Hampshire farming family, resided in the environs of New York City. He divided his time between practicing law and teaching at Columbia Law School, where he served as dean for more than a decade. In 1924, President Coolidge, looking for a new United States Attorney General, selected Republican Stone. Not a year later, the President selected Stone to become an Associate Justice of the Supreme Court. Justice Stone accumulated seniority on the bench and, in 1941, President Franklin D. Roosevelt placed him in the chair of Chief Justice, in spite of his not being a member of the President's party.

By temperament, by analytic ability, by intellectual training, Stone's career as a great lawyer and judge was predestined. He demonstrated this inchoate skill as an Amherst undergraduate when he wrote an opinion which devastated a faculty decision to expel a fellow student. His classmates at Columbia Law School saw that he would undoubtedly become a Supreme Court Justice. Stone did so without scheming or working for it but step-by-step, "as the dog went to Dover, leg by leg," he once said. And when

Harlan Fiske Stone finally became a Supreme Court Justice he knew he was in the right place. For two decades he was importuned to take a post in the Cabinet and to try to become President, but Stone did not wish to leave the Court. He was content with his calling, believing that it was the one work for which he was best suited.

Stone always demonstrated the outstanding qualities of a judge. He resolved all problems, legal or political, by carefully collecting the facts, weighing and evaluating them, and then resolving the open issues. Stone seemed to eschew popular causes or passions. When Stone became Attorney General in 1924, there was a clamor raised in the press and by the public against the man he had succeeded, Henry M. Daugherty. Stone refused to join in the complaints about the office before he assumed it, although he recognized its inadequacies. "After all," said Stone, "we're all human."

His formal education at Newburyport High School, at Amherst, and at Columbia Law School was directed to perfect the skills he was to employ later. He recalled, "I was also realizing then, in those days college and law school education did not grow on every bush for students in my position in life, and I was doing the best I could to get the full advantage of my college courses in the belief that diligence and loyalty to my immediate job would best serve to fit me for some useful achievement in the years ahead."

Stone sat on the Supreme Court from 1925 to 1946. During the early period of his tenure, constitutional controversy revolved about the extent to which state legislatures could intervene into rearrangement of existing property relationships. But before this issue was resolved completely, the Court was confronted with the question of whether the national government could supersede state action by passing its own legislation. During all of Stone's work on the Supreme Court, he had to cope with the shifting relationships between nation and state and between state and state—the problems of the federal system.

Stone's essential personality was without inherent rancor toward people and he was basically unflappable. This was fortunate since during his entire stay on the High Court he was plunged into a maelstrom of controversy. During the time that Stone served under Chief Justices Taft and then Hughes, he buffeted self-serving brethren who sought to impute their own economic and social predilections into their judicial interpretations. When he finally assumed the job of Chief Justice, he was subjected to pressure from those progressive colleagues who attempted to mold him in their image.

Stone accepted the idea that law must "be fitted to the life of a people." In the usual case, he was to be found joined with Holmes and Cardozo, supporting the idea that judges had an obligation not to impose on the legislative branch their pet social or economic or political predispositions for the solution of community problems. This latter conviction was critical to the way in which he voted on Franklin D. Roosevelt's New Deal laws. In *United States v. Butler*[1] the judges voted six to three in declaring the Agricultural Adjustment Act unconstitutional. It is fascinating to realize that neither Justice Roberts, who wrote the opinion for the majority invalidating the law, nor Republican Stone, who dissented because he thought the law should be upheld, believed in the policy of the law. Justice Stone chided the majority for holding that legislation they thought "undesirable" was, as a consequence, deemed "unconstitutional." He charged that the Supreme Court had come to regard itself as "the only agency of government that must be assumed to have capacity to govern." While the President and Congress are controlled by "the ballot box and the processes of democratic government, the only check upon our own exercise of power is our own sense of self-restraint. . . . Congress and the courts both unhappily may falter or be mistaken in the performance of their constitutional duty," said Stone, "but interpretation of our great charter of government which proceeds on any

[1] U.S. v. Butler, 297 U.S. 1 (1936).

assumption that the responsibility for the preservation of our institutions is the exclusive concern of any one of the three branches of government or that it alone can save them from destruction, can result in the destruction of the federal system."

Shortly thereafter, Stone was to reiterate his view of the judicial function in the second minimum-wage case.[2] He criticized the replacement of the commands of the Constitution by "personal economic predilections." Said he:

> . . . the legislature must be free to choose unless government is to be rendered impotent. The Fourteenth Amendment has no more imbedded in the Constitution our preference for some particular set of economic beliefs, than it has adopted, in the name of liberty, the system of theology, which we happen to approve.

Many resented the attempt by Stone to reveal that the Justices were all human beings capable of imputing to the words of the Constitution meanings that were compatible with their own beliefs. Argued Sutherland, "the blame must rest upon that instrument and not upon the court for enforcing it according to its terms. The meaning of the Constitution does not change with the ebb and flow of events."

Justice Stone was frequently allied with Holmes and Brandeis. It would be a mistake, however, to assume that the three represented an identical viewpoint, since they each brought to the law a distinctive philosophy of law. However, they had one conviction in common, which was the conception that judges had an obligation to restrain themselves in testing the validity of statutes. As Stone said: "Statutes were not to be held invalid, as long as anyone could find a reasonable basis for not ascribing them purely to envy or greed; and, as it was seldom, if ever, that this could not be done with any confidence, most statutes were upheld." Yet, Stone disagreed with Holmes, charging him with facile generalizations and

---

[2] Morehead v. New York *ex rel.* Tipaldo, 298 U.S. 587 (1936).

the omission of troublesome facts. He also disagreed with the willingness of Brandeis to be an activist, an advocate of his point of view; Stone would have preferred that Brandeis be a passive jurist.

Simply because Stone did not insist on finding his own intention mirrored in a statute did not mean that he did not probe the meaning of a statute. The Justice was not contemptuous of the technical skills of his craft. He refused to accept the easy cliché of presuming the validity or constitutionality of statutes. Instead, he would plow through the legislative history of a statute to hunt out the elusive "intention" of the legislation. His pride in his work as a legal craftsman, his sure-handed confidence in his conscious judicial role, and his mastery of analysis and language established him as a worthy associate of Holmes, Brandeis, and Cardozo.

From its earliest days, the Supreme Court had emphasized the safeguarding of property as its primary interest. After the judicial turnabout of 1937, the judiciary began to exercise self-restraint in approaching statutes that interfered with private property; a new "preferred freedom" emerged. Now the Court used its protective mantle against government action that encroached on free speech, religion, and other forms of individual expression. Paradoxically, although Stone was the apostle of judicial self-restraint toward legislation that threatened property rights, he was the creator of the concept of the so-called preferred freedom status for civil liberties.

The implication of a special sanctity for intellectual freedom was implicit in Holmes' belief in "free trade in ideas" and in Brandeis' underscoring of the need for "new legislation and new institutions." Even Chief Justice Hughes, in *Near v. Minnesota*,[3] refused to throw a blanket of presumed validity over statutes that threatened freedom of thought and expression.

In 1938 the case of *United States v. Carolene Products*

[3] Near v. Minnesota, 283 U.S. 697 (1931).

Company,[4] in effect, cleared the way for the abolition of child labor. Stone, writing for the majority, expressed the idea that the Court would not lightly interfere with the judgments of Congress as to economic policy. Then, he added a footnote that has now become famous. It suggested a different judicial responsibility in civil liberties cases, contrasted with that involving private property. He wrote:

> There may be narrower scope for operation of the presumption of constitutionality when legislation appears on its face to be within the specific prohibition of the Constitution, such as those of the first ten amendments, which are deemed equally specific when held to be-embraced within the Fourteenth. . . .
>
> It it unnecessary to consider now whether legislation which restricts those political processes which can ordinarily be expected to bring about repeal of undesirable legislation, is to be subjected to more exacting judicial scrutiny under the general prohibitions of the Fourteenth Amendment than are most other types of legislation. . . .
>
> Nor need we enquire whether similar considerations enter into review of statutes directed at particular religions . . . or national . . . or racial minorities . . . whether prejudice against indiscreet and insular minorities may be a special condition, which tends seriously to curtail the operation of those political processes ordinarily to be relied upon to protect minorities and which may call for a correspondingly more searching judicial inquiry.

World War II brought legal controversies that were to test the limits of freedom of expression in time of national crisis. In an eight-to-one vote, the Court upheld a compulsory flag salute as applied to Jehovah's Witnesses in Pennsylvania.[5]

Stone, consistent with his ideas expressed in the footnote to the Carolene Products case, dissented, the only dissenter on the Court. He deemed the statute a "vulgar intrusion" by the

[4] U.S. v. Carolene Products Co., 304 U.S. 144 (1938).
[5] Minersville School District v. Gobitis, 310 U.S. 586 (1940).

lawmakers into intellectual freedoms that the Justices were duty-bound to protect. Said he: "I am not persuaded that we should refrain from passing upon the legislative judgment as long as the remedial channels of the democratic process remain open and unobstructed. This seems to me no less than the surrender of the constitutional protection of the liberty of small minorities to the popular will."

Dissenter Stone ultimately triumphed. By 1943, Jackson and Rutledge, the two new Justices, together with Black, Douglas, and Murphy—who voted with the majority in the earlier case—changed their minds. They joined with Stone, and by a vote of six to three, they knocked out the compulsory flag salute.[6] Stone was, in the last analysis, conscious of his responsibilities as a judge rather than interested in pursuing some aspect of social policy that he regarded as sacred; thus, his record on civil rights is somewhat imposing. He was frequently, but not invariably, teamed up with Holmes and Brandeis on issues involving personal liberty. Yet, he was not decided on the hotly contested issue of whether pacifists who refused to take an oath to bear arms could be refused naturalization.[7] While he served as Chief Justice, he voted for governmental control in the Bridges,[8] Schneiderman,[9] and Yamashita[10] cases.

Stone was first to assert the doctrine of preferred freedom. But when the time came to accept it without reservation, Stone backed away. His formulation was merely suggestive in the Carolene Products case. He asked whether the rights protected by the First Amendment should not be "subjected to a more exacting judicial scrutiny," and whether in such situations there was presented a "narrower scope for the

---

6 West Virginia State Board of Education v. Barnette, 319 U.S. 624 (1943).
    7 U.S. v. Mackintosh, 283 U.S. 605 (1931); U.S. v. Bland, 283 U.S. 636 (1931).
        8 Bridges v. California, 314 U.S. 252 (1941).
        9 Schneiderman v. U.S., 320 U.S. 118 (1943).
        10 *In re* Yamashita, 327 U.S. 1 (1946).

operation of the presumption of constitutionality." In *Jones v. Opelika*[11] the Court held the statute as being unconstitutional "on its face." Wrote Stone:

> The Constitution, by virtue of the First and Fourteenth Amendments, has put those freedoms (speech and religion) in a preferred position. Their commands are not restricted to cases where the protected privilege is sought out for attack. They extend at least to every form of taxation which, because it is a condition of the exercise of the privilege, is capable of being used to control or suppress it.

Yet, a few years later, when the Court sought to presume that all legislation threatening the freedoms protected by the First Amendment was invalid, Justice Stone dissented.

Thomas v. Collins[12] invalidated a Texas statute that made it mandatory for persons organizing unions to register with the secretary of state of Texas. When R. J. Thomas came to Texas to speak for the United Auto Workers he was served with a restraining order before the speech, on the ground that he had not registered as a union organizer. He went ahead, and to test the law, proselytized a Pat O'Sullivan in the course of his remarks. The Texas act, on its face, seemed an economic regulation, rather than a state restriction directed to one of the preferred freedoms. But the Court majority invalidated the statute. According to Justice Rutledge who spoke for the Court, where it was necessary to decide whether a regulation was an incursion of free speech or free economic activity, "Choice in that border, now as always delicate, is perhaps more so where the usual presumption supporting legislation is balanced by the preferred position given in our scheme to the great, the indispensable democratic freedoms secured by the First Amendment."

Stone, joined by Roberts, Reed, and Frankfurter, dissented. They saw the statute as constituting economic regula-

---

[11] Jones v. Opelika, 316 U.S. 584 (1942).
[12] Thomas v. Collins, 323 U.S. 515 (1945).

tion rather than free speech entitled to protection as a preferred freedom. And the following year, 1946, the Court
sustained the distribution of religious tracts in a company
town.[13] Again Stone dissented, with Burton and Reed.

By 1950 Murphy and Rutledge had died. The Cold War
was a real threat to American security. The preferred freedom
doctrine did not seem so preferred. In *Dennis v. United States*[14]
it was expressly rejected by Justice Frankfurter. Black, in
dissent, expressed the hope that "when present pressures,
passions and fears subside, this or some later Court will restore the First Amendment liberties to the high preferred
place where they belong, in a free society." The dissent by
Justice Black found partial vindication on June 17, 1957,
when the Supreme Court dismissed the conviction of five
Communists and ordered a new trial for nine other Communists.[15]

Except for the interval between 1937 and 1941, Justice
Stone was steadfast—first against his colleagues on the right,
and later against his colleagues on the left—in adhering to his
work principle of judicial self-restraint. He would not go
along with the majority because it was expedient to do so.

In the field of tax immunity between the national government and the states, he said:[16]

> The problem is not one to be solved by a formula, but we may
> look to the structure of the Constitution as our guide to de-
> cision. In a broad sense, the taxing power of either government,
> even when exercised in a manner admittedly necessary and
> proper, unavoidably has some effect upon the other. The bur-
> den of federal taxation necessarily sets an economic limit to
> the practical operation of the taxing power of the states, and
> vice versa. . . . But neither government may destroy the other
> nor curtail in any substantial manner the exercise of its powers.

13 Marsh v. Alabama, 326 U.S. 501 (1946).
14 Dennis v. U.S., 341 U.S. 494 (1951).
15 Yates v. U.S., 354 U.S. 298 (1957).
16 New York v. U.S., 326 U.S. 571, at p. 589 (1946).

Hence the limitation upon the taxing power of each, so far as it affects the other, must receive a practical construction which permits both to function with the minimum of interference each with the other; and that limitation cannot be so varied or overextended as seriously to impair either the taxing power of the government imposing the tax . . . or the appropriate exercise of the functions of the government affected by it.

Stone refused to be intimidated by the expertise accorded the determinations of administrative agencies. "It is just ridiculous to say that the money collectors in the Treasury Department know better than we or the federal courts what Congress intended to do by the legislation here involved."

The Chief Justice felt that the Court had authority to correct its prior mistakes by new decisions only to a limited degree. He explained this thought in 1940, through *Apex Hosiery Company v. Leader.*[17] He reviewed those Court rulings which decided that "to some extent and in some circumstances" trade unions came within the operation of the antitrust laws. Although Stone did not agree with these decisions, Congress did not use its legislative power to overcome the effect of them. Stone reasoned that this inaction was a ratification by Congress of what the Court had decided. Nevertheless, he felt that the judiciary should not intervene if Congress chose not to exercise its authority to overcome a decision.

Stone was ready to employ this approach even in opposition to the views of Justice Black. Undaunted by a precedent of seventy-five years standing, Black decided that the insurance business came within the authority of Congress under the interstate commerce clause and was therefore subject to the Sherman Act.[18] Stone dissented from this decision.

In 1931 the Supreme Court agreed with a congressional

---

[17] Apex Hosiery Co. v. Leader, 310 U.S. 469 (1940).
[18] U.S. v. Underwriters Assn., 322 U.S. 533 (1944).

act that declared that the refusal to bear arms could bar naturalization.[19] Stone dissented. On April 22, 1946, Douglas, speaking for a different Court, declared that the early dissents were correct.[20] Stone, now Chief Justice, dissented from this decision based on the fact that Congress had not seen fit to pass new legislation in response to the Court's decision of 1931. Stone felt that it was not his place as a judge to change the public policy in which Congress acquiesced. He explained:

> It is the responsibility of Congress, in reenacting a statute, to make known its purpose in a controversial matter of interpretation of its former language . . . it is not lightly to be implied that Congress had failed to perform it and has delegated to this Court the responsibility of giving new content to language deliberately readopted after this Court has construed it. For us to make such an assumption is to discourage, if not to deny, legislative responsibility.

Chief Justice Stone had just about finished his statement when he experienced some difficulty in speaking. He was assisted from his seat. Then, the same day, after twenty-one years on that august bench, he died. He dissented at the end because of his self-respect as a judge.

Stone was not a "great" Chief Justice if that word entails the ability to weld the Court into a cohesive unit. The members of his Court quarreled and were often divided. He was incapable of the type of pressure that Taft and Hughes could exert in the conferences. He either could not or would not rely on comradeship or persuasiveness or political loyalties to bind his colleagues to him. He would not even seek to create this illusion for the public. The difference between the way Hughes or Taft ran the Court and the lack of management exhibited by Stone was striking.

Stone left a heritage for all judges to consider. He was

[19] U.S. v. Mackintosh, 283 U.S. 605 (1931); U.S. v. Bland, 283 U.S. 636 (1931).

[20] Girouard v. U.S., 328 U.S. 61 (1946).

steadfast in carrying out his obligation as a Justice without giving in to his personal philosophy or his public image. He conceded to the legislature its responsibility for making public policy when it acted in appropriate areas.

In his professional life Stone was often associated with Holmes, Brandeis, and Cardozo. But he was not conscious of vanity or status or aloofness. A former secretary tells with warmth how he would hail his chauffeur by using two fingers in his mouth to whistle shrilly. He expressed a simple, uncomplicated pleasure in his work and for the product, and even in praise for a job well done. When he became involved in the excitement of a good legal discussion with one of his young law clerks, it was on a plane of equality rather than a clerk and a Justice of the United States Supreme Court.

Stone was a whole man, "a person who turned neither to partiality on the one hand nor impartiality on the other."

IV

DECADE
OF NEW DEAL
AND DISSIDENCE

-10-

Benjamin N. Cardozo

"THE LAW IS A JEALOUS MISTRESS"

AT AGE NINETY, OLIVER WENDELL HOLMES, JR. SUBMITTED HIS resignation as Justice of the Supreme Court to President Hoover on January 12, 1932. There was virtual unanimity throughout the country as to who his successor should be: Benjamin N. Cardozo, chief judge of the New York court of appeals.

Cardozo was a superlative judge on the bench in New York. His reputation was tremendous during his short tenure as Associate Justice of the United States Supreme Court. After his death, he was acclaimed by workingman and aristocrat alike, by liberal and conservative, by people from every segment of American life. In the wake of his demise, the press, the learned journals, the courts, the officialdom, the churches, the trade unions, poured forth a flood of eulogy unparalleled in volume since the funeral of George Washington.

In his lifetime, he was compared to Abraham Lincoln, to a saint, to a scholastic monk. Without minimizing his extraordinary talents and character, it is fair to say that these descriptions do not give a balanced picture of the man. In 1925 Benjamin N. Cardozo wrote *The Paradoxes of Legal Science* but it is the great jurist himself who poses the most tantalizing of legal paradoxes.

Consider the following conundrums: For his entire life, Cardozo lived in the shadow of his family's dishonor. Yet no public servant ever conformed to a higher standard of ethical conduct. He was the very model of a proper Victorian, self-contained, punctilious, polite. But in his work Cardozo expressed and applied the psychology of the twentieth century, stressing the interrelation between society's institutions and the cultural forces that create them. He was unable to untangle the cords that bound him first to his mother and then to his sister. Yet, he was not afraid to wrench loose the legal principles that chained modern human needs to the obsolete principles of feudal law. To his dying day, Benjamin N. Cardozo was self-effacing, modest, shy. Somehow, without political involvement and without substantial community exposure he was catapulted into the New York court of appeals after sitting in a lower trial court for not more than a few weeks, and ultimately landed in the United States Supreme Court.

In countless law offices all over the United States a portrait of Benjamin Cardozo surveys the bustling affairs of life and law that are being conducted in these precincts. Cardozo stands slightly bowed, as if needing support, for he was lean and slight. His lips are compressed in a half-wistful smile, an enigmatic quality like the "Mona Lisa." In the words of an admirer: "although there was not a trace of weakness about him, he had an almost feminine charm." His nose is straight and proud. It culminates in a long drawn face, the jaw slightly unslung, just forward. Silver hair falls across his forehead. But the most arresting feature of his noble head are the eyes. Even in faded photographs or etchings, it is apparent that those eyes missed nothing. They peer out as if into the future, and, at the same time, they are clues to the unfathomed emotions that pulsated within the man.

Cardozo was the scion of a proud and ancient lineage.

The Cardozo family fled to Holland after their expulsion from Portugal, as Jews. In 1752 Aaron Nunez Cardozo emigrated to the American colonies where he met and married the daughter of Moses Seixas. As the organizer of the Bank of Rhode Island and a friend of George Washington, Seixas was a patriot of the American Revolution. Tragedy struck the Cardozo family when Michael, the son of this union, suddenly died, just before his election as a justice of the Supreme Court of New York.

He was survived by a second son, Albert Cardozo, who even as a young man exhibited legal virtuosity. Again tragedy befell the Cardozo family, but this time it took the form of dishonor. In the year 1862 the notorious boss of Tammany Hall proffered a seat on the New York State Supreme Court to Albert. He accepted, and like Faust, his soul was thereupon bound over to the devil. In his servitude, Albert rendered certain favors to the friends of Tammany Hall. He was part of a triumvirate that processed scads of illegal naturalizations to persons who became grateful citizens and voted the way of Tammany. Albert Cardozo had the power to designate referees in the Court, and, of the six hundred pieces of judicial largesse he distributed, he gave three hundred lucrative appointments to a nephew and one hundred to the son of Boss Tweed. It has never been established that Albert actually accepted bribes, but he did appoint a receiver for the Erie Railroad friendly to the financial wheeler-dealer Jay Gould, which enabled Gould to control the railroad. This act was so flagrant that the Judiciary Committee of the New York State Assembly instituted an investigation into it. Albert resigned from the bench before the report was rendered. Nevertheless, in the minds of members of the committee and in the eyes of the public, he was branded. Since he was not disbarred, he continued to practice law. Finally, in 1885, under the dark shadow of his dishonor, Albert died a broken man.

On May 24, 1870, twins had been born to the Albert Cardozos, a little boy and a little girl, Benjamin and Emily.

The family at the time of the twins' birth numbered three daughters and one son. Joy gave way to grief. A few weeks after Benjamin was born, the uncle for whom he had been named was mysteriously beaten and murdered in his bedroom. And three years later Albert was forced to resign from the New York State Supreme Court because of his misdeeds. All his life, Benjamin labored to cleanse the stain of his father's obloquy. Even in the circle of his most intimate friends he rarely discussed his father or the Tweed ring. Certainly they did not broach the subject to him. One indication of the intensity and persistence of Benjamin's feelings is shown by the fact that he was never willing to become a regular member of the bar association because it had preferred charges against his father.

Albert's career served as a warning to his son Benjamin. But it was his mother, Rebecca, from whom Benjamin sought solace and direction. She was a woman of culture who imparted much of her love for literature to Benjamin. The attachment was intimate and abiding. Rebecca's death, when the boy was just nine years of age, threw Benjamin into unconsolable grief. Then Nellie, an older sister, became materfamilias to the brood of brothers and sisters.

The Cardozo home on Madison Avenue in New York City was an unhappy one. A cousin wrote, "As a child, I was always trying to tread a path warily through the maze of family feuds." Both parents died, followed by the untimely passing of Grace, one of Ben's sisters, and Albert, Jr., his only brother. Another sister, Lizzie, was an invalid with a spinal affliction until her death, and there were times when her fantasies verged on hallucinations. It was Lizzie who had described Nell, the oldest of the children, as the "mother-sister." Ben's twin sister Emily was the only one of the female siblings to marry. But her marriage outside the faith was an additional source of unhappiness to her family. In the end, it was Benjamin and Nell who remained close together, alone in the Madison Avenue home.

It is fascinating to learn that Benjamin's early education was carried out at home. His tutor was Horatio Alger, the world famous author of those many books which invariably employed the same theme—the disadvantaged or handicapped boy persevering over adversity to become rich and famous by dint of honesty, hard work, and intelligence, and the spoiled rich boy receiving his just reward. At the turn of the century stories that fantasized about the ethos of a capitalist society were extremely popular; in fact, they served to inspire many people.

Horatio Alger was a roly-poly man. He had been an ineffectual minister. He was passionately devoted to young boys, perhaps as Lewis Carroll, author of *Alice in Wonderland,* was devoted to little girls. Cardozo once remarked that Alger "did not do as successful a job for me as he did with the careers of his newsboy heroes." But undoubtedly, their hours of study and discussion, their reading together of poetry, classics, the works of Thackeray, Dickens, and George Eliot, inculcated in the lonely Benjamin many of the values of his teacher and companion. Certainly, this relationship motivated him to mold his life in the pattern of the heroes of his tutor.

Not quite sixteen, Benjamin Cardozo enrolled at Columbia University as its youngest student. The self-effacing adolescent demonstrated very soon that he was a superb student. One of the professors said of him, "there goes the man who writes the most powerful English of any Columbia student since Alexander Hamilton." His brilliance, coupled with his modest manner, captured the affection and admiration of his classmates. Because of these qualities, it is not too surprising that he graduated from Columbia College with the highest scholastic record in its history. At the same time, he was elected permanent class vice-president by the young men in the class.

Chosen to be commencement valedictorian, he selected as his theme "The Altruist in Politics." In his address he rejected "the substitution of the community in the family's present position . . . the absolute dominion of the State over the actions and property of its subjects." He quoted from Matthew Arnold, emphasizing the primacy of individual initiative and "the instinct of expansion" as a factor in human progress. The classical erudition, the felicity of style, and certainly the emphasis on private enterprise and personal initiative must have warmed old Horatio Alger's heart.

Like his ill-starred father and grandfather before him, Benjamin Cardozo chose law as his vocation. He registered for classes at Columbia Law School. But he terminated his formal training in law at the end of the second year. He applied for admission to practice law in New York. Then, he formed a partnership with his older brother, Albert Cardozo, Jr. The firm of Simpson, Werner, and Cardozo was organized and it continued until Albert's death in 1909.

The young lawyer was recognized very rapidly for his legal virtuosity. As a "lawyer's lawyer," he was soon busy handling cases referred to him by other lawyers. The story is told that shortly after Cardozo was admitted to practice, he argued a case before the New York Court of Appeals. The nervousness and insecurity of the novitiate was apparent to the judges. His apprehension was increased tenfold when, at the conclusion of his argument, an attendant handed him a note from the chief judge asking him to come to chambers. When Cardozo nervously presented himself the chief said to the young man: "I just wanted to tell you, speaking for my associates as well as myself, how well you argued your case."

Such outstanding legal exploits became his stock in trade. He developed a reputation as the lawyer to retain for difficult appeals. He was recognized by the bench and bar as the man to answer intricate questions of law, for his memory for cases and authorities was incredible. Charles Evans Hughes, Jr., once remarked that Cardozo's success at the bar was largely due to his being a "walking encyclopedia of the law." So prodigious was his memory that he could write a brief and supply the volume and page numbers of the cases cited from memory.

For the next two decades Benjamin Cardozo toiled tirelessly at his chosen profession. It constituted his entire life. He left no time for such frivolities as sports, hobbies, cards, or dancing. After office hours, when all his other work was completed, he devoted himself to researching material for his treatise, *The Jurisdiction of the Court of Appeals of the State of New York*. This authoritative work was published in 1904 and soon became the definitive text in the field.

The young lawyer had no time for women. To a cousin who once referred to the possibility of Ben's marrying someone, he carefully replied, "I can never put Nell in second place." His mother and then his sister Nell were the only two women he ever loved. It has been said that "the law is a jealous mistress." Cardozo, then, except for his mother and sister, was never unfaithful to the law, his chosen mistress.

One of the periodic waves of civil reform that wash over New York City from time to time struck in 1913. It is difficult to accept the concept of a spontaneous germination of the judicial career of Benjamin N. Cardozo, but, according to all of his biographers, that is exactly what took place. It is reported that only after the good government leaders and outstanding members of the bench and bar urged him to be a candidate did Cardozo permit his name to be proposed by the Fusion Party for the New York State Supreme Court.

The initial returns on election night showed Cardozo running behind the rest of the Fusion ticket, headed by John Purroy Mitchell, their candidate for mayor. He went to bed unperturbed by the probability that he was defeated. By sunrise, though, Cardozo discovered "that my name led all the rest when the returns from the Bronx came in. Our good Italian citizens took my name for one of their own." This insight seems more that of a political pro than that of the neophite Cardozo has been represented to be. Perhaps it was more than a curious coincidence that Governor Al Smith of New York referred to Cardozo as "my personal lawyer."

Cardozo had actually been working as a Supreme Court judge for a few weeks when the governor appointed him to sit as a temporary judge on the New York Court of Appeals. Governor Glynn disregarded the judges available on the Appellate Division, the intermediate court between the supreme court and the Court of Appeals, and positioned Cardozo in the highest court of the state. So, at forty-four years of age, he joined the judicial body of which he was to become a superlative member for eighteen years. In 1917, Cardozo, a Democrat, received a bipartisan endorsement for an additional fourteen-year term on the court. After completing thirteen years as an associate, Cardozo was designated as chief judge of the New York Court of Appeals.

Over the next two decades Cardozo gradually matured. He dominated a "household" consisting of seven black-robed men. He was advisor and friend, as well as molder of the legal ideals and ideas of his brethren. Cardozo's personal life began to bud in the circle of his judicial intimates of the Albany court, and his career flowered. Yet the interests and ties of his boyhood and the traits that had impressed themselves on his character persisted. On weekends he returned to the shelter of Nell's company in New York City. Even the fascination of his library or the spirited discussions with his fellows could not serve as a complete substitute for the companionship of his sister. During the work week he telephoned her frequently from Albany, and when the schedule of the court was not too hectic, he traveled to New York City to visit her.

In Albany, his cavernous chambers were a suitable retreat. His rooms were colorless and devoid of charm or human warmth; they reflected Cardozo's disdain for popular taste and his disregard for personal indulgence. His chambers immediately reflected his scholarly interests, his indefatigable industry, and his dedication to the law: heavy drapes in an ambiguous amalgam of green and yellow; a ponderous, ornately carved oak desk, strewn with open volumes of the law reports, miscellaneous legal papers, assorted law journals, and a black upright telephone. The only concession to human frailty was the old worn rocking chair near the window, with cane back and seat. The expanse of the nondescript colored walls were broken by row on row of the shelved leatherbound legal treatises. On the wall hung an etching of Chief Justice William Howard Taft of the United States Supreme Court, and an engraving of the judges of the first New York State Court of Appeals showing the members lined up in full judicial regalia complete with muttonchops, wing collars, and elasticized gaiters.

Austere though he was, there are few Cardozo stories in circulation. President Robert C. Clothier of Rutgers University offered Cardozo a cigarette after each was awarded an honorary degree at Princeton. When Cardozo declined the cigarette, Clothier smiled and said, "I suppose that Justices of the Supreme Court have no bad habits." Cardozo answered, "None that people know of."

He was a man without patent vices, except his indulgence of a sweet tooth. Cardozo was essentially a lonely man without hobbies. Music, reading, and art were his principal relaxations. His friends induced him to take up golf but he could not learn the game, perhaps because he did not permit himself to enjoy golf, or any game. He was punctual to the minute and precise about his commitments. The courses of his meals, as well as his eating times, could be predicted by friends; he imbibed alcoholic beverages infrequently, and not at all during Prohibition.

While he enjoyed a hearty laugh or good joke (but not an off-color one), his personality had a deep and underlying strain of melancholy. He did not use his position to ridicule or castigate lawyers who appeared before him, although there were instances in which he invoked a subtle ironic wit in putting down obstreperous attorneys. As a rule his demeanor expressed a beatific and pervasive calm that affected those before him. His friends were hard-pressed to understand how Cardozo suffered those who impinged upon his privacy or otherwise took advantage of his generosity. His acceptance seemed to border on masochism.

If Cardozo had been born a few generations earlier, he might well have been a rabbinical scholar, a scholastic recluse. All his life he retained a strong identification with his Jewish heritage, especially with his Portuguese ancestors. He was a member of the Spanish-Portuguese synagogue, as had been his family, since its founding. He took particular pride in the fact that his great-uncle, Rabbi Seixas, had been the first Jewish trustee of Columbia University. He was the second. Cardozo was not Jewish in that he adhered to ritual or dogma, but, like Baruch Spinoza, the great philosopher of the seventeenth century, he expressed Judaism's most exalted religious sentiments.

Not only was Benjamin N. Cardozo the greatest judge of the New York Court of Appeals, but under his leadership, that great court became the matrix of common law throughout America. It should be noted that the common law is the vast repository of the rules that govern disputes concerning property, contracts, purchase and sale of goods, crimes, wrongful acts that are compensable in money damages, and many others. Common law comprehends the myriad legal rules that make up the fabric of the day-to-day lives of ordinary men and women. It is in the state courts rather than the federal courts that most legal disputes are usually decided. And it was in this area that Cardozo made his greatest contributions.

More than any other court, the New York Court of Appeals serves as a clearing house for the critical issues that relate to current legal problems of business or commerce. Its decisions in the commercial areas therefore, as in the other matters of substantive concerns, are followed closely by the courts in other states. Cardozo's rulings in these fields have been followed more closely than those of almost any other American jurist.

The genius of Cardozo lay in his impeccable historic scholarship. He had a profound interest in the origins of common-law principles and the social environment in which they developed. He theorized that ancient justification for the continuance of a legal rule was not enough. The ultimate test was its ability to serve present human needs. He understood that just one legal principle was not a single strand but was interwoven into the fabric of the entire social system. The great legal philosopher, Professor Morris R. Cohen, pointed out that Cardozo emphasized law as "an essential part of the process of adjusting human relations in organized society." According to Cohen, Cardozo realized that "to meet his responsibility for making the law serve human needs the judge cannot rely on legal authorities alone but must know the actual facts of life around him, the psychologic and economic factors which determine its manifestations, and must thus keep abreast of the best available knowledge which those engaged in various social studies, researches or investigations can supply."

Always retiring and conservative in his habits of dress, decorum, and moral standards, he did not strike out for social reform as did Brandeis or Holmes, nor was he an avid dissenter. His work on the bench is distinguished by humanism and scholarship.

Immersed in his books, Cardozo was insulated from the pressures of life. Books were his natural habitat, rather than people. As he once confided to a friend, "I do love words, more, probably, than a wise man should." The law was the principal beneficiary of this affection.

Every law school graduate can recognize a Cardozo opinion by a quick perusal. His style is unmistakable: limpid clarity, conciseness suffused with a moral almost spiritual luminosity, and a command of historical material that is unrivaled in the entire common-law tradition. The beauty of his prose must be rated with those of the Greek and Roman classicists whose works he read in the original language for his own pleasure. His opinions and his writings had a lasting impact on the Anglo-American law and on the nature of legal writing.

The Storrs lectures delivered at Yale University in 1920 served as the content of a slender book entitled *The Nature of the Judicial Process*. It was a great success because of the beauty of its style, its clarity, and above all, because of the way in which Cardozo used his incisive mind to lay bare the inner workings of legal decision-making. It accurately exposed some of the underlying considerations—conscious and subconscious—that affect a jurist in arriving at a decision in a given case. Most lawyers and jurists assumed that legal decisions were logical analyses from accepted premises. Cardozo made it clear that the common law was not just a sterile extension of rules first formulated in feudal days, but a complex system of social rules capable of responding to present human needs. Using historical material he employed his genius as a catalyst to supply a new understanding to the judicial process.

A few years later, in another lecture series, published under the title *The Growth of the Law* he supplemented the earlier lectures and reinforced its message. In *The Paradoxes of Legal Science*, Cardozo analyzed the relationship between justice and the law, and the entire work is enriched by his erudition. The book demonstrates also how his early intellectual training, steeped in Greek philosophy, shaped and sharpened the Socratic approach he was to use for the rest of his professional work.

In 1930 his last book, *Law and Literature*, was published. In this hegemony of lectures and various writings, he included an essay that has frequently been quoted. One outstanding paragraph described the various judicial styles for writing opinions:

> There is a type magisterial or imperative; a type laconic or sententious; a type conversational or homely; a type refined or artificial; smelling of the lamp, verging at times on preciosity or euphemism; a type demonstrative or persuasive; and finally a type tonsorial or agglutenative, so called from the shears and paste pot which are its implements and emblem.

Cardozo recognized that law did not have the certainty of mathematics or engineering—"my bridges are experiments, I cannot span the tiniest stream in a region unexplored by judges and law givers before me, and go to rest in the secure belief that the span is wisely laid." Nevertheless, he saw the necessity of trying to reconcile the conflict in law occasioned by a system of numerous state courts and legislative bodies spewing forth a cascade of statutes and decisions, often conflicting. To further unity in the law (a major drive in his life) and to keep it responsive to social needs, he helped organize the American Law Institute. In addition, he proposed the formation of a ministry of justice to foster cooperation between the courts and the legislatures.

Cardozo had only been a judge eight years when a vacancy occurred on the Supreme Court of the United States. At that time, although three law school deans proposed his name to President Harding for consideration, he was not appointed. Later, President Coolidge tendered him a seat on the Hague Court of International Arbitration, but Cardozo turned down the offer.

In 1932, when Justice Holmes resigned from the Supreme Court of the United States, President Hoover, a conservative Republican, initially responded to the demand for Cardozo's appointment by pointing out that there were already two New Yorkers in the Court. Justice Stone, one of these New Yorkers, offered to resign to provide a place for Cardozo. Another seat was held by Louis D. Brandeis, also a Jew, and considerable opposition was voiced to his appointment on that count. The President feared that the appointment of Cardozo might encourage anti-Semitism. Senator Borah of Idaho countered by telling Hoover that "there is only one way to deal with anti-Semitism, that is, not to yield to it."

The legal profession responded from all parts of America. They felt that the man whose father had exiled himself in disgrace from the bench was the one lawyer in the United States capable of filling the seat left by Holmes. And it seemed that the view expressed by the leaders of the bench and bar echoed the feelings of men and women in all walks of American life. Somehow this retiring scholar, this very private person, had become for the multitudes the embodiment of the sanctity and humanity of the American legal system. To his credit, President Hoover submitted the name of Cardozo to the Senate. They confirmed it.

But the next six years, during which Cardozo was a member of the United States Supreme Court, in "homesick exile," were not happy years for him. The sixty-two-year-old Cardozo was away from his old family lodgings in New York. "I have always looked upon a change of home as one of the severe crises of a lifetime." Cardozo missed the noncommittal no-nonsense atmosphere of his Albany chambers. Being away from the Albany circle of intimates was a painful dislocation for a person of his temperament. Cardozo was separated from his beloved sister Nell. She had been fearful, in his younger years, that he might be married and taken from her. But as the years went on Cardozo was to say, "I am nervous as soon as I am out of her sight." Not only was he away from Nell, but during Cardozo's tenure in the Supreme Court, Nell passed away. This experience was most traumatic for Cardozo, and he in turn suffered a series of heart attacks. However, he did not slow down in his work. He said, "I have not much interest left in life now except to work."

The change that faced Cardozo in Washington involved more than his life style. His legal work now focused on public law rather than private common law; he dealt with statutes and the job of interpretation and application of the Constitution. Holmes led the fight to permit legislatures to enact social policy into law to meliorate the onerous conditions of life faced by many people. In 1916 he was joined by Brandeis. In 1930 they were joined by Stone. And in 1932 the group was joined by Cardozo. The great Depression and the election of Franklin D. Roosevelt as President shifted the primary concern of the Court from state laws designed to overcome the hardships that stemmed from the bad economic situation to the flow of New Deal legislation passed by Congress under the aegis of President Roosevelt. The struggle for the survival of the American economic system occurred in front of the Supreme Court, in the full glare of public scrutiny. It caused President Roosevelt to try to pack the Court with men sympathetic to his designs. The court-packing plan was rejected, and it followed that, in the 1936 term, a number of shattering decisions were then handed down by the Supreme Court. The controversy, legal and political, was one into which Cardozo was plunged. It took its toll on him both physically and emotionally. Cardozo, as his associates Brandeis and Stone, and as his predecessor, Holmes, believed that the legislative branch had the primary responsibility to formulate the public policies necessary to meet community problems, and the Court was not to substitute lightly its own judgment for that expressed in a particular law. Holmes, Brandeis, and Cardozo cannot be measured by the same yardstick; each approached the cases before him differently. Brandeis had a fully developed philosophy of economics and a view of society that he applied as a social reformer. Cardozo, instead, applied a judicial test, a view in which the judge was passive and the courts respectful of the legislature, which was entitled to formulate public policy.

This deference to laws passed by Congress and by state legislatures was not shown by the majority of the High Court. The history of the Supreme Court during the 1930's is replete with cases in which legislation was held invalid as violating the commerce clause, the Tenth Amendment, or the Fourteenth Amendment. And usually the majority opinion was countered by dissents from Cardozo, Brandeis, Stone, and, sometimes, Chief Justice Hughes.

At the time Cardozo was reaching the end of his career, the Court was in serious trouble. The public and President Roosevelt were outraged by its attacks on the New Deal legislation. The landslide reelection of Roosevelt and the court-packing scare caused the Court, in April 1937, to restrict its review of a whole series of cases. The Court was trying to protect itself from criticism in view of Roosevelt's widespread support. In effect, the Court was assuming what Cardozo conceived to be its proper judicial role. As a result, Cardozo had the opportunity to write the majority opinion in upholding an important New Deal legislative accomplishment, the Social Security cases.[1]

Only in the area of free speech did Cardozo feel that legislative action should be carefully limited. "Only in one field is compromise to be excluded, or kept within the narrower limits." Said he, "There shall be no compromise of the freedom to think misthoughts and speak them, except at these extreme borders where thought merges into action."

Cardozo reached this conclusion not as a result of his passion for freedom, as did Holmes, or his burning sense of social justice, as did Brandeis. He studied the dictates of the Fourteenth Amendment and the Bill of Rights in the context of the entire Constitution, and his approach represented a lawyer's considered judgment on how the system had to work. Thus, when the New York Criminal Anarchy Act was applied to convict Benjamin Gitlow for the publication of the left-wing manifesto,[2] Cardozo dissented.

The critical issue of how many provisions of the Bill of Rights were incorporated into the Fourteenth Amendment to be applied against the States was placed before the Court in the Palko case.[3] This involved a Connecticut law that gave the prosecuting attorney, with the permission of the judge presiding, the right to appeal issues of law in a criminal case. Cardozo's formulation is still widely quoted:

> We reach a different plane of social and moral values when we pass to the privileges and immunities that have been taken over from the earlier articles of the federal bill of rights and brought within the Fourteenth Amendment by a process of absolution. . . . If the Fourteenth Amendment has absorbed

---

[1] Steward Machine Co. v. Davis, 301 U.S. 548 (1937); Helvering v. Davis, 301 U.S. 619 (1937).
[2] People v. Gitlow, 268 U.S. 652 (1925).
[3] Palko v. Connecticut, 302 U.S. 319 (1937).

them, the process of absorption had its source in the belief that neither liberty nor justice would exist if they were sacrificed. This is true, for illustration, of freedom of thought, and speech. Of that freedom one may say that it is the matrix, the indispensable condition of nearly every other form of freedom.

Cardozo joined in Justice Roberts' opinion for the majority that set aside the conviction by a Georgia court of Angelo Herndon[4] for attempted insurrection. He decided that the application of the statute to the particular facts of the case was an illegal invasion of free speech and the right of assembly. Yet, when the University of California required all students to take military science courses and refused to exempt conscientious objectors, Cardozo voted to sustain the regulation. The policy of not permitting his human instincts to interfere with what he conceived to be his legal obligation was the same policy he seemed to use in his own personal life. The uncomplicated principles of constitutional law and the proper role of the judiciary as articulated by Cardozo do not seem entirely adequate today as they did in the 1930's. Thus, while the approaches to due process of law derive from the views of Holmes, Brandeis, and Cardozo, they differ from each other and from the views held by the majority in the 1930's. Cardozo will always be the great common-law jurist of America who clutched the torch from the hands of Justice Holmes. His was the voice of the present. He spoke of the way the Constitution should be approached and the proper job of the judiciary in the American system.

At the conclusion of the term of the Court, in May of 1938, Cardozo was ill and slipped out of Washington in his characteristic way. He found a resting place at the home of his close friend, Judge Irving Lehman of the New York Court of Appeals, at Port Chester, New York. He lingered for two months in the company of the person closest to him, now that his mother and sister Nell were gone. On July 9, 1938, his heart stopped beating.

[4] Herndon v. Lowry, 301 U.S. 242 (1937).

Felix Frankfurter

THE "HAPPY HOT DOG"
GOES TO WASHINGTON

FELIX FRANKFURTER SUCCEEDED TO THE SUPREME COURT SEAT once inhabited by the great Holmes and then his worthy successor, Cardozo. Frankfurter unquestionably was a brilliant lawyer. But his role on the New Deal Court was marked by bitterness, acrimony, and perhaps not the fullest employment of a rare talent.

Frankfurter came to the United States at age twelve from Vienna. Brought up with middle-class advantages, he represented a rigorous continental tradition of erudition and culture. He effortlessly mastered the public schools, the College of the City of New York, and attended Harvard Law School. Spiritually and intellectually, Frankfurter would remain forever in Cambridge. He was secure enough and had sufficient insight to realize that, after an experience of just two months, Wall Street law firms were not for him. So, until 1914 when Harvard recalled him to teach law, he employed his legal talent in government service, specializing in antitrust work. At Harvard for the next twenty-five years, he spent most of his time bedeviling, stimulating, and inspiring the thousands of embryonic lawyers, who sat in his classes. He also spent his time wheedling, cajoling, and prevailing upon Washington officials to hire his ex-students, the "happy hot dogs" from Harvard law. Frankfurter was anxious to place his former students in Washington.

He demonstrated a willingness to act on behalf of his beliefs by throwing his efforts and abilities and reputation into the fight to save Sacco and Vanzetti, the anarchists who were bullied into a conviction for murder. But his deep passion was the United States Supreme Court. He was well known to many Justices and a friend and confidant of the two other Harvard men, Holmes and Brandeis. The men on the Supreme Court felt Frankfurter's influence through the ideas and opinions of the law clerks whom he supplied to them and the many former students who, as lawyers, populated Washington.

A clue to the way Justice Frankfurter approached legal questions of the Supreme Court is found in his academic interest in form and procedure almost more than in substance. This interest was founded years before: "Jurisdiction and Procedure in the Federal Court" was his favorite course at Harvard. The first time he was offered a post as Justice on the United States Supreme Court he declined. But when President Franklin Roosevelt offered him the "scholar's seat" on the Supreme Court, he was happy to accept. His many former students, the tremendous circle of friends, and his intellectual admirers in public life and throughout the world were pleased for him and for the country.

As a neophyte on the Court, his vote helped convert the dissenting views of Holmes and Brandeis into majority opinions. His views, however, expressed in separate opinions, demonstrated that Professor Frankfurter had simply moved his teaching lectern to the bench of the Supreme Court. He used his staccato wit, his emotion and knowledge, his verbal skill, to electrify those who were before him. The lawyers, like his students, were captive audiences. Critics accuse Frankfurter of being "the Supreme Court's Emily Post." They contend that he frequently refused to become engaged in the substance of an issue (for example, the matter of public policy), but rather directed his skills to a pedant's legal technicalities, the subtle questions of practice and procedure.

He persisted in being the model continental professor—a martinet, confident of his intellectual superiority, condescending and secure. While he kept proclaiming the gospel of judicial self-restraint and justifying interference with governmental action on that ground, simultaneously his convictions did not stop him from leading the majority when the Court set aside a number of state taxes that may have remotely interfered with the carrying on of business in interstate commerce.[1] This sort of double standard caused Justice Black to express heatedly in one case that he was writing only "in order that silence may not be understood as acquiescence in the views expressed by the dissenting opinion of Mr. Justice Frankfurter." Black, usually phlegmatic, wrote: "The dissent in question . . . mentions no statute at all. Instead the chief reliance appears to be upon . . . the writer's personal views on 'morals' and 'ethics.' . . . And for judges to base their interpretation of statutes on nothing but their own conceptions of 'morals' and 'ethics' is, to say the least, dangerous business."

Ironically, Frankfurter has been denounced as a radical by those on the right; yet, in the most controversial cases before the New Deal Court, his opinions frequently reflected a conservative viewpoint. Only where the approach laid out by Holmes and Brandeis was clear and inescapable, or where the substantive answer accorded with his idealized conception of what the federal courts should be doing, did Frankfurter join the liberal wing in its decision. Thus, rather than predictable, he was more often than not the weathervane. Frankfurter did not misunderstand the critical issues before the Court; he just seldom allowed these issues to influence his deliberation. At the present time, Frankfurter's popularity is higher than for a long time, perhaps because of the low level

[1] New York v. U.S., 326 U.S. 571 (1945).

of intensity of the present Court or because his approach is
more compatible with the jurisprudence of some now sitting.
However, Frankfurter was a tragic disappointment and an
unhappy source of contention to his peers. In view of his
potentialities, he did not carry any great weight in helping
them bear the load.

Felix Frankfurter was a self-appointed guardian of consistent interpretation of the Constitution. Explained he, in
1949:

> Those liberties of the individual which history has at-
> tested as the indispensable conditions of an open as against a
> closed society come to this Court with a momentum for re-
> spect lacking when appeal is made to liberties which derive
> merely from shifting economic arrangements. Accordingly,
> Mr. Justice Holmes was far more ready to find legislative in-
> vasion where free inquiry was involved than in the debatable
> area of economics.[2]

Actually, Justice Frankfurter was just as ready to make
allowances for the values he deemed most important as
Holmes was for the rights he deemed sacrosanct. The two did
not always agree as to which values deserved most protection.
Frankfurter urged "restraint" on his judicial brethren and the
idea that the Supreme Court should uphold statutes whenever possible, yielding the policy-making function to legislators. At the present time, Frankfurter is highly respected
for this view by President Nixon.

Curiously, for all Frankfurter's insistence on judicial restraint, he did not follow his own advice when he felt strongly
about a particular problem. For example, Frankfurter did not
like wire-tapping. He agitated to have certain wire-tapping
prohibited as unreasonable search and seizure under the
Fourth Amendment, contrary to a decision of 1928. This view
was not adopted until after Frankfurter died. His strong feelings about police searches and seizures were expressed in a

[2] Kovacs v. Cooper, 336 U.S. 77 (1949).

1952 opinion he wrote for the majority in reversing a conviction for narcotics.[3] The conviction was predicated upon evidence pumped by the police from the stomach of the suspect. Frankfurter did not seem to be much of a strict constructionist in that case. Without relying on a specific provision in the Constitution, he decided that pumping the suspect's stomach breached the due process requirement of the Fourteenth Amendment simply because it was "conduct which shocks the conscience." On the other hand, Frankfurter went along with invasions of free speech that would have repelled Holmes and Brandeis.

Frankfurter supported the prosecutions of Communists under the Smith Act of 1951 for conspiracy to advocate the overthrow of the government by force.[4] He explained that the Communist party presented such a substantial threat that Congress should treat its members as a danger to the safety of the nation. This stance justified legislative action that might otherwise appear "illiberal because repressive and envenoming." The same Frankfurter became enraged in 1957 when he would not allow New Hampshire to encroach on academic freedom by jailing a lecturer for refusing to answer inquiries concerning the Progressive party.[5] And because of his concern with separation of church and state, Frankfurter queried the validity of tax exemptions for church property, release time for religious studies, and state aid for bussing to parochial schools. Thus, the apostle of strict construction picked those issues and cases to which he applied this philosophy of restraint and those to which he did not, based on some deep personal hierarchy of values.

From the vantage point of the long history of the Court, only a handful of cases from this period remain as significant contributions to public law. The ground had been broken for the New Deal before Franklin D. Roosevelt was able to ap-

---

[3] Rochin v. California, 342 U.S. 165 (1952).
[4] Dennis v. U.S., 341 U.S. (1950).
[5] Sweezy v. New Hampshire, 354 U.S. 234 (1957).

point a single judge. The Court of New Dealers followed the leads that their predecessors laid down. Because their function seemed anticlimactic, there was little excitement in 1941 when they overturned ten established precedents, some of which stretched back a third of a century.

The decisions that seemed so newsworthy in the 1940's do not seem so important today. The latitude permitted unions by the Supreme Court under the Roosevelt Wagner Act was sharply limited under the later Taft Hartley Act. The issue of whether giving public school pupils "released time" for religious training violated the First Amendment seems stale in the light of today's controversies concerning the division between church and state. Many of these decisions were not based on constitutional grounds. Some simply called for interpretation of statutes or regulations governing the NLRB, or the FCC, or the FTC, or the ICC, or some other agency.

The Justices were handing down decisions in which majorities were narrow, frequently with multiple opinions and dissent. An example is the case in which John L. Lewis was cited for contempt.[6] Justice Vinson who said he "spoke for the court" based his result on two grounds. Only Reed and Burton went along with both. Frankfurter and Jackson accepted only one ground. Black and Douglas accepted the other, and also dissented as to the penalty imposed. Rutledge and Murphy dissented together. A legal decision that is made by a bare majority for different reasons, and accompanied by several dissents could hardly convince the government or the public that the legal body is destined to endure for all times.

As time passed and the membership of the Court changed, its political flavor changed. Only Black, Reed, Frankfurter, Douglas, and Murphy sat for the entire decade. The term of 1940 to 1941 supported national government and New Deal all the way. By the 1948 to 1949 term the Court

[6] U.S. v. United Mine Workers, 330 U.S. 258 (1947).

was out of tune and it turned out little in the way of harmonious decisions.

The heritage of the New Deal decade may be illuminating if the different issues are reexamined. The approach to the regulation and taxation of business by Congress or state legislatures shifted from a judicial veto based on a determination of unconstitutionality to the technique of finding the "intention" of the legislature. The Court would declare what the statute (usually an act of Congress) intended. An example is the case[7] in which the Court decided that the insurance business was within the scope of the anti-trust laws, by a four-to-three vote. The sharply contested issue involved what the statute meant, since it was silent on the coverage intended. To reach the result it did, the Court had to expressly overrule its own precedent, seventy-five years old, which held that insurance was subject to state control since it was of local concern. Another set of decisions, with disagreement among the Justices, treated certain dividends on corporate stock as not taxable when paid in stock rather than cash. The decision involved the construction of a statute, which amended the income tax law and which was designed to overcome the effect of an earlier case. Then there were a number of cases involving the influence of one or another of the government agencies over business; these concerned "rate-making" by public utilities, the patent office, and the Federal Power Commission. Sometimes the government won, sometimes it lost. None of these decisions was unanimous.

The Warren Court has been credited (or charged) with making strides in protecting individual liberty. What has been overlooked were the contributions made by the New Deal Justices. Perhaps the record of that Court has been overstated with regard to its protection of the individual from oppressive government practices. However, the Court took significant steps in protecting those accused of crime from brutality or coercion by state or local police. It also took

[7] U.S. v. South-Eastern Underwriters Association, 322 U.S. 533 (1944).

preliminary steps to protect the voting rights of black people and their physical security. But Black, Douglas, Murphy, and Rutledge were not enough without additional consistent support to effect the tremendous changes that had to be made. They decided a number of civil rights cases, many of them involving the Jehovah's Witnesses; but these free speech, free religious practice, free thought cases did not face up to the basic issues. That would be left to other times.

The Justices had difficulty in coming to terms with the concept expressed in Stone's famous footnote in the *United States v. Carolene Products Company* case,[8] which suggested that, in regard to free expression, there were "preferred freedoms" that were entitled to special protection from the Supreme Court. Another problem that agitated the Court in cases of individual freedom was the extent to which the Fourteenth Amendment incorporated the first ten amendments. A faction of four, headed by Black, took the position that the entire Bill of Rights was to be enforced against state and local action. The rest of the Justices picked and chose specific guarantees of the Fifth Amendment to be funneled through the Fourteenth Amendment.

The New Deal Court devoted considerable attention to the separation of church and state provisions of the First Amendment. They decided cases involving the right to refuse to salute the flag, to release children from school for religious instruction, to proselytize the faith, to have the state pay for transporting youngsters to parochial schools by bus. The decisions were usually close and divided. The Court voted five to four to overrule an earlier determination that immigrant conscientious objectors could not become citizens.[9] This case was memorable in that Stone dissented on the day he died, although he had also dissented, for different reasons, when the Court reached the opposite result years earlier.

The Court gave support to the idea of free speech until

[8] U.S. v. Carolene Products Co., 304 U.S. 144 (1938).
[9] Girouard v. U.S., 328 U.S. 61 (1946).

the pressures of the Cold War raised fears of Communism and the demand for "loyalty." The Court was not now the same guardian of free speech as it had been in the earlier New Deal days. The Justices were ambivalent and divided in issues of freedom of the press. The principal cases concerned the right of reporters to criticize judges without being punished, and the attempt by judges to protect themselves from undue pressure by reporters and publishers affecting their decision-making.

Other cases related to the treatment of issues about those suspected of crime, the investigation of crimes, and the conduct of criminal trials. The cases went both ways, the Justices were even more divided. It is almost impossible to reconcile certain of these decisions. The issues of criminal justice raised questions of search and seizure, interrogation by "third-degree" tactics, the right of grand jury indictment, the right to be represented by counsel, the right to a speedy and public trial by an impartial jury, protection against self-incrimination, double jeopardy, and cruel and unusual punishment.

It was in the protection of rights of black citizens that the New Deal Court reached almost complete agreement. It broke the ground that the Warren Court was to sow and reap. It outlawed, as contrary to the Fourteenth Amendment, states' devices that prevented people from voting because of race or color; states devised a gimmick allowing the state legislatures to leave the management of the primary elections to the political parties. In reality, the primary elections in the Democratic party in the South determined the outcome of the actual elections. The Democratic party regulated its primaries so that the blacks could not vote in them. This effectively meant that the blacks were disenfranchised. To dislodge this device, the Court had to overrule a unanimous precedent of less than ten years before (when Holmes, Brandeis, and Stone sat in judgment). South Carolina tried to preserve the "lily white" primary by then converting its Democratic party into a private club. The lower federal court refused to permit this subterfuge, and the Supreme Court upheld this ruling.[10]

Using the Interstate Commerce clause, the Supreme Court prohibited discrimination on buses making interstate trips and sustained a state law that forbade this sort of segregation.[11] Then, by several decisions, the Court ruled that the state courts could not enforce "restrictive covenants" by which property owners were agreeing, in contracts, not to sell or rent real estate to non-Caucasians.[12] The enforcement of such contracts by the state courts violated the Fourteenth Amendment.

Faced with a number of civil-rights cases arising out of World War II, the Court responded with a greater effort to be objective than it had been during earlier wars. It reversed several convictions for treason and espionage.

The most shameful decision of the Court was its six-to-three ruling[13] permitting the evacuation from the West Coast of all those of Japanese descent, without regard to their citizenship or loyalty. On the other hand, for the third time in its history the Court invalidated an act of Congress in order to protect individual liberty: Congress approved a rider to an appropriations measure that removed three non-Communist employees with important positions from the payroll of the federal government. The Justices set aside this congressional action as constituting a "bill of attainder," which is prohibited by the Constitution. This was the only time during the New Deal decade that the Court held an act of Congress unconstitutional.

Freedom of expression and economic rights overlapped in the cases that involved labor union activity. The problem became most pressing and yet most difficult to resolve when it involved "peaceful picketing" in labor disputes. Initially, the

10 Smith v. Allwright, 321 U.S. 649 (1944).
11 Morgan v. Virg:nia, 328 U.S. 373 (1946).
12 Shelley v. Kraemer, 334 U.S. 1 (1948).
13 *In re* Yamashita, 327 U.S. 1 (1946).

Court treated picketing simply as free speech. Later, it came to feel that this definition was not always appropriate. The sensational prolabor cases were those which permitted union newspapers supported by union funds, in spite of the prohibition of the Taft-Hartley Act, to promote political issues and candidates; the approval of "portal to portal" pay; the outlawing of the "closed shop." Usually, in the labor field, the Court validated acts of legislatures and then enforced the administrative regulations and decisions made under these acts. The results, however, were often inconsistent, for the Justices often disagreed. Two aberrational decisions were made when John L. Lewis was held in contempt, over Rutledge's forceful dissent[14] and Murphy's opinion deciding that peaceful picketing is free speech.[15]

One of these cases stimulated the most explosive and colorful event during the decade of New Deal control. It was the vitriolic blast leveled by Robert Jackson from Nuremberg in 1946, where he was a prosecutor in the war crimes trials, against the temperate Justice Black. The attack was precipitated by the way Black participated and voted in an appeal in which one of the parties, the United Mine Workers, had as their lawyer a man named Harris, who at one time had been a law partner of Black. Jackson's attack was surprising since other Justices, including Butler, Roberts, and, on one occasion, Stone, had similarly sat on cases argued by their former law partners. Disqualification had always been left to each Justice's own sense of propriety. Jackson's outburst was especially difficult to justify since Black had hardly seen Harris during the nineteen years that passed after their brief partnership came to an end. Black's fine sense of ethics led him to disqualify himself from all cases involving the Federal Communications Commission on the ground that his brother-in-law was a member of that agency. It also seems worthy of

14 U.S. v. United Mine Workers, 330 U.S. 258 (1947).
15 Thornhill v. Alabama, 310 U.S. 88 (1940).

note that the decision in the United Mine Workers case would have been the same even without Black's vote.

Undoubtedly, Jackson's intemperate outburst was the flaring of a smoldering resentment against Black. It reflected his disappointment over not being designated Chief Justice when Stone retired, and was fired by reports reaching Jackson that Black had been responsible for the rejection. Jackson felt that the position was due him as a result of a promise allegedly made by President Roosevelt before his death. His chagrin was the culmination of past disappointment at failing to obtain the governorship of New York, disappointment at being held back from a try at the Presidency by Roosevelt's third term and now this final ignominy.

It may well be that Black helped undermine Jackson's chances to become Chief Justice. Frankfurter did frustrate any attempt to name Douglas. So President Truman designated as Chief a man he had named to the Court. Fred Vinson was a Democrat, a soothing and conciliatory member who had come out of the New Deal. Truman felt that his mediating talents could be well used on the Court. Vinson came to the Court one year after President Truman appointed Harold Burton to the traditional "Republican" seat, which had been occupied by Roberts before him. Three years later both Murphy and Rutledge passed away, and Truman filled their places with Tom Clark of Texas and Sherman Minton of Indiana. In this natural way, the New Deal decade of personal pyrotechnics, irrepressible geniuses, and discordance amid unity became part of history.

–12–

Robert H. Jackson

THE ORDEAL OF
THE NEW DEAL

IN THE END, THE PLAN OF PRESIDENT ROOSEVELT TO DILUTE THE
majority of the Supreme Court by the addition of Justices of his
own choosing succeeded. But it did not succeed through his
scheme of packing the Court. It succeeded through the effects
of time and death.

After the eventful 1936 term of Court had concluded,
Van Devanter, then seventy-eight years of age, still mindful of
the sanctity of property and the value of money, decided to
take advantage of a new act of Congress that permitted the
Justices to retire at full pay. Roosevelt, always sensitive to the
impact of drama, took the opportunity during the summer
recess to designate Senator Hugo Black of Alabama as Van
Devanter's replacement.

This move accomplished as much as his court-packing
scheme, since the President was rid of one archconservative
and he had added a rabid New Dealer. The reactionaries
throughout America, and especially in the Senate, were furious. But, because of the inhibitions of "senatorial courtesy,"
they were frozen from intervening.

Next of the "four horsemen" to retire was Sutherland. In
his place, President Roosevelt put a Kentuckian, Stanley

Reed. As Solicitor General of the United States, Reed appeared before the High Court many times, pleading the cause of New Deal legislation with a passionate conviction so intense that in one case he fainted during his presentation.

The reoriented bench was now grinding out decisions consistently against big business and pro-New Deal in a way that would have been unthinkable just two years before. They upheld the Securities and Exchange Commission, the National Labor Relations Board, and the Federal Power Commission in short order. They cast off a few old chestnuts of tax law, weighed down by age and precedent; for example, they invalidated the doctrine that exempted federal judges from income taxes.[1] They set aside a chain of precedents that excused state workers from federal income taxes and federal employees from state income taxes (going back to the landmark case of *McCulloch v. Maryland*[2]). So, in a way that Franklin Roosevelt never anticipated, he was breaking down the hostility of the old Supreme Court to the New Deal.

Then between 1935 and 1939, Brandeis resigned and Cardozo died. To fill the awesome voids resulting from their departures, President Roosevelt plucked two ornaments from ivy league schools. From Harvard Law School he recruited Felix Frankfurter to occupy the "scholar's seat" vacated by Cardozo. From Yale he pulled William O. Douglas, who, at forty years of age, was the youngest Justice to be seated for over a hundred years, since Justice Story. Brandeis, more than twice the age of Douglas, told him, "I wanted you to be here in my place." Douglas, like Brandeis, was a financial wizard.

By the end of 1939 Butler was dead, leaving McReynolds as the last of the conservative quartet. President Roosevelt, who by now had learned the time-tested recipe for a political stew, selected Attorney General Frank Murphy for one of these seats. A Catholic, Murphy had established himself as a friend of labor while he was mayor of Detroit and later as the

---

[1] O'Malley v. Woodrough, 307 U.S. 277 (1939).
[2] McCulloch v. Maryland, 4 Wheat 316 (1819).

liberal governor of Michigan. It seemed as if the Roosevelt new order was firmly entrenched and would endure at least for many, many years. Stone, as Chief Justice, sat as the cornerstone of a leftward-facing coalition of the reconstituted majority of five.

When the liberals were in the minority, they were bound together by common cause into a band of dissenters. Now that they were in the majority, they began to splinter off in six or seven different directions. What became apparent was that they were different individuals, highly articulate, critical, of varying intellectual convictions and persuasions, all lumped under the liberal rubric. By the 1940 to 1941 term, lawyers and others closely following Supreme Court affairs could catch the rumbling, the disagreements, and the personal antagonisms that were manifesting themselves. Stone circulated above the acrimony between Douglas and Frankfurter. From Nuremberg, Germany, where he was serving as prosecutor in the trial of alleged war criminals, Justice Jackson let loose a blast at Justice Black. Black did not respond, but he certainly reacted to the assault on his reputation which was released by Jackson to the newspapers against the importuning of President Truman. The animosities of certain members of the Court for certain of their colleagues was more than harmless gossip.

Once the New Deal majority took over, many of the big controversies disappeared. Times were changing. New legislation that once seemed so daring was now passé and longstanding precedents were all but wiped away. Laws long on the books were expanded by means of a "liberal interpretation." Property rights were, after more than a century, subordinated to personal liberties. And now the Court with a unanimous voice was willing to outlaw child labor,[3] which in 1918 was opposed by the single voice of Holmes, in dissent. Concededly, government could regulate business enterprise in

---

[3] U.S. v. Darby, 312 U.S. 100 (1941).

spite of the due process clause or the prohibition against the impairment of contracts.

Yet, problems seemed to multiply rather than diminish. The Court was called upon to explain the meaning of acts of Congress. The Court was in favor of civil liberty but had to determine the latitude and longitude of the rights of individuals. Conflicts over the extent of individual freedoms were exacerbated by the dark clouds of war and then by the war itself. Federal and state statutes were not frequently cut down as being unconstitutional, but judicial interpretation often rendered acts impotent. Was a "liberal" always for expansion of national legislative power or for the protection of state legislative power? Was liberal always prounion or did it intend protection of "little" business against "big" labor? What if legislative power was being asserted for the business, industrial, or agricultural tycoons against the small plant or dirt farmer, or just the consumer? Should the same yardstick be applied against economic legislation as against legislation that threatened individual rights? Should the Court be more vigilant against excesses by Congress in the civil rights field than against such action by state legislatures? Does civil liberty mean one thing when applied to the intellectual freedoms of the First Amendment and another when applied to the rights of criminal suspects? Should the guarantee of freedom be more searching in peacetime than in time of "cold war" or "hot war"? Reasonable "liberal" Justices of the Court differed on these tough questions.

All these problems were compounded by the many facets of the human personalities involved. Two of the members of the Court felt that their liberal credentials were so well established that they should be given automatic respect in this regard from the newer Justices. They expected due deference as veterans of the wars to establish the Court philosophy. They were Chief Justice Stone and Felix Frankfurter (the pedant from Harvard, always the authoritarian Vienna professor). Piqued at the refusal of Black and Douglas to "follow the leader," they retreated into noncooperative conservatism. The New Deal patina quickly rubbed off Reed and Jackson, and the security of judicial tenure brought to the surface a firm foundation of conservatism. Black, the self-educated lawyer in the Marshall tradition, compensated by lengthy exposition of legal history and citation of authority in his opinions. Douglas, quick to leap to the jugular of a problem, at times neglected to elucidate the steps that led to his conclusions. Murphy was sometimes berated for a failing of scholarship in the law because his warm and generous impulses for people made him seem to respond emotionally rather than intellectually. And Wiley Rutledge was scholarly but his almost neurotic concerns with microscopic details at times tried the patience of his colleagues without successfully influencing them.

The Roosevelt team was all different, all human. The ninth member was James Byrnes of South Carolina. The Supreme Court for Byrnes was a resting place between administrative jobs for President Roosevelt; his one-year stint on the High Court seemed to be no more than a hiatus in his life. The fragmentation of the Court during the period from 1939 to 1949 was aggravated by the fact that it was presided over by three successive Chief Justices: Charles Evans Hughes until 1941 when he resigned; then Stone until 1946; then Fred Vinson. McReynolds and Roberts lingered on into this decade; theirs was a different period and philosophy. Roberts was replaced by Republican Harold Burton of Ohio, a dull conservative. The heart of the New Deal Court consisted of Stone with his seven individualists: Black, Reed, Frankfurter, Douglas, Murphy, Jackson, and Rutledge.

Stanley Reed could never have been a hero of Horatio Alger. Born into the comfortable middle class of Kentucky tobacco-growing gentry, he was the son of a well-established physician. His roots were in that middle state, deep in the soil of a substantial farm. Open and big-hearted, devoted to the outdoor life, Reed was neither a scholar nor an intense intel-

lectual, although his schooling was impressive. He was educated at Kentucky Wesleyan and Yale; he studied law at the
University of Virginia and Columbia. He spent a year in
France at the Sorbonne. He was a moderate in politics and
had done a creditable job as a member of the Kentucky
legislature. The Hoover administration, rather than the New
Deal, took him from a lucrative law practice to work for the
federal government in Washington, although he had been a
hereditary Democrat. He did a competent job as counsel to
several administrative agencies, including the Reconstruction
Finance Corporation before Roosevelt took over. He remained on the job when the Democrats came in and landed
up as Solicitor General in the Justice Department. In that
spot, he handled the New Deal cases before the Supreme
Court. And he ended upon that bench as a Roosevelt appointee. It is not easy to piece out Reed's jurisprudence. On
ascending the High Court, he joined the ranks of New Deal
dissenters. When the liberal group put together a majority,
Reed's support pivoted this swing. From 1943 to 1946, at the
zenith of the Roosevelt Court (coinciding with the period
between the appointment of Wiley Rutledge and the death of
Stone), Reed moved politically to the right of center. Thereafter, he moved slightly to the left of center.

One must evaluate Reed's record with respect to issues in
the light of Reed himself to find consistency in his career. He
was consistently for national power against the thrust of state
action or individual freedom or local taxes. Because of his
professional background and farming tradition, he did not
seem too upset when business interests were threatened. His
boast of having supported a number of prolabor bills in the
Kentucky legislature reflects some sympathy on his part with
such efforts by state legislatures. He was quite ready to
permit both state and federal action in the civil-rights area,
out of deference to his belief that legislative power should not
cut down national power. In cases involving the voting rights
of black people, Reed, almost as if to belie his background,

voted to outlaw white primaries and decided in favor of blacks in other racial issues.

Frank Murphy had a sense of moral commitment to advance the human condition, a quality which often led his colleagues and legal commentators to understate his skill as a judge. The pun "Justice tempered with Murphy," acknowledged the priest-like devotion of that Irishman from Michigan. He established an impressive record as Assistant United States Attorney, law professor, local judge, mayor of Detroit, High Commissioner of the Philippines, and governor of Michigan.

He came known nationally when, in 1937, after just having been elected governor, he would not order the state troopers to pull out workers who were engaged in "sit-ins" in automobile factories because of bad economic conditions. He was defeated because of his unceremonious disregard of the interests of the automobile industry, although the way he handled the sit-ins, without brutal force and with tolerance, brought him expressions of thanks from labor and from Ford and General Motors as well.

This almost saintly man, with his mop of red hair and heavy eyebrows, who did not drink or smoke, was almost directly appointed by Roosevelt to be Attorney General. There he shook the Justice Department. He created the civil-rights section, fought for human rights, and landed in the Supreme Court.

No judge in the history of the Supreme Court of the United States ever burned with such a passion for human freedom as Frank Murphy. Nor was he selective. He argued for the rights of wartime foes, Nazi and Japanese. A devout Catholic, he nevertheless advocated the rights of Jehovah's Witnesses to proselytize,[4] to be anti-Catholic, and those of Harry Bridges, a Communist labor leader, in his resistance to being deported.[5] In spite of his experience as prosecutor, he

[4] Jones v. Opelika, 316 U.S. 584 (1942).
[5] Bridges v. Wixon, 326 U.S. 135 (1943).

demanded that those accused of crime be afforded every protection. He was as firmly committed to the interests of laboring men and women as he was to free speech. It was hardly a coincidence, then, that the first important opinion to be written by Murphy held that peaceful labor-picketing was to be protected as free speech.[6] Lawyers did not have any trouble in predicting where Murphy stood on any issue.

Another member of the Court was just as direct as Frank Murphy but with a different set of interests. Robert Jackson wrote with a sharp tongue that was as forceful and direct, in nontechnical language, without legal frill. He could cut through to the core of the problem before the Court. The story of Robert Houghout Jackson is not one of unrelenting boyhood poverty or a struggle to manage an education and then legal training. Jackson was the scion of a pioneer family. He was born in Silver Creek, Pennsylvania, and first saw a city, Pittsburgh, when he was fourteen years old. He was not the product of a deprived background, yet Jackson never graduated from a college. He never graduated from a law school, stopping after just one year of formal law studies. A brilliant youngster, he picked up his legal training as an apprentice in an upstate New York law office. Before long he developed a highly successful practice of his own. He soon made enough as a lawyer to be able to support himself as a gentleman farmer. Both his interests grew; he developed a substantial corporate practice and a stable of five horses as well.

As an upstate Democrat, he took on some assignments for another upstate Democrat, Franklin D. Roosevelt, then governor of the state. And in 1934 another upstater from New York and friend of now-President Roosevelt, Secretary of the Treasury Henry Morgenthau, called Jackson to Washington for a few months to untangle some legal problems of the Internal Revenue Bureau. The "six to eight" months of government work ended up as a lifetime commitment of his facile

[6] Bakery & Pastry Drivers v. Wohl, 315 U.S. 769 (1942).

mind and rapier tongue. Gone was his life as a country
gentleman in Jamestown, New York, except for a rare trip to
see friends or relax. Jackson entered the jungle of tax and
antitrust law and cut a path of coherence through each, and,
at the same time, brought the Mellon interests to its knees.

In the spring of 1938 Jackson moved into the second slot
in the Justice Department, resulting from the appointment of
Reed to the Supreme Court. But in January of 1939 Frank
Murphy was given the job of Attorney General, bypassing
Jackson. The two did not work compatibly in the Department
of Justice. One year later Murphy went to the Supreme Court
and Jackson became Attorney General, but there was no love
lost between the two men. A forensic genius, he won twenty-
three and lost only one of the appeals he argued as Solicitor
General before the 1938 to 1939 term of the Court. Then,
with war approaching, he became Attorney General. On the
eve of World War II, President Roosevelt appointed him to
the Supreme Court. There, Jackson continued his hard-hitting
and scintillating advocacy of New Deal programs for a time.

A number of factors intervened to make him turn into a
conservative. First, conservatism was not hard for an upstate
gentleman farmer with a lawyer's dexterity at advocating the
cause of the moment. Second, Jackson was both unfettered
and independently wealthy. Third, Jackson was miffed, to say
the least, when Roosevelt had broken precedent to run for
President a third time, thereby depriving another upstate
New Yorker of the opportunity to do so.

Initially he put his nimble use of language to service for
the liberal view. Then he shifted on economic questions.
Finally he switched even on civil rights. More and more, he
joined Justice Frankfurter in dissent. However, he was a good
foil, as well as friend, to the peppery Frankfurter. Once, when
a young man looking for a job told Jackson that he studied at
Harvard Law School under Frankfurter, Jackson chided him:
"If you have learned your legal history under Felix Frankfurter thoroughly and are willing to unlearn most of it under

me, I think there is hope for you." While Frankfurter wrapped himself in his robe in a posture of righteous impartiality, Jackson was direct and brutally frank.

Never afraid to be himself, or to show the man beneath the robe, he took a leave of absence from the Court when President Roosevelt asked him to prosecute the Nazi war criminals in the Nuremberg trials. Jackson's handling of the trials caused a stir, as compared with the calm that attended the investigation of Pearl Harbor by Justice Roberts, also at the urging of President Roosevelt. Many lawyers in the United States were annoyed that they had to wait for Jackson's return for his vote in cases that were being held for him.

He returned burning angry at the fact that the President had not named him Chief Justice at Stone's death. He let loose a thunderbolt of invective against Black, blaming the Alabamian for his failure to be given the appointment. Whether his attack was justified or not is irrelevant, but such a diatribe caused him to lose the respect of his colleagues. He lived on for eight more years. Shortly before he died, doctors warned him that if he continued at his pace, with his serious heart condition, it would be fatal. Characteristically, Jackson chose to plunge on relentlessly. In 1954 his heart gave out and he died.

Robert Jackson showed himself to be conservative in economic affairs and in those areas involving human rights. In 1950, *The New York Times Magazine* reprinted one of his concurring opinions word for word. Significantly, it expressed a position against labor and civil liberties. A revealing clue to Jackson the man is a picture that he clipped and saved from a very old periodical. It showed a solitary young student doing work at a beat-up desk. The caption, quoting Kipling, read: "He travels fastest who travels alone."

The last appointment to the Supreme Court made by President Roosevelt was Wiley Rutledge. In sharp contrast with Jackson, he presented the stereotyped ideal of a judge.

To Rutledge, decision was not an innate expression but rather the searching out of the considerations presented by the appeal, the weighing of these various factors, and then the striking of a balance. Although Rutledge was charged, as it is said in politics, to Iowa, his pattern of life pierced almost every section of the United States. Rutledge, like Douglas, was born the son of an itinerant minister. Although born in Kentucky, he spent his boyhood years in North Carolina and Tennessee. He attended and graduated from the University of Wisconsin. He started his academic career by teaching law in Colorado and Missouri, and later served as dean of the Iowa Law School. Rutledge, transported from academic life, brought Midwestern slow speech and outgoing warmth to the federal circuit court of appeals in Washington. President Roosevelt appointed him to replace Byrnes who had gone back to his real love, politics.

For six years, Rutledge was a solitary and dependable member of a four-man team, including Black, Douglas, and Murphy, which was dedicated to using the law as an instrument for humanism. Less given to flights of fancy or whim, he provided the ballast of sound legal precedent and painstaking, albeit sometimes boring and ponderous legal analysis to the views of this group. At times, especially with respect to civil liberties or labor, glimmerings of emotion would seep into his words. He always exhibited the traditional lawyer's caution and verbal decorousness to construct his opinion. When the majority, aided in part by Black and Douglas, yielded to the furies of public opinion and hit John L. Lewis and the striking United Mine Workers with a tremendous fine, Rutledge and his ally Murphy refused to give in.[7] With the skill of a good lawyer and the feelings of a great human being, Rutledge dissented. In a magnificent dissent of forty-four pages, he decimated the majority position and argued that the Court's approval of a civil and criminal suit in one case was incomprehensible.

[7] United States v. United Mine Workers, 330 U.S. 258 (1947).

The first significant opinion written by Jackson[8] was overshadowed by the Axis powers' declaration of war against Germany and Japan. The team of Jackson, Black, Douglas, and Murphy did not have much of a common future, since they rarely joined in such ventures after the first session. As a neophyte Justice, Jackson did not concur or dissent often.

The next year, 1942, Jackson wrote four majority opinions, from which, significantly, Black, Douglas, and Murphy dissented. In the "wheat penalty" case, the Court unanimously stretched the power of Congress to regulate interstate commerce to new lengths.[9] Jackson also wrote an emotional opinion that cited historic episodes in which persons were persecuted for refusing to pay obeisance to symbols of authority, reversing an earlier decision of the Court to sanction mandatory flag salute.[10]

"Compulsory unification of opinion achieves only the unanimity of the graveyard," warned Jackson. "It seems trite but necessary to say that the First Amendment to the Constitution was designed to avoid these ends by avoiding these beginnings." Jackson concluded that, "If there is any fixed star in our constitutional constellation, it is that no official, high or petty, can prescribe what shall be orthodox in politics, nationalism, religion, or other matters of opinion or force citizens to confess by word or act their faith therein."

That term, his other significant stands were primarily dissents. When the majority set aside the application of municipal license taxes as applied to Jehovah's Witnesses,[11] he chided, "the Court has, in one way or another, tied the hands of all local authority and made the oppressive methods of this group the law of the land." Rejecting this extension of civil rights, he wrote: "This court is forever adding new stories to

[8] New York Central and St. Louis Railroad Co. v. Frank, 314 U.S. 360 (1941).

[9] Wickard v. Filburn, 317 U.S. 111 (1942).

[10] West Virginia State Board of Education v. Barnette, 319 U.S. 624 (1943).

[11] Douglas v. City of Jeannette, 319 U.S. 157 (1943).

the temples of constitutional law, and the temples have a way of collapsing when one story too many is added. . . . Civil liberties had their origin and must find their ultimate guaranty in the faith of the people. If that faith should be lost, five or nine men in Washington could not supply its name." Yet during the same time, in another civil rights case, Jackson complained about the Court's refusal to help a draftee who argued that he was a conscientious objector and had not been allowed to see draft board records.[12]

By 1943 Jackson was attracting attention for the vigor and phraseology of his opinions, as well as their increasing conservative orientation. In economic matters, it was readily apparent that he was not on the same side as Black, Douglas, and Murphy; in civil rights matters his stands were both ways. He spoke for the majority in setting aside a Florida statute that the Court ruled was equivalent to peonage and involuntary servitude.[13] In another case, the Court held that in a prosecution of so-called religious leaders for using the mails to defraud, the truth or falsity of the religious doctrines must be excluded.[14] Jackson wrote: "Religious symbolism is even used by some with the same mental reservation one has in the teaching of Santa Claus or Uncle Sam or Easter bunnies or dispassionate judges."

By 1944, the war cases were tormenting the Justices. In two important decisions, he certainly did not sound like a man who was shortly to leave the Court in order to prosecute war criminals. He wrote for the majority in favor of the defendant who had been charged with treason for aid to Nazi saboteurs.[15] Jackson reviewed the law of treason in a forty-five-page opinion, a case of novel consideration in the Supreme Court. He concluded that the evidence adduced did not meet the exacting standards set out by the Constitution.

12 Bowles v. U.S., 319 U.S. 33 (1943).
13 Pollock v. Williams, 322 U.S. 4 (1944).
14 U.S. v. Ballard, 322 U.S. 78 (1944).
15 Cramer v. U.S., 325 U.S. 1 (1945).

In the Japanese relocation case, Jackson dissented in favor of those interned.[16]

In four labor cases, all decided five to four, he joined with Stone, Roberts, and Frankfurter. A fifth case dealt with whether travel time should be considered work time for the purpose of computing pay. The majority decided that the wages-and-hours law of Congress should govern. Jackson dissented. The Jewell Ridge case is important because of its import on "portal to portal" pay, but also because the decision was later disclosed by Jackson to be the basis of his feud with Black.[17]

[16] Korematsu v. United States, 323 U.S. 214 (1944).
[17] Jewell Ridge Coal Corp. v. Local No. 6167, U.M.W., 325 U.S. 161 (1945).

V

INTO THE POLITICAL THICKET

-13-

Hugo L. Black

FREEDOM RIDER
IN A WHITE SHEET

THE APPOINTMENT OF FRED VINSON AS CHIEF JUSTICE AND THE addition of other Truman appointees had little effect on the team of Black and Douglas. Hugo Black was Franklin Roosevelt's first appointee. His designation as the fighting liberal Senator from Alabama infuriated the conservatives and delighted the liberals, at least until the controversy over his early membership in the Klan came to light.

Black was admired by some and despised by others, as the intellectual dean of the New Deal Court. His life seems like a tableau in a tapestry of American history. He was born the eighth child of a Confederate Army volunteer in a tiny cabin at a red-clay crossroads town in the cotton-chopping farmlands of Alabama.

Hugo Black is an educated man, but not by standards of formal schooling. Few of his days have been spent in classrooms, and less than two years were spent in a law school. Like those judicial giants John Marshall and Samuel Miller, Black has been engaged in a continual process of self-education, rigorously and vigorously, throughout his entire career. This educative process has enabled Black to cut through to the core of a tough intellectual problem; he is not lost in superfluous layers of erudition. As he rose in prominence and personal success, he never insulated himself from the poor, the downtrodden, or the minorities.

As a practicing lawyer in Alabama, he used his extraordinary talents to oppose the establishment. His early career was successfully maintained by his ability to outmaneuver and outsmart the corporate interests in court. As a United States Senator, his views, his fights, and his interests were well in tune with those New Deal politicians running the country. Black was feared and despised by big business for his painstaking and penetrating investigations of the tentacles of lobbyists in legislation and of the shipping interests, which resulted in regulatory statutes. By temperament, Black is a mature person, with a warm, slow Southern manner; yet his mild exterior hides a steel-trap mind. He has the rare faculty of being objective enough to separate his strong ideological convictions from his personal relationships with those who dispute them.

In the summer of 1937 after Roosevelt named Black to the Supreme Court, an event occurred that had all the makings of a first-class scandal. A reporter, digging through the back issues of an Alabama newspaper, came across an item that established beyond all doubt something that was common knowledge in that town. As a young politico and for a brief time, Black was a member of the Ku Klux Klan. The reporter's story, reprinted throughout the country, earned him a Pulitzer Prize as well as the approbation of the Republican paper by which he was employed. The entire country was aghast. But, upon analysis, it was quite clear that the stirred-up excitement of the naming of Black was not based on his current membership in the Klan. Among the Justices, Black appeared safe. McReynolds, who had strong ethnic and racial prejudices (he rarely spoke to Cardozo), scarcely elicited a word. But Black was a thoroughly professional politician. He went to the people via national radio; he convinced the American public that he did not hold a single feeling of prejudice and that his record proved the veracity of his statement. Black was successful. He actually relied on the communications media a great deal. In 1969 Justice Black used television to explain the way in which the Court works. Flourishing a copy of the Constitution, he proudly explained that all the answers are to be found right in the unadorned text.

Black is a self-styled strict constructionist. In discussing the Constitution recently, he explained: "I believe the Court has no power to add to or subtract from the procedures set forth by the Founders. . . . I shall not at any time surrender my belief that the document itself should be our guide, not our own concept of what is fair, decent, and right."

He expressed this view with respect to a case[1] that questioned whether a juvenile court, in the trial of a minor for what would be an adult criminal offense, must establish guilt beyond a reasonable doubt. The majority decided yes. Justice Black took the position that the Constitution does not require proof beyond a reasonable doubt for either a child or an adult. He argued that, unlike the right to trial by jury or the right to counsel, this standard of proof cannot be found in any part of the Constitution. Thus, if there is no basis in the language of the Constitution for treating this test as part of due process, Black denied it.

When Frankfurter wrote in a case[2] that rejected evidence obtained through stomach pumping as being a violation of due process because it was based on conduct that "shocks the conscience," Black dissented. He rejected what he described as "the accordion-like qualities of this philosophy." The majority judges, claimed he, were projecting their own notions into the due process clause. "What avenues of investigation," queried Black, "are open to discover canons of construction so universally favored that this Court should write them into the Constitution?"

[1] Matter of Winship, 397 U.S. 358 (1970).
[2] Rochin v. California, 342 U.S. 165 (1952).

Black has been able to utilize his strict-construction approach to the Constitution as a strong force in the Court. Through his keen reasoning, the Court has become an agency for social change in America. By being "strict" Black has led judicial action to read precisely the language of the Constitution. Thus, when the First Amendment says that: "Congress shall make no law . . . abridging the freedom of speech," Black argues that it means "positively." This rationale means Black is against restrictions on obscenity, is against loyalty oaths, and does not believe in the suppression of Communists.

Yet, Black has considered some mass demonstrations as being entitled to the protection of "speech" and others outside that character and hence subject to official control.[3] Similarly, he has taken the position that the First Amendment did not prevent New Jersey from paying for parochial school buses.[4] This does not seem to be strict construction, in spite of Black's analysis: "The First Amendment has erected a wall between church and state. That wall must be kept high and impregnable. We could not approve the slightest breach. New Jersey has not breached it here."

The incongruity is best illustrated by Black's insistence on "one man, one vote." This is a cause he espoused as early as 1946,[5] in dissent. By 1964 the majority of the Court, through Chief Justice Warren, enunciated the rule that each legislative district must be approximately equal in population.[6] This judicial action brought about a reconstitution of almost every legislative body in the nation. The constitutional basis of the decision was the provision of the Fourteenth Amendment that guarantees to each person "the equal protection of the laws," nothing more specific than that provision. As Justice Harlan observed in his dissent, there was not even judicial precedent applying the Fourteenth Amendment to malapportionment of state legislatures. Black faced up to the issue of legislative

[3] Adderley v. Florida, 385 U.S. 39 (1966).
[4] Everson v. Board of Education, 330 U.S. 1 (1947).
[5] Colegrove v. Green, 328 U.S. 549 (1946).
[6] Baker v. Carr, 369 U.S. 186 (1962).

misrepresentation not by strict construction but rather as judicial improvisation necessary to meet a national problem.

Vinson was named Chief Justice of the Court in 1946. But until Tom Clark and Sherman Minton were added to support him, and Burton, too, in 1949, Vinson did not have many followers. Before acquiring support, Vinson was not successful in using his skills to mediate among the judges or to focus on the issues. He lacked the intellectual capacity to resolve the basic jurisprudential differences between the Black-Stone alliance and the Jackson-Frankfurter liaison. Of course, these differences were extremely important, and their nonresolution sustained periods of inactivity. It is interesting that Reed, who was held in the lowest esteem during the New Deal decade, became the head spokesman for the Vinson quartet. Both Vinson and Reed held almost identical views almost all the time: both Kentuckians shared a view on individual rights, for example, except as it related to the civil rights of black people.

After four judges were appointed by President Truman, the Court seemed to grind to a halt. The only comparable period in its history was twenty-five years earlier, when President Harding added Taft, Sutherland, Butler, and Sanford. Whereas the Court during the New Deal decade directed itself toward tempering the authority of government in its dealings with individuals, the Vinson Court slowed down, and in some cases, even turned back this trend. As evidence of this regression, the Vinson Court overruled two decisions that reinforced individual liberty; these cases were decided by Murphy less than one year earlier. And, in a more objective evaluation, it is a matter of record that the Vinson court produced only one hundred complete opinions after one term of Vinson's tenure as Chief Justice. This output was far below that of the Hughes Court over a comparable period. (The Hughes Court rendered about two hundred full opinions.)

Fred Vinson was the son of a county jailer, born in a remote Kentucky town. He was a typical American boy, lucky enough to play shortstop as a semi-pro in the Blue Grass baseball league. He was an excellent mathematics student, but he finally chose law and became very successful. He went to work for the federal government and secured top positions rapidly in the days when government functions and agencies were proliferating. He won many friends and influenced various people. He was both powerful and resolute, on the one hand, and weak and cunning, on the other. When he went to Congress, although a Democrat, he was accorded recognition by all his colleagues, without respect to party lines, as the expert on matters of taxation. He was effective enough as judge in a circuit court of appeals to have President Roosevelt select him to serve at the same time as head of an emergency court to decide OPA appeals. More significant positions came along: the President took him from the bench to make him economic stabilizer; then he was named Federal Loan Administrator; then he was designated Chief of the Office of War Mobilization and Reconversion, or "assistant President." Finally, he was picked by President Truman to be Secretary of the Treasury, and then, one year later, the President named him Chief Justice. Certainly, Vinson's experience was conducive to his support of the national government policies and his training as administrator of many agencies gave him what seemed to be invaluable experience for running a tight Supreme Court.

To Vinson, federal action was always good. During his seven years on the Supreme Court, his major decisions were directed against state action. In defending the civil rights of blacks, he decided that the enforcement of "restrictive covenants" were violative of the Fourteenth Amendment,[7] and he decided against so-called equal but segregated law school facilities in the South.[8] He sought to protect federal supremacy by limiting state taxes on federal bonds,[9] and by

[7] Shelley v. Kraemer, 334 U.S. 1 (1948).
[8] Sweatt v. Painter, 339 U.S. 629 (1950).
[9] New Jersey Realty Title Insurance Co. v. Division of Tax Appeals of New Jersey, 338 U.S. 665 (1950).

deciding against a state law that limited the ability of trade unions to strike.[10] Yet when the federal government proceeded against labor by setting fines for the formidable John L. Lewis and his United Mine Workers, Vinson supported the tremendous fine imposed,[11] leading the first of four opinions by members of the Court. He also wrote the majority opinion authorizing Congress to require union officials to take oaths that they were not Communists.[12] Then when President Truman wanted to seize the steel plants in a labor dispute against which the majority ruled,[13] Vinson, in a gesture unusual for him, dissented vociferously.

Vinson's profederal-government bias was most clearly manifested in the "loyalty" or "security" cases. During his tenure issues arose concerning the "loyalty oath" or program[14] and the handling of aliens or those suspected of crimes.[15] Vinson was always on the side of governmental authority. In a state case,[16] he enunciated the rule that a speaker, who is threatened by his listeners with violence as a result of expounding his views, may be silenced, rather than those who threaten him. Said Justice Black, dissenting: "I will have no part or parcel in this holding which I view as a long step toward totalitarian authority."

But Vinson's lasting monument will probably be his decision in the Dennis case,[17] which dealt with the Smith Act, roughly the twentieth century counterpart of the Sedition Act of the Federalists. Vinson authorized sending Communists to prison because they tried to sell the "party line" to convert people to communism. It is characteristic that the final judi-

[10] International Union of United Automobile Workers v. O'Brien, 339 U.S. 454 (1950).

[11] U.S. v. United Mine Workers, 330 U.S. 258 (1947).

[12] American Communications Ass'n. v. Douds, 339 U.S. 382 (1950).

[13] Youngstown Sheet & Tube Co. v. Sawyer, 343 U.S. 579 (1952).

[14] Garner v. Board of Public Works of Los Angeles, 341 U.S. 716 (1951); Bailey v. Richardson, 341 U.S. 918 (1951).

[15] Wong Yang Sung v. McGrath, 339 U.S. 33 (1950).

[16] Feiner v. New York, 340 U.S. 315 (1951).

[17] Dennis v. U.S., 341 U.S. 494 (1951).

cial act of Fred Vinson was to call the Court together to jam
through a reversal of the stay of execution that had been
granted by Douglas to the Rosenbergs, a couple convicted of
being spies.[18] Even Frankfurter, who was himself no Douglas
partisan, dissented in protest. And the Rosenbergs were elec-
trocuted according to schedule. The three Truman Justices—
Minton, Burton, and Clark—slavishly followed the lead of
"Fair Deal" Vinson.

Harold Burton, who was once described as the least able
Justice in a century, was born in Massachusetts into a comfortable bourgeois home. He received a fine education, established a traditional law practice in corporate law (a
conscientious and well-meaning venture), and then plunged
into Republican politics and conservative government service.
He served as mayor of Cleveland for three terms before being
elected to the United States Senate. His middle-of-the-road
and conscientious work as Senator induced then-Senator
Harry Truman to seek to have Burton as the ranking minority
of the Truman Committee to look into the defense contracts.
Truman and he became friends, and were drawn closer together. When Roberts, the only Republican of the Court,
retired, President Truman decided to yield to the sentiment
for a Republican replacement. So, his first appointment to the
Supreme Court was the upright yet pleasant Harold Burton
from Ohio, who with a shock of white hair looked like the
amiable proprietor of the village general store.

When he first began, it was clear that plodding Burton
was submerged in the taxing and overwhelming work of the
Court. He hunted for precedents from which to expand his
mind securely and appropriately. But somehow he never
came to grips with the real issues. Working hard, he only
managed to compose five or six opinions for the majority in
one term (at a time when Douglas and Black were managing
almost thirty apiece). But as the level of the entire Court
sunk, Burton's stock went up. By experience and application

[18] Rosenberg v. U.S., 346 U.S. 273 (1953).

his production rose to about ten opinions per term, which has become standard for the Court. And he did manage to grow in the job.

Thomas Clark, who changed his first name to Tom like that of his first mentor in political life Senator Tom Connally, has always been one of that distinctive breed, a Texas Democrat. The two dominant influences of his career have been political and prosecutorial. Clark was but five years out of law school when he landed the post of district attorney for Dallas County. In the heyday of the New Deal, he moved to the Justice Department. There he was assigned to antitrust matters and later to investigating war frauds. He oversaw the corraling of the California Japanese into detention camps during World War II. Apparently President Roosevelt was not too happy with his work and was about to remove him, when the President died. Truman, who had had a few amicable contacts with him, promoted him instead of firing him. As Attorney General, he ran the loyalty program with a vigilant eye for the government. Always the extrovert politico, wearing a bowtie and a perennial smile and handshake, he fitted the Truman pattern.

When an opening in the Supreme Court occurred, it was assumed that Clark would be asked to fill it. Vinson was receptive to the appointment. Prior to that time it was rumored that Vinson wanted someone on the Court who knew less law than he did. Certainly, Clark's career on the Court had not been outstanding. He served as "hatchetman" against all those who did not conform to his stereotype of an American. Alleged radicals, aliens, and criminal suspects received scant help from him. Furthermore, he expressed himself through language that was pedestrian and dull, aiming at his conclusions in a maze of illogical reasoning.

Clark finally had an opportunity to pen an exciting and important majority opinion in a long-awaited decision to overturn an old ruling of almost a half-century standing to the effect that the infant movie industry was not within the protection of free speech. He labored mightily to produce a turgid and boring field manual.[19] Clark rarely bothered to deviate from the group and infrequently expressed even a murmur of dissent. Clark seemed aware of his shortcomings as a lawyer and Justice and may have even been unhappy with his role. Perhaps this is why he depended so much on his judicial brethren or on the clerking law school graduates to do so much of his work. When his son, Ramsey Clark, was designated United States Attorney General, Justice Clark resigned to avoid any appearance of conflict of interest, and perhaps with a sigh of relief.

The humility of Tom Clark may be more desired than the brash self-confidence of Sherman Minton. Minton served one term in the Senate during which time he was Democratic whip, pushing New Deal measures. He became friendly with Senator Harry Truman. With his squat head, solid and square build, his flashing temper and quick tongue, he looked and was a formidable fighter for the program of the national administration. In 1940 he was defeated for his bid to be reelected to the Senate. He was hired for a short time as administrative assistant to President Roosevelt. Then he landed a job as a judge of a circuit court of appeals. For eight years in that capacity, he issued opinions that were not always directed to the issue, nor did they invoke the precedents in point, but they were always confident.

In any court Black and Douglas would be stellar attractions, but in this company they were stars of the first magnitude. Since October 4, 1937, when Black first began his duties as Associate Justice of the Supreme Court, his production has been overwhelming in quantity, encyclopedic in subject matter, and superlative in quality. His dominant concern for the last third of a century has been human rights. He believes in a freedom that takes many forms. He does not agree with Holmes' famous formulation that free speech may be silenced if there exists a "clear and present danger" of some evil that government has the right to prevent.

[19] Joseph Burstyn, Inc. v. Wilson, 343 U.S. 495 (1952).

Black believes that speech without action should not be restrained. For that reason, during the McCarthy crusàde against communism, in the 1950's, he dissented sharply in a number of cases.[20] "Ultimately all the questions," dissented Black in the Barenblatt case, "boil down to one—whether we as a people will try fearfully and futilely to preserve democracy by adopting totalitarian methods, or whether in accordance with our traditions, and our Constitution we will have the confidence and the courage to be free."[21] Black has persistently argued for more freedom of expression.[22]

Thus, in *Talley v. California*,[23] Black, for the majority, decided that the provision of the Los Angeles Municipal Code forbidding the distribution of anonymous leaflets was unconstitutional. His position was that free speech includes the right to be anonymous. In *Bridges v. California*,[24] he ruled that the right of Courts to control a newspaper's contents was markedly limited. He believes that even publications that are obscene are protected under the Constitution as free speech,[25] which follows from his literal reading of the free speech provisions of the Constitution. While speech alone is to be completely protected, it may lose its sanctity when coupled with illegal action. Thus, he held picketing unlawful when used to violate the antitrust laws.[26] And similarly, in *Adderley v. Florida*,[27] he upheld the conviction of student demonstrators who entered prison grounds, stopped traffic, and refused to disperse, while protesting arrests and municipal segregation policies.

Contrary to his earlier position, in 1944 Black came to believe that the Constitution protects school children who

[20] Dennis v. U.S., 341 U.S. 494 (1951); American Communications Association v. Dowds, 339 U.S. 382 (1957).

[21] Barenblatt v. United States, 360 U.S. 109 (1959).

[22] Yates v. U.S., 354 U.S. 298 (1957).

[23] Talley v. California, 362 U.S. 60 (1960).

[24] Bridges v. California, 314 U.S. 252 (1941).

[25] See Justice Black's opinion in Ginsburg v. United States, 383 U.S. 463, (1966).

[26] Giboney v. Empire Storage Co., 336 U.S. 490 (1949).

[27] Adderley v. Florida, 385 U.S. 39 (1966).

refuse to salute the flag because of their religion. In *Board of Education v. Barnette*,[28] Black and Douglas wrote that we "cannot say that a failure, because of religious scruples to assume a particular physical position and to repeat the words of a patriotic formula creates a grave danger to the nation. Such a statutory exaction is a form of test oath, and a test oath has always been abhorrent in the United States."

Writing for the majority in *Engel v. Vitale*,[29] Black held that it was unconstitutional for public schools in New York to start the school day with a prayer by the children. In another case he supported those who gave out religious tracts, even within the confines of private company towns.[30]

When the issue revolves about spending public money to help religious institutions, Black has made a distinction between expenditures that are primarily for the promotion of religion and expenditures that are primarily for the social welfare. Thus, writing for the majority in the Everson case,[31] Black ruled that public funds could be used to transport pupils to parochial schools as well as to public schools.

Since his early days as a lawyer, Black has opposed "third-degree" tactics often employed by the police. When he became a Justice of the Supreme Court, his dislike of the procedure persisted.[32] He has been concerned with fair trials for those accused of crime. Many years ago, Black argued in dissent that the privilege against incrimination protects such persons in state prosecutions[33] as well as federal. Ultimately, his view prevailed.[34]

In 1938 the Court, through Black, held that an accused had a right to counsel in all federal prosecutions.[35] Yet the Court, with Black dissenting, would not go so far as to require

[28] Board of Education v. Barnette, 319 U.S. 624 (1943).
[29] Engel v. Vitale, 370 U.S. 421 (1962).
[30] Marsh v. Alabama, 326 U.S. 501 (1946).
[31] Everson v. Board of Education, 330 U.S. 1 (1947).
[32] Chambers v. Florida, 309 U.S. 227 (1940).
[33] Adamson v. California, 332 U.S. 46 (1947).
[34] Malloy v. Hogan, 378 U.S. 1 (1964).
[35] Johnson v. Zerbst, 304 U.S. 458 (1938).

lawyers in state prosecutions.[36] More than two decades later, Black scored a personal triumph by being permitted to write the majority opinion in *Gideon v. Wainwright*,[37] which required that attorneys be provided for indigents in all criminal cases.

Curiously, with respect to the requirement of the Fourth Amendment that searches and seizures be reasonable and upon a warrant, Black has voted in accordance with the view of law enforcement officials.[38]

Justice Black has been in the forefront of the judicial efforts to erase segregation and to more equitably apportion the state legislatures. In *Griffin v. County School Board*,[39] he wrote for the majority that it was illegal to close the public schools in order to thwart integration and unlawful to contribute public funds to private segregated schools. In *Gibson v. Florida Legislative Committee*,[40] a duly appointed state committee was not permitted to compel a branch of the National Association for the Advancement of Colored People to disclose its membership.

In two important cases, Black wrote opinions defining the limits on martial law.[41] He also has supported the rights of public employees to their jobs and extensively reviewed the history of bills of attainder in *United States v. Lovett*.[42]

Because of the preeminence of Justice Black in the civil-rights field, his work in other problem areas is at times overlooked. He has argued that corporations are not "persons" entitled to the protection of the due process clause.[43] He has attacked the standards applied by the Court to the review of

[36] Bates v. Brady, 316 U.S. 455 (1942).

[37] Gideon v. Wainwright, 372 U.S. 335 (1963).

[38] See dissent, Berger v. New York, 388 U.S. 41 (1967).

[39] Griffin v. County School Board, 377 U.S. 218 (1964).

[40] Gibson v. Florida Legislative Committee, 372 U.S. 539 (1963).

[41] Duncan v. Kalanamoki, 327 U.S. 304 (1946); Reiv v. Covert, 354 U.S. 1 (1957).

[42] U.S. v. Lovett, 328 U.S. 303 (1946).

[43] Connecticut General Life Insurance Co. v. Johnson, 303 U.S. 77 (1938).

public utility rates,[44] in fact, to all social legislation.[45] From the time Black came on the Court, no state attempt to regulate its economic affairs has been deemed to violate due process because of its subject matter. Black has joined with those who believe that Congress can freely use the commerce clause to deal with national economic problems. Thus, in *United States v. South-Eastern Underwriters Association,* [46] he validated the sweep of the antitrust laws to cover the insurance business. He has had enormous influence in the antitrust field and has supported congressional regulatory statutes such as the Fair Labor Standards Act, the National Labor Relations Act, and others. At the same time, he has approved of nondiscriminatory state legislation that regulates commerce or invokes taxes not contrary to action by Congress.[47]

In the late spring of 1970, Hugo Black was still on the side of those espousing unpopular causes. He wrote the opinion for the unanimous Court in reversing the conviction of a man who wore an Army uniform to perform a piece of "guerrilla theater" meant to dramatize American brutality in Vietnam. The man was convicted of violating federal law that forbids wearing a distinctive part of a military uniform in theatrical productions if the role "discredits" the armed services. Wrote Black, a double standard cannot be applied to free speech. A law cannot survive that "leaves Americans free to praise the war in Vietnam but can send persons like Schacht to prison for opposing it."[48]

In June of 1970, the Supreme Court exempted from military service all young men who have strong moral or ethical objections to military duty, so long as their beliefs are

[44] McCart v. Indianapolis Water Co., 302 U.S. 419 (1938); Federal Power Commission v. Hope National Gas Co., 320 U.S. 591 (1944).
[45] Lincoln Federal Labor Union v. Northwestern Iron & Metal Co., 335 U.S. 525 (1949); Ferguson v. Skrupa, 372 U.S. 726 (1963).
[46] U.S. v. South-Eastern Underwriters Association, 322 U.S. 533 (1944).
[47] Southern Pacific Co. v. Arizona, 325 U.S. 76 (1945); dissent in Givin, White and Prince, Inc. v. Heuveford, 305 U.S. 434 (1939).
[48] Schacht v. U.S., 90 S.CT. 1555 (1970).

deeply held and not based on expediency.[49] Interpreting the draft law section that provides for conscientious objectors, Justice Black wrote: "That section exempts from military service all those whose consciences, spurred by deeply held moral, ethical, or religious beliefs, would give them no rest or peace if they allowed themselves to become a part of an instrument of war."

Justice Hugo L. Black, at eighty-five, is not thinking of retiring from the Supreme Court. "I have no plans to retire or not to retire," said he on his birthday.

Only four men have served as long as Black: Joseph Story and the first John M. Harlan, thirty-three years; Chief Justice John Marshall, thirty-four years, and Stephen J. Field, a few months under thirty-five years.

Recently, Black has said that "The layman's constitutional view is that what he likes is constitutional and that which he doesn't like is unconstitutional." Some critics of the Justice's recent rulings complain that this criticism may be applied to Black. They accuse him of becoming increasingly conservative and uncharacteristically crochety. But such carping is mere piddling. This polite and considerate gentleman of the South is one of the great Justices of the United States and has left a permanent and important impress on its constitutional history.

[49] Welsh v. U.S., 90 S.CT. 1792 (1970).

–14–

William O. Douglas

THE LAST OF THE FRONTIERSMEN

PRESIDENT TRUMAN, WHO DID NOT SUFFER FROM UNDERCONFI-
dence, decided to name his confidant, Minton, a Democrat of
the old school, to the Supreme Court. He found his place in the
Fair Deal quartet very quickly. In his very first year, he wrote
an opinion that overruled one of Murphy's civil Liberties decisions.[1] (Reed wrote the other one.)[2] Minton soon became the
foremost opponent against the extension of individual rights.
His illiberal votes even exceeded those of Vinson, and certainly
those of Reed and Clark. In Vinson's last term, the Court struck
down the attempt by the Texas "Jaybirds," an all-white club,
to hold their private elections before the regular state primary
as a method of determining the clube vote in the official primary.[3] The only dissenter was Minton. He wrote the opinion
in the case and used the Constitution to protect a previously
established precedent of guilt by association, as used by the
New York Court of Appeals in upholding the firing of school
teachers.[4] Uncharacteristically, he dissented in a case in which

[1] U.S. v. Rabinowitz, 339 U.S. 56 (1950).
[2] Carlson v. Landon, 342 U.S. 524 (1952).
[3] Terry v. Adams, 345 U.S. 461 (1961).
[4] Adler v. Board of Education, 342 U.S. 485 (1952).

the majority upheld the arrest of a speaker who was threatened with violence by his audience.[5]

The Vinson Court, in Truman's administration, managed to breach the defensive walls protecting individual liberty that were constructed by the New Dealers. This Court is also remembered because its work product fell to the lowest in this century. Court procedures bogged down. For example, Frankfurter's philosophy of judicial restraint was put into practice. At one time, Black and Douglas could count on Murphy and Rutledge to provide the four votes necessary to bring up a case for review by granting certiorari. Now, the Vinson four plus Frankfurter were able to figure a way to block the review of many, many lower court decisions. Further, in some instances, where certiorari was granted because four votes were found, Frankfurter resorted to a new tactic. After the appeal was heard, he would argue that it be dismissed on the ground that certiorari had been "improvidently granted." Such summary dismissal required five votes; Frankfurter usually had them. Thus, in ten years, the number of cases the Court would consider in one term was reduced by half. Furthermore, many important civil liberty issues were not being considered by the Supreme Court.

The perennial problem of the regulation of business or labor by government came up before the Truman Court, but in less numerous cases. At the top of the list of such appeals was the steel seizure case[6] in which Black wrote "for the court," with six of the Justices concurring with him, each writing his own opinion, and three dissenting. The opinions are spread over one hundred thirty-two pages of the official reports.

The refusal of the steel companies to meet the demands of the workers for higher wages made it appear that a strike throughout the country was to be expected. The Korean hostilities created an urgent demand for steel. President Truman

[5] Feiner v. New York, 340 U.S. 315 (1951).
[6] Youngstown Sheet & Tube Co. v. Sawyer, 343 U.S. 579 (1952).

did not wish to invoke the Taft-Hartley Act, the symbol of antiunionism, to stop the imminent strike. Instead, he signed the necessary papers, had the flag of the United States raised over the steel plants, and thus symbolically "seized" them. He received no mandate from Congress. The President was following the example of Franklin D. Roosevelt when, before World War II, Roosevelt seized factories to forestall strikes. The Supreme Court, with Vinson, Burton, and Reed strenuously dissenting, invalidated the President's action. The strike was thereby instated. The Court once more asserted the right to its last word on who can do what under the Constitution.

The Court in this period threw out fair trade laws that forbade pricecutting on products sold nationally, thus helping discount houses and cut-rate drugstores.[7] The Court undermined administrative expertise by supporting the Federal Communications Commission's selection of one of two types of competing color television systems.[8]

In the areas of civil liberties, the Court was undistinguished. President Truman was inveighing against the McCarran Act of 1952, which was enacted into law over his veto, characterizing it as "worse than the infamous Alien Act of 1789." But at the same time, the Supreme Court was applying the McCarran Act of 1940 in a repressive way. An example was the case of the alien who had been a Communist twenty-three years before and was deported to Italy, with his family left behind in America.[9] Douglas and Black complained by means of their dissent. Jackson implied that the Court should not get involved since the issue involved an exercise of political judgment. Frankfurter, with his usual restraint, suggested the place to handle such laws is "Congress, not this Court."

But even Jackson and Frankfurter joined forces with Black and Douglas in two cases in which the injustice was overwhelming. Their efforts, however, were to no avail

[7] Schwegman Brothers v. Calvert Distillers Corp., 341 U.S. 384 (1950).
[8] Radio Corporation of America v. U.S., 341 U.S. 412 (1950).
[9] Mascitti v. McGrath, 342 U.S. 580 (1951).

against the votes of the other five. In one appeal, the Attorney General of the United States had caused the arrest on unsubstantiated charges of a number of aliens, among them a waiter who had been living in the United States for thirty-nine years, had been a blood donor seven times during World War II, and whose sons had served in the United States Army. They also supported a man named Meyer who was being detained at Ellis Island indefinitely because he was denied readmission into the United States after going to Rumania to visit his mother who was dying. When he reached Ellis Island after his trip, he was sent back to Europe, but no country, twenty in all, Western or Communist, would admit him. He was thereupon compelled to return to the prison of Ellis Island. Meyer, who resided in Buffalo, had lived in the United States for twenty-five years. He was never advised of the "confidential" charges filed against him and never afforded a hearing. Wrote Jackson, in dissent: "This man, who seems to have led a life of unrelieved insignificance, must have been astonished to find himself suddenly putting the government of the United States in such fear that it was afraid to tell him why it was afraid of him. . . . No one can make me believe we are that far gone."

In the area of civil liberties, the Vinson group made Frankfurter and Jackson, and at times Burton, look liberal, at times forcing them to join Black and Douglas.

When the Los Angeles "loyalty" oath, which was required of all employees of that city, was sustained five to four, Jackson joined the majority. Frankfurter and Burton joined the dissent, terming it an invalid "bill of attainder." Douglas charged that the ordinance punished the workers for their past, "by legislative act and not by judicial process."[10] And when the Bailey case,[11] concerning the "loyalty" program of the federal government with its secret inquiries and its

[10] Garner v. Board of Public Works of Los Angeles, 341 U.S. 716 (1951).
[11] Bailey v. Richardson, 341 U.S. 918 (1951).

paid informers came before the Court, Frankfurter and Jackson joined Black and Douglas to decry the action.

Justice Clark did not participate since he had played a major role in the loyalty program as Attorney General. There was no indication how the other Justices voted because the vote was four to four; thus, the lower court decision was "affirmed by an equally divided Court." However, later in the same term, when the listing of subversive organizations by the Attorney General, without a determination by a hearing, was prohibited, the lineup became clear.[12] The vote was five to four, with Burton against the listing on the ground that this procedure went too far. Six of the eight Justices wrote individual opinions that revealed how they felt about the programs as a whole. Douglas denounced the entire loyalty program as being a fifth column tactic itself. This time, Vinson, Minton, and Reed were forced to dissent.

Then the Court decided on the Dennis case.[13] In that case, a few leaders of the Communist party in the United States were sent to jail, which improved their status as martyrs within the party. But what was more serious was that the Supreme Court was willing to uphold a law that so blatantly violated the guarantees of free speech guaranteed by the First Amendment. Dennis and the others were not convicted and sentenced for committing a crime. They were imprisoned for "teaching and advocating" communism. Vinson, for himself and his henchmen, Minton, Reed, and Burton, resorted to a somewhat twisted "clear and present danger" test to get around the First Amendment. He did concede that the threat to America posed by the defendants' "known and nonsensible Communist activities" was not very present or clear. Jackson went still further. He rejected the "clear and present danger" test whenever there existed a "conspiracy" at large. In a mammoth but timid opinion, Frankfurter deplored the viola-

---

[12] Joint Anti-Fascist Refugee Committee v. McGrath, 341 U.S. 123 (1951).

[13] Dennis v. U.S., 341 U.S. 494 (1951).

tion of civil liberties yet said the Court could do nothing about it. Douglas, in dissent, sharply pointed out that there was no showing of a "clear and present danger." Black, reaching the same result, argued that the First Amendment's right of free speech covered the defendants' activities. He expressed the hope that "in calmer times, when present pressures, passions and fears subside, this or some later Court will restore the First Amendment liberties to the high preferred place where they belong in a free society."

The alliance of Vinson, Minton, and Reed was again joined by Burton and Jackson after the principal Dennis case, when the six-month sentences that Judge Medina imposed upon the lawyers for the Communists for contempt of court came up for review.[14] Frankfurter joined with Black and Douglas. In a comprehensive, thoughtful dissent, with a forty-seven-page appendix, they criticized Medina for "incontinent wrangles" between the judge and the attorneys, which "weaken the restraints of respect" for Medina, whose "self-concern pervades the record."

In two other areas, the Vinson Court retreated to a position held by the Supreme Court before the accomplishments of the New Deal Court. It weakened the restraint of the Bill of Rights on police treatment of those accused of crime.[15] In one case, the Vinson Court sustained the conviction of two New York suspects who were held privately by the police until they were actually coerced into confessions. Only Black, Douglas, and Frankfurter dissented.

But one area of marked difference was the approach of Vinson's Court as compared with the New Deal Court on the issues of racial segregation. A half-century before, in 1896, the Fuller bench institutionalized segregation with the legal fiction of "separate but equal."[16] The first Harlan then dissented by commenting that "Our Constitution is color blind."

[14] Sacher v. U.S., 343 U.S. 1 (1952).
[15] U.S. v. Rabinowitz, 339 U.S. 56 (1950).
[16] Plessy v. Ferguson, 163 U.S. 537 (1896).

The Vinson Court was presented with several cases that sought the admission of black students into an all-white law school in Texas,[17] and a white graduate course in Oklahoma.[18] The main point urged was the overthrow of the "separate but equal" doctrine. The Court would not meet the larger issue and decided that the blacks had to be admitted on the factual ground that the facilities offered them were not equal. But it would not face those cases in which the physical facilities might actually be better for blacks, but where there was segregation of the races. The Vinson Court refused to consider such latter cases, avoiding them by all sorts of technicalities, by delays and postponement. That the responsibility must be placed at Vinson's door is clear since the situation radically changed the first year the new Chief Justice, Earl Warren, came to the Court.

Together with Hugo Black, William O. Douglas was ready, intellectually and spiritually, for the coming of Earl Warren. Although born in Minnesota, Douglas represents the expansiveness of spirit, the sense of adventure, and the indomitable will of the frontiersman.

The Douglas family chanced to be in the State of Washington at the time that the boy's circuit-riding preacher father passed away. Douglas had to support himself through high school and then Whitman College. He did so with menial jobs ranging from newsboy, berry picker, window washer, sheep herder, and a miscellany of other jobs. In his spare time, he conquered the effects of polio by climbing mountains. Since then he has roamed around the world finding the highest peaks and most rugged terrain to overcome.

His formative years in Tacoma, Washington, left a permanent impression on the boy. "Bill used to tell me," an old friend explains, "what it was like living on the wrong side of the tracks in Tacoma. The kids didn't make fun of him just because he was weak. They also taunted him because he was

---

[17] Sweatt v. Painter, 339 U.S. 629 (1950).
[18] McLaurin v. Oklahoma State Regents, 339 U.S. 637 (1950).

poor, and Bill never forgot it. I've had many conversations with him about the 'establishment' in Tacoma and how contemptuously it treated him. . . . Bill has never forgotten that he was once poor. Maybe the memory keeps him a little frightened. But unlike so many men who make it big, he has never ceased to identify with the poor. Bill hated the Tacoma 'establishment' and, when he left town to go to law school, he vowed he would cut those people down to size. He worked ever since—with a widening horizon—to keep that vow."

He came to New York to enter Columbia Law School by riding the roads and freight cars and staying at hobo camps with only a few cents in his jeans. While studying law, he managed to keep clothed and fed by the odd jobs Dean Harlan Stone found for him. Graduating second in his class, he entered Wall Street, where he was inducted into the cabala of complex corporate transactions. After a few years of unraveling and putting together such financial mysteries, Douglas went back to Columbia to teach. Always an independent thinker, he resigned in protest when Nicholas Murray Butler, Columbia's president, named a new law dean—in violation of academic democracy, according to Douglas. Yale hired him in less than five years after his graduation from law school. He shook up the orthodox concepts of business law and got right in to work with the students, although this did not make him as popular as Professor Frankfurter was at the rival law institution, Harvard.

President Roosevelt made Douglas a member of the new Securities Exchange Commission, a New Deal innovation, after the uproar his investigation and report of corporate financing brought out in its authoritative and information-packed report. His forthrightness and brilliance soon made him the chairman of that agency. Heralded as the most skillful and fearless New Deal administrator, it was regretted by many that after only three years in Washington he went to the Supreme Court. Yet, with Brandeis retiring, the Supreme Court sorely needed a member who understood the advan-

tages and the evils of big business. "One day in 1939," as
Douglas tells it, "I was out on the golf course when a caddy
ran up to me and said the President wanted to talk to me on
the phone. I knew there was a vacancy on the Federal
Communications Commission and I really thought Franklin
Delano Roosevelt was going to offer it to me. But he didn't.
That's when he told me he was going to put me on the
Court. . . ."

Ironically, four Senators voted against his confirmation
on the assumption that, since he had been employed on Wall
Street, he had to be reactionary.

⟨ The two living American success stories, Black and
Douglas, immediately gravitated to each other. For three
terms they voted the same way in every case. There were
some differences between them during World War II; there
are some more marked differences today, but the team of
Douglas and Black connotes much as Holmes and Brandeis
did about half a century ago.

Much furor has been made of the differences that have
come between Black and Douglas. To some extent, their disputes have sprung from the legal positions each has expressed. Black has in recent years taken the more conservative
road. For a quarter of a century the two companions have
disparaged each other on the bench, and, it is reputed, off the
bench as well. Certainly, personal reasons must be involved as
well as different legal philosophies. But in any event they will
always be linked together in the history of the Supreme
Court. ⟩

Before long, Douglas was writing the tough opinions in
the field of corporate finance. Even his denigrators concede
his outstanding abilities in this area. Thus, in an important
freight-rate case, sustaining the Interstate Commerce Commission, he virtually wrote a monograph on the economics of
setting rates, replete with a graph and seventeen titles. It is a
felicitous coincidence that Douglas shares the mistrust that
Brandeis felt of corporate bigness. He explained this view by

way of dissent in a case that permitted the United States Steel
Corporation to expand its holdings in the far west:

> Power that controls the economy should be in the hands
> of the elected representatives of the people, not in the hands
> of an industrial oligarchy. Industrial power should be decen-
> tralized. It should be scattered into many hands so that the
> fortunes of the people will not be dependent on the whim or
> caprice, the political prejudices, the emotional stability of a
> few self-appointed men. The fact that they are not vicious men
> but respectable and socially minded is irrelevant. That is the
> philosophy and command of the Sherman Act. It is founded on
> a theory of hostility to the concentration in private hands of
> power so great that only a government by the people should
> have it.

In the area of civil rights, Douglas is a strong advocate of
individual freedom. Although in the cases that arose out of
World War II Douglas sided completely with the national
government on issues of spies, treason activity, and the
evacuation of the Japanese citizens from the coast, today, as
in the loyalty cases, he is the most consistent champion of
freedom.

Advancing age and a heart that requires a pacemaker
implanted in his chest do not seem to stifle Douglas' exuberance or his ability to leap into controversial matters. He has
been threatened with impeachment on several occasions. In a
lengthy speech on the floor of the House of Representatives,
the nine-year association of Justice Douglas and the Albert
Parvin Foundation was reviewed. While this foundation as-
sists students from underdeveloped areas of the world (a
project close to Douglas' heart), it has been linked to Las
Vegas gambling interests. Douglas resigned from the foundation and denied that he gave legal advice to Albert Parvin or
committed any other improprieties.

Douglas was also criticized for his connection with the
"leftish" Center for the Study of Democratic Institutions.
Congressman Ford, in his House speech, expressed indigna-

tion at Douglas' book, *Points of Rebellion*, on the ground that it added "legitimacy to the militant hippie-yippie movement," but mainly because portions of the book appeared in a magazine also containing pictures of nudes, which Ford described as "hard core" pornography.

Points of Rebellion is a hard-hitting polemic against the status quo. "Violence has no constitutional sanction," writes Douglas, "but where grievances pile high and most of the elected spokesmen represent the Establishment, violence may be the only effective response." In 1776, George III of England was "the symbol against which our founders made a revolution now considered bright and glorious. We must realize that today's Constitution is the new George III. Whether it will continue to adhere to his tactics, we do not know. If it does, the redress, honored in tradition, is also revolution." Actually, Douglas called for "political regeneration" rather than revolution, but the indictment of the system was serious and the language shrill.

But Douglas, now over seventy, may be the last of the robust and lusty pioneers; certainly he is the last on the Supreme Court bench. His career has always been surrounded by the crack and spark of his activities. Within a month, his twenty-six-year-old wife divorced him and he married an even younger woman, then twenty-three years old. He has never silenced his personal opinions on issues ranging from the recognition of Red China to the rape of nature.

In 1953, there was talk of impeachment when he granted a brief stay of execution to the Rosenbergs, convicted spies. Their petition for habeas corpus raised a substantial issue that was not presented earlier. Impeachment charges were considered then, but, undismayed, Douglas and Black continued to take up cudgels in defense of underdogs. Douglas has gone on record against violence but in First Amendment cases he has steadfastly held to his belief that free speech and assembly should be protected even for "miserable merchants of unwanted ideas."

In the face of demands to censor pornography, Douglas has rejected the role of guardian of morality for the Court. As he explained in a recent dissent, not "because I relish 'obscenity' but because I think the First Amendment has prohibited all kinds of censorship." He applies the same fundamentalist approach to the constitutional requirement of separation of church and state. In 1962, Douglas not only went along with the ruling of the Court that prohibited prayers in public schools[19] but would have extended the decision to remove all religious symbols from public life, such as prayers which open legislative sessions or the motto "In God We Trust" from currency.

Many Americans do not like the views and lifestyle of William O. Douglas. But Douglas has often pointed the way to important shortcomings in the law to meet the needs of society. Certainly, he has been a strong ally to Hugo Black in the successful campaign to incorporate most of the guarantees of the Bill of Rights through the due process clause of the Fourteenth Amendment so as to protect individuals from oppression by state as well as federal officials. Nowhere in the Constitution is the right of privacy expressed. Yet Douglas found it there by implication. In *Griswold v. Connecticut*,[20] in 1965, writing for the majority, Douglas used the "right of privacy" concept to strike down state prohibitions on the use of contraceptive devices by husband and wife. This right of privacy is now serving as a protection against statutes that dictate personal relations and moral conduct, such as sex acts between consenting adults. In his typical affirmative manner, he wrote: "Specific guarantees in the Bill of Rights have penumbras, formed by emanations from those guarantees that help give them life and substance."

The criticism hurled at Justice Douglas for his nonjudicial activities seems to be irritating him. In autographing *Points of Rebellion* for someone's friend, he wryly joked,

[19] Engel v. Vitale, 370 U.S. 421 (1962).
[20] Griswold v. Connecticut, 381 U.S. 479 (1965).

"Your friend had better stop quoting me, or he'll soon be cited for some kind of criminal violation." His inability to display emotion, his aloofness, and his lack of concern with appearance, have not helped endear him to his critics. Unlike Holmes and Frankfurter, Douglas has not enshrined himself with his former aides and secretaries. While he often won their admiration, he has not always won their abiding friendship. As one secretary said: "I kept thinking that Douglas was another of those liberals who loved humanity in the abstract, but couldn't stand people in particular."

In the late spring of 1970, he defended the right of a judge to live his own life off the bench: "Federal judges are entitled, like other people, to the full freedom of the first amendment," he wrote in a dissent to a decision. "If they break the law they can be prosecuted, if they become corrupt or sit in cases in which they have a personal or family stake, they can be impeached by Congress."

The dissent was based on a decision in an appeal from a judge in Oklahoma, seeking review in the Supreme Court of the authority of other judges to restrict his judicial role.[21] "Our tradition," wrote Justice Douglas, "bars political impeachments as evidenced by the highly partisan, but unsuccessful effort to oust Justice Samuel Chase of this Court in 1805." He went on to say, "there is no power under our Constitution" by which a group of federal judges can censor or discipline one of their colleagues. "The mood of some Federal judges is opposed to this view, and they are active to make Federal judges walk in some uniform step." He added that the attempt to limit a fellow judge by other judges "has happened to other Federal judges who have had perhaps a more libertarian approach to the Bill of Rights than their brethren."

"The result is that the non-conformist has suffered greatly," said Justice Douglas. "How under the Constitution can one judge's lips be sealed because of the predestined view

21 Chandler v. Judicial Council, 398 U.S. 74 (1970).

of other judges?" Douglas might just as easily have been thinking of himself.

Douglas' work is a good example of how questionable the distinction between strict construction and loose construction is. Douglas is as strict in reading the Bill of Rights as another judge is in reading the provisions of the Constitution which spell out state's rights. He is as much a strict constructionist when the issue is the right of a poor person accused of crime, under the provisions assuring the equal protection of law. "Certainly he who has a long purse will always have a lawyer, while the indigent will be without one. I know of no more invidious discrimination based on poverty."

No Justice is more strict than Douglas when he rules on obscenity as measured by the First Amendment. In explaining his decision in the case involving the ban of the movie, *I Am Curious Yellow*, he said, "I have consistently dissented," in such cases, "not because, as frequently charged, I relish obscenity. I have dissented before and now because I think the First Amendment bars all kinds of censorship. What can be done to literature under the banner of obscenity can be done to other parts of the spectrum of ideas when the partisan or majoritarian demands mount and propagandists start disclaiming the law."

He declared: "We are judges, not literary experts or historians or philosophers. We aren't competent to render an independent judgment as to the worth of this or any other book, except in our capacity as private citizens."

Certainly, Douglas' place in the history of the Court will rest on his conviction that the law must be relevant to the conditions of life to which it is to be applied. The prodigious volume of his work and his openness about his methods and goals have at times been at the expense of careful scholarship. His work has chiefly been expressed in dissent, like some of the other great Justices, ferreting out new areas of personal liberty.

Earl Warren

KNIGHT-ERRANT FROM THE SMOKE-FILLED ROOM

EARL WARREN, WITH A HERITAGE FROM ANCIENT NORSEMEN, has a ruggedly handsome appearance and a strapping figure. His father was a railroad mechanic, who apparently passed along to his son Earl the practical turn of ingenuity in handling matters and the ability to face problems directly in order to devise answers. Earl Warren's tendency to deal with the problems directly before him, without reference to consistency with the past, is pointed up by a remark made by a political adversary intending harsh criticism, that Warren "never had an abstract thought in his life."

The Justice exhibits an easygoing gregariousness reminiscent of most Western politicians. He deals equally with all people, regardless of status in life or political persuasion. Warren is a politician who has been living this role all of his adult life. He has climbed the ladder of state politics. Shortly after graduating from law school, he progressed from deputy city attorney in the county district attorney's office to the attorney general of the State of California. Although he was a successful prosecutor, he has related that it made him ill to succeed in obtaining a murder conviction.

The governorship of California was a position close to his

personality and interests. He succeeded in being elected, and later broke precedent by being reelected to that office for three terms and with substantial bipartisan support. His interest in balancing the state budget did not prevent him from increasing the old-age-pension rates or from working for a compulsory state-wide plan for health insurance or from brooding about the imposed broad loyalty tests for teachers.

He grew up in the fertile and integrated San Joaquin Valley of the south central portion of California. Perhaps because of his childhood or perhaps because of his later convictions, he was not prejudiced. As governor, he sent a Negro to sit on the Superior Court of the State of California, for the first time in the history of that state. He also became sufficiently aroused, without being solicited to do so, to write a sympathetic letter of concern to a Chinese family who were prevented from residing in an all-Caucasian neighborhood of San Francisco by the citizens' vote to bar them.

Warren ventured for national elective office when he ran for the Vice-Presidency in 1948 with Thomas E. Dewey. He was powerful in the councils of the national Republican party because of his command of the significant California delegation. And he was always a potential nominee for the Presidency. Warren threw the weight of his California delegation behind the candidacy of Dwight D. Eisenhower in 1952. This certainly did not adversely affect Eisenhower's feelings about him once elected. President Eisenhower selected the widely admired Earl Warren to sit as Chief Justice on the Supreme Court. Warren seemed to represent the solid, down-to-earth, middle-of-the-road respectability that typified the Eisenhower years.

From the first, however, it was apparent that Warren could not be forced into any mold. In closely controverted civil-rights cases, he was compelling Reed and Minton to dissent rather than Black and Douglas. As a matter of fact, Justice Warren voted with the Black-Douglas team about fifty percent of the time.

The outstanding decision of the Warren Court, of course, has been its direct, no-nonsense prohibition of segregated schools. The unanimous Court held[1] that separate facilities for black and white children violated the equal protection of laws provision of the Fourteenth Amendment. It is a tribute to Warren's administrative skill and forceful personality that he was able to speak for the entire Court without a single dissent or even a separate opinion concurring. He aimed directly at the target without the evasion offered by old precedents and without pseudohistoric legal scholarship. He simply declared that the day of "separate but equal" no longer was the law. Arguing that "we cannot turn the clock back to 1868," he rejected the efforts of those who sought to establish what the Fourteenth Amendment "intended." To separate school children, "from others of similar age and qualifications solely because of their race generates a feeling of inferiority as to their status in the community that may affect their hearts and minds in a way unlikely ever to be undone. . . . We conclude that in the field of public education the doctrine of 'separate but equal' has no place."

Justice Warren had as his associates Hugo Black, William Douglas, Tom Clark (succeeded by Thurgood Marshall), John Harlan, William Brennan, Potter Stewart, Byron R. White, and a seat shared by Arthur Goldberg and then Abe Fortas.

After considerable dawdling, the Senate confirmed the man President Eisenhower chose to replace Associate Justice Jackson. It is unlikely that Justice John Marshall Harlan will ever exhibit the same humanism or bold and passionate independence of his grandfather who sat on the Court. He represents a new breed of Eastern Republicanism. Although he was actually born in Chicago, Harlan is a product of Princeton and Oxford, polished by his experiences in a Wall Street firm. He comes from a financially secure and socially prominent background. As a Rhodes scholar, he brings a new type of

[1] Brown v. Board of Education of Topeka, 347 U.S. 483 (1954).

expertise to the Court, but perhaps not a unique view. Like Warren, he did not have extensive federal experience except for a short term on a federal court of appeals. His public service has otherwise consisted of an amalgam of state prosecuting and investigating.

Brennan resembles the stereotype ward politician of the old days. He even possesses the warmth and gregariousness of that political tradition. But he was the most experienced of all the judges who came to the Warren Court. He is a Catholic in religious conviction and also a man of broad cultural and humanistic interests. He is doctrinaire only in his commitment, as was Frank Murphy, to the values of intellectual freedom and the other safeguards afforded by the Bill of Rights. However, Brennan reaches his conclusions through thorough research and tight logic; he is a modern scholastic. What is remarkable is that after employing traditional values such as hard work, logic, and research, he is likely to emerge with a moral approach. Brennan is a man of good will and humor, who is serious and painstaking, an indefatigable worker in the cause of liberty.

Justice Stewart is an Ohio conservative who yet manages to maintain a mind that still looks for answers. He is not afraid to stand alone, and his philosophy may well be the dominant one on the Court in the years to come. He has a simple and direct wit that is his own. He was the first of the World War II generation to reach the Court. A judge of strong convictions, Stewart espouses, for instance, the idea that the separation of church and state is overdone. It may be said about him that he is willing to examine with fairness, yet is not afraid to express his own views.

Byron R. White exemplifies the Greek ideal of a sound mind in a sound body. No one better personifies the administration of President John F. Kennedy than this appointee: a former football player, Phi Beta Kappa, Rhodes scholar, and an experienced and capable lawyer. A clear example of the cool and dispassionate "New Frontiersman," he is not a zealot for the radical right or left. White's personality exudes competence and the ability to make close and practical judgments. Someone once quipped that Jack Armstrong, the All-American Boy, was modeled after Byron R. White.

Justice White seems to grasp the dual job assigned to the Court: to allow government to extend its reach to meet the needs created by an increasingly complex society; to worry about the growing power of officialdom over the life, liberty, and property of ordinary men and women. White refuses to accept or act in accordance with a pat approach to constitutional interpretation. He possesses a keen analytic ability coupled with maturity, honesty, and imagination, a sense of national destiny and knowledge of its past; the ability to state, clearly and persuasively, the basis for a ruling. All the important ingredients for a Justice of the Supreme Court are in the person of Byron R. White. Dissenting in the Miranda case[2] White seemed to have an almost intuitive grasp of what was required—neither loose nor strict construction. The Court held that a criminal suspect must be advised by the police detaining him that he has the right to stand mute; that if he makes a statement it may be used against him; that he has the right to the assistance of a lawyer, free, if he does not have the money to hire one. White disagreed:

> That the Court's holding today is neither compelled nor even strongly suggested by the language of the Fifth Amendment (self-incrimination provision), is at odds with American and English legal history, and involves a departure from a long line of precedent does not prove either that the Court has exceeded its powers or that the Court is wrong or unwise. . . .
>
> What it has done is to make new law and new public policy in much the same way it has in the course of interpreting other great clauses of the constitution. This is what the Court historically has done. Indeed, it is what it must do and will continue to do until and unless there is some fundamental

2 Miranda v. Arizona, 384 U.S. 436 (1966).

change in the constitutional distinction of governmental powers. . . .

But it is wholly legitimate to examine the mode of this or any other constitutional decision in this Court and to inquire into the admissibility of its end-product in terms of the long range interest of the country. At the very least the Court's text and reasoning should withstand analysis and be a fair exponent of the constitutional process which its opinion interprets. Decisions like these cannot rest alone on syllogism, metaphysics or some ill defined notions of natural justice, although each will perhaps play its part.

To sit on the Supreme Court essentially requires an understanding of the spirit of the country rather than conformity to a formula. Justice White recognized this requirement.

Arthur Goldberg, who left the bench to represent the United States at the United Nations, was a Justice who sparked ideas. Earlier, as Secretary of Labor, he threw himself into any situation that his attention or his energies might benefit. A typical example of his enthusiasm for his work occurred when the Metropolitan Opera was shut down. The Secretary of Labor jumped onto a plane to New York City to personally intervene in the dispute.

Thurgood Marshall was as much at home before the mahogany bench of the Supreme Court as sitting behind it. In his role of advocate for the N.A.A.C.P., he was so quick to tell a story or make some flip joke that his considerable legal talents were not always apparent. It was easy to believe that this genial, cigar-chomping, handshaking man was a local politico rather than a sophisticated constitutional lawyer.

Anyone who does not appreciate Justice Marshall's legal talent or understand his compassion for the underprivileged or oppressed misses Marshall's contribution to the Supreme Court. His simple, straightforward questions on the Bench go right to the jugular of complex legal problems. As an example,

in the course of an argument on the constitutionality of requiring paupers to work off their fines in jail, Marshall, in a
deceptively naive way, asked, "As I understand it, the State of
Illinois' argument here is that the poor person goes to jail and
the rich man goes free. Now, that's it, isn't it?" And that was
that.

Although Earl Warren made a marked contribution to
the Supreme Court in improving its administration, his public
image reflects his influence on the substance of the law.
Warren's attitude was markedly different from that of his
predecessor, Chief Justice Vinson, who was a staunch supporter of official action. Earl Warren began with a strong bias
in favor of personal rights. Under Vinson's leadership, the
Court was ready to minimize asserted incursions of individual
rights by officialdom. Warren was more responsive to complaints about the acts of public servants.

This emphasis on individual freedom caused the Warren
Court to think more closely about the scope of the Bill of
Rights. The striking judicial shift in this century has been the
changing emphasis of the Supreme Court from property
rights to individual rights. In the first quarter of this century,
a judge could state: "of the three fundamental principles
which underlie government, and for which government exists,
the protection of life, liberty and property, the chief of these
is property." Certainly, the strength of the Warren Court's
popularity rested on its support of individual freedom rather
than the protection of traditional rights of property. The
Court extended the Bill of Rights and the Fourteenth Amendment so as to increasingly encompass the states as well as the
federal government. The freedoms of speech, press, religion,
the rights of blacks and other minorities, the rights of those
accused of crime, the inequalities of legislative representation, all came under the attention of the Warren Court.

An important commitment of the Warren Court was the
fostering of civil liberties of black persons. Until recently, the
post-Civil War amendments to the Constitution were actually

ignored by the executive and legislative branches, and were given scant support by the courts. But in 1944, the Southern Democratic primary, which in effect limited participation to whites, was held unconstitutional.[3] In 1948 the enforcement of covenants that restricted the sale and use of land on a racial basis was declared a violation of the Fourteenth Amendment.[4]

The landmark case of *Brown v. Board of Education*,[5] however, by a unanimous decision held that the enforcement of segregation in the public schools was violative of the equal protection of law to the black citizenry. It has already had and will continue to have an impact on the basic way of life of all Americans.

The legal foundation of compulsory school segregation in the South, before the ruling in Brown, was the fiction of "separate but equal" facilities, expressed in the 1896 case of *Plessy v. Ferguson*.[6] Beginning in 1937 the Supreme Court started to emphasize individual freedom, and began to take a hard look at the "separate but equal" educational facilities that were given to blacks.[7] For a decade, the Court tried to decide whether facilities met the test on a factual basis. It soon became apparent that, with respect to the college and postgraduate level of education, the blacks were being discriminated against.[8] And it could no longer be denied that all segregated facilities were in fact unequal by the very nature of things. The very fact of segregation implies inherent discrimination. In fact, even if the facilities were virtually equal, separation simply on the basis of skin color would constitute a "badge of servitude" that had to inculcate a feeling of inferiority, which nothing could eradicate. On this rationale, the Brown decision held that segregated schools were discrimina-

[3] Smith v. Allwright, 321 U.S. 649 (1944).

[4] Shelley v. Kraemer, 334 U.S. 1 (1948).

[5] Brown v. Board of Education of Topeka, 347 U.S. 483 (1954).

[6] Plessy v. Ferguson, 163 U.S. 537 (1896).

[7] Missouri *ex rel* Gaines v. Canada, 305 U.S. 337 (1938).

[8] Sweatt v. Painter, 339 U.S. 629 (1950); McLauren v. Oklahoma State Regents, 339 U.S. 637 (1950).

tory, depriving black citizens of the equal protection of law as required by the Fourteenth Amendment.

A field of continuing concern for the Warren Court was the attempt to reform the administration of criminal justice. Much of the criticism of the Warren Court stemmed from its attempt to protect those accused of crime from lawless police officers, district attorneys, and judges. But what is overlooked is that its rulings were not radical departures from the past. Justice Black, in 1966, ruled for the majority that where the defendants were poverty-stricken and sought free transcripts of the trial hearings so that they could effectively take an appeal from criminal convictions, it was a denial of the Fourteenth Amendment to refuse them.[9] The effect of a state law imposing a fee for transcripts, without providing relief for the impecunious, meant in effect that those convicted, but who lacked funds to order a transcript of the trial minutes, were denied a trial, for all practical purposes. The Court, accepting the reality of economic disparity, held the state law violated the Constitution. Wrote Black: "There can be no equal justice where the kind of trial a man gets depends on the amount of money he has. Destitute defendants must be afforded an adequate review as defendants who have enough money to buy transcripts."

The doctrine of the Griffin case, the willingness of the Court to pierce the fiction that rich and poor stand equal before the bar of justice, has had ramifications running far beyond the case and the criminal law. In fact the Griffin case revolutionized procedure and substance in dealing with the poor. It served as the basis for the landmark case of *Gideon v. Wainwright*,[10] which held that, at the request of indigent defendants in criminal cases, the state had an obligation to supply free lawyers. Under the Gideon case and the cases that later spelled out its implications, the right to counsel is

[9] Rinaldi v. Yeager, 384 U.S. 305 (1966).
[10] Gideon v. Wainwright, 372 U.S. 335 (1963).

guaranteed at every point in the criminal procedure, from initial arrest to appeal.

The Gideon case, by dictating the right to a lawyer, has stimulated the protections of criminal suspects in *Escobedo v. Illinois*[11] and *Miranda v. Arizona.*[12] In these decisions, the right to be represented by a lawyer starts when the police bring a custodial interrogation. The law enforcement agent must give a full warning to the accused that he is entitled to stand mute and to the help of an attorney, his own or one appointed by the court, or the confession may not be used. It is probable that this rule has resulted in eliminating many of the objectionable practices that have characterized arrest procedures.

Perhaps the most important cases decided by the Warren Court have been those in the field of legislative apportionment. In the 1962 case of *Baker v. Carr*[13] the Court decided that the federal courts had the authority to consider an action challenging a law apportioning legislative districts as violative of the equal protection of laws. As a consequence, the Supreme Court has taken upon itself the responsibility of policing unfairness of legislative apportionment throughout the federal courts. The effect of the many cases applying precepts of *Baker* has been to change significantly the way in which legislative districts are apportioned.

In 1964 in *Reynolds v. Sims*[14] the Supreme Court decided that the equal protection clause enunciates an "equal protection" test for the apportionment of state legislatures. What is required is nothing less than the substantial equality of population in each legislative district. Where population equality is missing, the result is an unconstitutional vitiation of the right to vote. "The fact that an individual lives here or there is not a legitimate reason for overweighting or diluting

[11] Escobedo v. Illinois, 378 U.S. 478 (1964).
[12] Miranda v. Arizona, 384 U.S. 436 (1966).
[13] Baker v. Carr, 369 U.S. 186 (1962).
[14] Reynolds v. Sims, 377 U.S. 532 (1964).

the efficacy of his vote." The ultimate effect will be the elimination or diminution of the effect of rural voters in constituting legislative majorities or determinating legislative policy. Reapportionments ordered by the Court have resulted in giving cities and suburbs a louder voice in state legislative halls. The Supreme Court has also imposed the requirement of "one man—one vote" on local units of government such as municipal councils or town and village bodies.[15]

The leadership of Earl Warren is most reminiscent of the style of John Marshall in the early days of the republic. Thus, shortly before Warren was appointed in 1953, the nine Justices took up the problem of school segregation. The Justices argued, hot and heavy, behind the closed doors of the conference room. The division was five to four in favor of perpetuating segregation. Before the Court had a chance to announce its decision, Chief Justice Vinson died and was succeeded by Earl Warren.

Chief Justice Warren, in his low-keyed, warm manner, took on the job of persuading his new associates to adopt his views on segregation. With a quiet, sincere approach, he asked each of his colleagues to study a draft of a vigorous opinion against school segregation, written in his own hand.

One after another, Frankfurter, Black, Clark and Reed did an about-face. In the prior conferences, each of them had indicated that they would vote to continue school segregation. Warren managed to convert the then ailing Justice Jackson. The Chief Justice carried his draft to the hospital where Jackson was a patient to explain his position, and to convince the last holdout. It seemed incredible, but the Supreme Court decided against segregation in a unanimous opinion.

By the same gentle and personal appeal, Warren brought about the seven to two decision which ordered State Legislatures to reapportion on the basis of one-man, one vote.

[15] Avery v. Midland County, 390 U.S. 474 (1968).

VI

THE FORK IN
THE ROAD

–16–

"LOWERING THE PROFILE"

WHEN EARL WARREN RELINQUISHED HIS CENTER SEAT AS CHIEF Justice on June 23, 1969, one of the most active and ambitious eras in the history of the Supreme Court came to an end.

Characteristically, Warren departed on a strong note. He had just issued a historic opinion in the case of Congressman Adam Clayton Powell,[1] declaring that the House of Representatives acted unconstitutionally in 1967 when it refused to seat Powell, a long-time spokesman for the black people. The seventy-eight-year-old Chief Justice asserted for the first time that the Supreme Court had jurisdiction to settle constitutional questions involving internal congressional matters.

President Nixon lavishly praised Warren for his role in keeping the nation "on the path of continuity and change" during the sixteen years of his leadership in the Supreme Court. The remarks of the President contained no trace of the criticism leveled at the Warren Court during Nixon's presidential election campaign. The appointment of Chief Justice Burger fulfilled a campaign pledge of President Nixon to appoint a strict constructionist as Chief Justice of the Court.

It is hard to believe, from the tenor of the President's

[1] Powell v. McCormack, 395 U.S. 486 (1969).

remarks at the swearing-in ceremony of Chief Justice Burger, how vituperative the criticism of Warren and his Court had been. The agitation of the John Birch Society to "impeach Earl Warren" was muted just a few years before. However, the congenial but iron-willed Warren has remained a symbol of judicial activism. The controversy over the liberal Warren Court fed on opposition—mostly from political conservatives against the decisions that hobbled government loyalty-security programs, banned prayer and Bible reading in the public schools, outlawed segregation and reapportionment, and restricted the action of the police.

President Eisenhower was said to have called his appointment of Earl Warren the "biggest damnfool mistake I ever made." On the other hand, President Lyndon B. Johnson assessed Justice Warren as the "greatest Chief Justice of them all." Yet, one complaint about the Court has had the widest circulation: it has been asserted that the Supreme Court has acted too much like a legislature and not enough like a court; that is, that the Court translated its own notions of wise public policy into constitutional dogma. Much of this doctrine could not be enforced because the Court lacked the administrative and other enforcement facilities to make them work.

In the opinion of many experts, the reapportionment decisions have been a success in the sense that reapportionment has been achieved without as much difficulty as might have been expected. Despite the warnings that the Court would become bogged down in the "political thicket," redistricting has been widely accomplished and the initial outcry has died down. "The word even among politicians is that the decisions are acceptable; the accomodations have largely been made," Robert B. McKay, an expert in reapportionment law, has opined.

School segregation is a much more subtle matter. The number of integrated schools is increasing. In the minds of many who are against the idea, integration is seen as inevitable and efforts are being made to minimize the pain of transition. But resistance to desegregation is also arising in many Southern communities, where the belief is strong that the South is being ordered to achieve levels of integration that are not being required in the North. This has been a rallying cry augmented by such officials from the North as Senator Abraham Ribicoff of Connecticut. The Nixon administration, while formally subscribing to the idea of integrating the schools, has encouraged a slow down in the efforts of the Supreme Court to outlaw segregation in the South.

The idea that criminal defendants should be represented by lawyers at their trials had already been accepted by all but five states when *Gideon v. Wainwright*[2] was announced. The importance of the decision was to establish the principle that poor people must be furnished the means to exercise their legal rights, in addition to being entitled to the rights themselves. This ruling has led to the creation of public defenders and legal aid offices across the country, and other offices to provide legal assistance to poor people.

The cases flowing from the Gideon decision have precipitated a controversy over counsel in the police station and the authority of the police to question suspects. The Supreme Court has tacitly acknowledged some of the problems by declining to apply the Gideon decision to misdemeanor cases. As a result of charges in some quarters—including some respected legal ones—that the Warren Court made criminal procedures too rigid, President Nixon made a point of selecting a Chief Justice who rejects much of what the Warren Court introduced on the subject of defendant's rights. Thus, Warren left the Court amid a rising chorus of complaints that the landmarks of the Warren Court—bold, aggressive moves on behalf of society's victims—were carried to excess in the criminal field and that the Court's idealism outstripped its practical sense in this regard.

Chief Justice Warren's departure was also tarnished by a

[2] Gideon v. Wainwright, 372 U.S. 335 (1962).

public controversy over the private activities of former Justice Abe Fortas and Justice William O. Douglas. Warren hoped to persuade the Court to adopt restrictions on extrajudicial conduct before he left, but he failed. Many observers feel that, in the long view, history will treat the Warren Court well.

"Generations hence," Professor William M. Beasy of Princeton recently said of the Warren Court, "it may well appear that what is supposedly the most conservative of American political institutions, the Supreme Court, was the institution that did the most to help the nation adjust to the needs and demands of a free society."

Regardless of the verdict of history, Earl Warren seems obviously satisfied with the results of his tenure. At the final news conference, Warren was asked to comment on the problems which had frustrated him. He paused for a long moment, then broke into a wide smile and replied that he could not think of any. "It has not been a frustrating experience," he said.

Immediately after Warren introduced the new Chief Justice, Warren E. Burger, the latter shook hands with Justices Hugo L. Black and William O. Douglas, who were to sit with him on the bench. The others currently on the Court are William J. Brennan, Potter Stewart, Byron R. White, Thurgood Marshall, John M. Harlan, and Harry A. Blackmun.

One day in the summer of 1967, a mutual friend of Richard M. Nixon and Warren E. Burger stopped to see Burger. The friend mentioned that Nixon had been impressed by a speech made by Burger criticizing some of the protection afforded defendants in criminal cases. Neither Nixon nor Burger knew it at the time, but that speech, which Nixon had come across while paging through a publication where it had been reprinted, was the first step for Burger on the road to the post of Chief Justice. Burger, a federal court of appeals judge in Washington, D.C., for thirteen years until the Senate approved his nomination as the fifteenth Chief Justice, thought little about Nixon's comment at that time. Burger had been active in Republican politics before he became a judge; he had even met Nixon casually several times previously and a few times thereafter. He impressed the President with his views, and he also had admirers close to the President.

Born in St. Paul, Minnesota, of Swiss and German heritage, Burger was one of seven children (five boys and two girls). The family never had much money, partially because his father tried many different employments. From the age of twelve, Burger knew he did not have enough money to go to college. He went to work as a bookkeeper for an insurance company, to night classes offered by the University of Minnesota, and then to a night law school. After graduating, he accepted a clerk's job in a respectable law firm in St. Paul and became involved in Republican politics. Herbert Brownell met Burger during the 1952 Republican convention. After the election, Brownell, the new Attorney General, brought him to Washington. During his three years at the Justice Department, he was noticed for successfully pressing a case against Aristotle Onassis and other Greek shipowners who were charged with taking over some American tankers without paying for them.

He agreed to argue a loyalty case before the Supreme Court, which Simon Sokeloff, then United States Solicitor General and now an appeals court judge, said he could not in good conscience argue. Burger lost the case, but he endeared himself to the right people. When an opening occurred in the court of appeals in Washington, Brownell suggested Burger to President Eisenhower and he was appointed.

Burger is about six feet tall and weighs about two hundred pounds. He wears his white hair fairly long. His face is serene and hardly wrinkled. His eyes are clear blue, his eyebrows prominent, his countenance open. He has a deep resonant voice, a firm handshake, and warmth reflects the man and recalls his folksy origins. It is easy to have confidence in him.

Burger came to the Supreme Court when, according to

the Gallup Poll, there was declining confidence in it. A major factor in this decline was the disclosures about the outside activities of some of the Justices. It came as a distinct shock for Americans to learn that Supreme Court Justice Abe Fortas, an appointee and long-time confidant and private counsel to Lyndon Johnson, had accepted a twenty-thousand-dollar fee from the family foundation of a stock speculator who wound up in jail. Fortas held the money for almost a year, returning it three months after the speculator was indicted. Although Fortas had not broken any law, he had clearly been guilty of a gross indiscretion.

Many felt that Nixon was right in using his considerable influence as a presidential candidate to block Fortas' nomination as Chief Justice when Warren announced his retirement. Fortas resigned under pressure, the first Justice to do so. Only one—Samuel Chase in 1804—had been impeached, but on such blatantly political grounds that he was later acquitted. Several years ago, it was disclosed that Justice William O. Douglas was receiving twelve thousand dollars a year in fees from a foundation linked to Las Vegas gambling interests. However, Douglas was not involved with any principal seeking improper influence.

The Nixon administration was itself jolted when the President's designee for the Fortas opening, Clement F. Haynsworth, Jr., was rejected by the Senate. It was claimed that Judge Haynsworth, a Southern federal circuit-court judge, had heard cases while he had a financial relationship with the corporation or parties appearing before him. The confirmation was denied by the Senate, in addition, because of charges that his decisions have been anti-labor or lacked impartiality in civil-rights matters. His law work was criticized as being pedestrian, even careless. Detractors argued that he devoted an injudicious amount of his time to personal business.

The next person whose name was submitted by President Nixon to the Senate was that of Judge G. Harrold Carswell, of Tallahassee, Florida. But a few days after Carswell was nominated, the press uncovered the text of a campaign speech he had made in 1948, when he first ran for office in his native Georgia. "I yield to no man," he had then stated, "in the firm vigorous belief in the principles of white supremacy, and I shall always be so governed. I believe," he went on, "that segregation of the races is proper and the only practical and correct way of life in our states. I have always so believed, and I shall always so act." When this statement came to light, twenty-two years later, Carswell vehemently repudiated it. He informed the Senate that he was "aghast" at having uttered those words. "These notions," he said, "are obnoxious to me." He stated for the press, "I denounce and reject the words themselves and the thoughts they represent."

Many observers felt that Carswell had a less impressive record than Haynsworth. As a district judge, sixty percent of his twenty-three decisions concerning civil rights were set aside by the Fifth Circuit Court. His cause was not helped by some of his Senate proponents, especially Senator Hruska, who urged that "mediocrity" deserved representation on the Supreme Court. Carswell took a beating after he answered, "No sir," in response to a question asking if he had been an incorporator of the Capital City Country Club (which was organized as a private club in 1956 to escape a desegregation order). It turned out that only the evening before this testimony, he admitted his incorporator's role to two representatives of the American Bar Association. Carswell was rejected by the Senate. The President was irate. He viewed this as a repudiation of the South and his constitutional perogatives.

Judge Carswell resigned from the Fifth Circuit Court of Appeals to run for the Republican senatorial nomination in Florida, as a foe of "racial balance" in the schools. He was defeated in the primary.

With what amounted to a collective sigh of relief, the Senate confirmed the third man nominated by President Nixon. Minnesotan Harry A. Blackmun has stated that he has "the utmost respect, almost a reverence," for the Supreme

Court and that any man who sits on it, "ought to be without sin." Blackmun is a reserved man who is zealous of his personal life, yet appreciative of his new job: "It's overwhelming and humbling."

His main interests have been lawyering and judging, his wife and three grown daughters, plus a lively concern with professional football and baseball. Although the Fifth Circuit is based in St. Louis, Blackmun has felt most at home in Rochester, Minnesota. There he was counsel to the Mayo Clinic from 1950 to 1959. Possessed of a dry wit, frequently directed against himself, he has always been a student. While in grammar school, he helped his father in a grocery and hardware store, and at Harvard he majored in math. Although he earned his expenses at college as a milkman, janitor, boat driver, and house painter, he also managed to earn a Phi Beta Kappa key, and to graduate summa cum laude. After Harvard Law, he clerked for a federal judge, went to work for a leading Midwest law firm, and, a lifelong Republican, was appointed by President Eisenhower to the federal bench in 1959.

Justice Blackmun's former associates say that it is difficult to put him into any category, except that he is independent and "not predictable," a man with a receptive mind. He refused to tie any label on himself except to say that he subscribes to the Frankfurter tradition. Certainly, Frankfurter was not an activist nor a wild-eyed radical. He denies "knowing what it means," when reference is made to strict construction. He has in the past been a careful adherent of past precedent, but, with reference to his work on the Supreme Court, Blackmun says: "Who is to say five men, ten years ago, were right and five men today are wrong?"

Blackmun was his Chief's schoolmate and best man at Burger's wedding in 1933. Blackmun admits "there will be some hard going if we disagree, but I'm sure we can do it without any rupture in our relationship." Says he, "I've greatly respected him all my life."

Justices Burger and Blackmun have voted together in almost every case in which they have both sat. Under the aegis of the "Minnesota Twins," as they are dubbed by some, the Court has definitely veered to the right. Their own views represent a distinct departure from the philosophies of the justices they have replaced: Burger for Earl Warren, and Blackmun for Abe Fortas and Arthur Goldberg.

This was evidenced very clearly by their dissents against the legislation passed by Congress to enable the eighteen-year-olds to vote.[3] A straw in the wind was their view in two cases involving the rights of criminal defendants. The first decision was a rejection of the defendant's argument that a plea of guilty was invalid if induced by fear of a death sentence.[4] In the second,[5] they rejected the contention that the defendant had a constitutional right to be confronted by "witnesses against him" where damaging admissions by an accomplice, unavailable for cross-examination, were used at defendant's trial. In the latter case, they concurred in separate opinions, expressing the view that the testimony used in the trial was so incredible on its face that no "normal" jury could have accepted it. Therefore, its introduction at the trial was "harmless beyond a reasonable doubt."

Justice Blackmun has revealed himself to be even more law-enforcement oriented than Justice Burger. In a case[6] decided early in 1971, Justice John M. Harlan, who is not exactly soft on crime, wrote the opinion supporting the double jeopardy claim of a defendant in a federal criminal prosecution. Justice Burger joined Justice Harlan "not without some reluctance," but Justice Blackmun voted to reject the defendant's plea, in spite of his friend's position.

What is even more indicative of Justice Blackmun's philosophy is his first full-scale majority opinion.[7] It sustained

[3] United States v. Arizona, 91 S.Ct. 260 (1970).
[4] North Carolina v. Alford, 91 S.Ct. 160 (1970).
[5] Dutton v. Evans, 91 S.Ct. 210 (1970).
[6] United States v. Jorn, 91 S.Ct. 547 (1971).
[7] Wyman v. James, 91 S.Ct. 381 (1971).

the authority of New York to cut off a welfare recipient from benefits because of her refusal to allow inspections of her home. It evoked a cutting dissent by Thurgood Marshall, joined by Justice William Brennan, and another dissent by Justice William O. Douglas. In some of its language, Justice Blackmun seemed to disagree sharply with precedents of recent years extending protections to welfare recipients.

More than a year of activity of Chief Justice Burger, Nixon's first "strict construction" Justice, furnishes some clues as to how he will function. Burger has said: "There is no reason why we as judges should regard ourselves as some kind of Guardian Elders, ordained to revise the political judgments of elected representatives of the people." Clearly, he would prefer less of an activist role for the Court than it assumed during Warren's tenure, a less controversial stance, and a greater reluctance to interfere with the work of other branches of government.

Paradoxically, the new Chief Justice has at least in one instance probably surprised President Nixon. In 1969 he joined his colleagues in applying the previous decisions of the Warren Court in order to desegregate the public schools in Mississippi "at once."[8] Nevertheless, Burger has more recently emphasized the need to understand the problems facing Southern school districts. In January of 1970, he and Justice Stewart added a "memorandum" to one decision, suggesting that the Fifth Circuit Court of Appeals might have well been allowed to interpret the meaning of "at once" in light of "the various situations of several school districts."[9]

The Chief Justice seems to particularly relish the role of efficient overseer of the judicial establishment and lobbyist for reform of the courts. He has worked hard, using energy and hours, to get silver water goblets and more law clerks for his brethren. In August of 1970, he presented a "State of the Judiciary" message at the American Bar Association's conven-

[8] Alexander v. Holmes County Board of Education, 396 U.S. 19 (1969).
[9] Carter v. West Feliciana Parish School District, 396 U.S. 290 (1970).

tion. His ambition is to make such annual reports before joint sessions of Congress. Burger has openly admitted that he spends more of his time in such activities than he does in deliberating. This is in sharp contrast to his predecessors who did not seem to have a flair for court administration.

In many speeches, he has put the prestige of his high office behind the growing call for reform of the nation's crime-breeding jails. In the attempt to streamline archaic court structures and procedures, he is sponsoring a new institute in Washington to train court administrators in management techniques.

Burger has been quite willing to use technical grounds to drop a case from the docket of the Supreme Court. In his speeches, the Chief Justice has also complained about the burden that many appeals put upon the appellate courts, and he has suggested that many of them are without merit.

"Six months ago," Burger told a friend recently, "if you had asked me what the Supreme Court should and should not do, I probably could have given you a quick answer. But now I'm not so sure. New problems arise that the authors of the Constitution did not anticipate. But the answers to the problems ought to be made to fit an existing pattern; a new pattern should not be made. The hardest question, though, is always: when should the Court step in?"

Chief Justice Burger has not been reluctant to state his disagreement with the legal precedents laid down by the Warren Court. In a little-noted suit brought by a longshoreman against a ship owner, the question of adherence to precedent was put squarely. Justice Harlan asserted that "past decisions" of the Court (over his own vigorous dissents) had decided the legal dispute in favor of the longshoreman and that the case could not "in good conscience" be distinguished from these precedents. The majority, which included the Burger-Blackmun team, decided the case[10] against the longshoreman. Justice Douglas, dissenting, stated that it was

---

[10] Usner v. Luckenbach Overseas Corp., 91 S.Ct. 514 (1971).

"surprising to find how law made by new judges takes the place of law made by prior judges."

Two other cases suggest that the Burger Court is not too respectful of the past. In the first of these, the Court reconsidered the effect of an appeal[11] decided in 1965. That case seemed to stand for the proposition that when a state defendant sought help from the federal courts on the ground that their rights were being violated, the federal courts should stay the prosecutions and decide the constitutionality of the state procedures or laws.

The district courts responded to the mandate of the Supreme Court with such enthusiasm that state statutes dealing with vagrancy, abortion, adultery, obscenity, homosexuality and other problems, began to be thrown out by the Supreme Court.

The Burger Court as constituted in the early part of 1971 decided that the interdiction of state prosecutions by federal judges was undercutting the federal-state relationship. It directed the federal courts to interfere with state action only when state authorities were using their powers to intimidate defendants.[12]

Perhaps the most significant indication of the trend of the Supreme Court was its five to four decision[13] restricting the effect of *Miranda v. Arizona*,[14] the famous 1966 decision of the Warren Court that ordered policemen to warn all suspects in custody of their rights to a lawyer and to remain silent. Writing for the majority, Chief Justice Burger offered prosecutors an escape valve when the police had neglected to give the warnings required by Miranda. Until the Burger Court spoke, such failure was deemed to make the incriminating statements of the defendant wholly inadmissible at his trial.

Under the new ruling, if the subject is not advised of his

11 Dumbrowski v. Pfister, 380 U.S. 479 (1965).
12 Younger v. Harris, 39 LW 4201, decided February 23, 1971.
13 Harris v. New York, 39 LW 4281, decided February 24, 1971.
14 384 U.S. 436 (1966).

rights when taken into custody and later testifies in his own defense, his pretrial admissions to the police may be used to undermine his courtroom testimony. The effect of this ruling, argued Justice William J. Brennan, is that the police may now "freely interrogate an accused incommunicado." In spite of Miranda, if the defendant "has the temerity to testify in his own defense," he may be convicted by his own pretrial statement. Burger rejected "the speculative possibility that impermissible police conduct will be encouraged."

In cases[15] coming from Arizona and Ohio, the Court decided five to four that bar applicants need not list all of the organizations they have joined, or swear that they have never belonged to groups that advocate violent overthrow of the government. Yet, by the same vote, in a New York case, the court made a distinction that was somewhat subtle. It held that New York may compel bar applicants to disclose whether they have ever belonged to a subversive group with actual intent to advance its aims of overthrowing the government.

However, the fact that only Justice William O. Douglas dissented from the decision limiting the power of the federal courts to halt state action, shows that even some of the Warren Court activists are reconsidering their old decisions. As an example, Justice Thurgood Marshall was quite irritated with the way in which federal courts had extended one of his obscenity rulings to invalidate a number of state and federal obscenity control laws. When the appeals involving such decisions were argued before the High Court, he complained about those who stretch the law beyond its intent.

It is rumored that there is dissension behind the facade of the great marble temple. Apparently, the Court has lost some of its easy affability and casual informality. Insiders indicate that the private sessions of the Justices are stiffly formal. The Chief Justice expresses his opinion followed by the others in

[15] Baird v. State Bar, 39 LW 4194; Law Students Civil Rights Research Council, Inc. v. Wadmond, 39 LW 4177; In re Stolar, 39 LW 4191; all decided February 23, 1971.

order of seniority. After the conference, Burger decides who shall write the decisions and sends the assignments on a printed sheet to each member. The warm personal relationship which existed in the Warren Court, responding to the personality of Warren, does not seem as enveloping in the present Court. Nevertheless, a Burger majority seems to be developing. It consists of Burger, Blackmun and three Justices who often dissented during the Warren period—John M. Harlan, Potter Stewart and Byron R. White. It may be that the major decisions of the recent years will not all be directly overruled. However, it is not necessary to overturn legal cases in order to blunt their effect. The Burger Court, as earlier courts, has already demonstrated that it can find the distinctions it needs in the appeals before it, so that it is able to skirt the famous past precedents with which it disagrees.

The new coalition was illustrated when the Court barred draft exemptions for men who claim they object in conscience to the Vietnam war but not to all wars. The vote was eight to one.[16]

Justice Marshall, delivering the court's opinion in two draft cases, said: "We hold that Congress intended to exempt persons who oppose participating in all wars . . . and that persons who object solely to participation in a particular war are not within the purview of the exempting section."

Marshall said that this was true even if the objection to a particular war had "roots in a claimant's conscience and personality that is 'religious' in character."

Justice Douglas dissented.

The decision dismissed claims brought by Guy P. Gillette of Yonkers, New York, a self-described humanist, and Louis A. Negre, of Bakersfield, California, a Roman Catholic. Both men contended that their consciences did not permit them to fight in Vietnam.

Marshall emphasized what he called "the interest in maintaining a fair system." He also rejected the argument

[16] Gillette v. United States, 39 LW 4305, decided March 8, 1971.

that individual religious viewpoints were discriminated against when exemptions were not granted for objectors to particular wars. Douglas, in dissent, said the draft system involved "invidious classifications" that segregated men on the basis of their consciences. "Yet, conscience and belief are the main ingredients of First Amendment rights," Douglas said. "They are the bedrock of free speech as well as religion."

Yet, the Burger Court has held unanimously that an affluent person can be thrown into jail for failing to pay his fine, but some other method of collection of fines from the poor, perhaps installment payments, must be tried first.[17] Here, the Burger Court created a right for the poor which does not exist for the rich.

In another case[18] the Court ruled, with only Justice Black dissenting, that people who want divorces, but are too poor to pay filing fees and court costs, must be accorded cost-free divorces by the states. Thus, the Court extended the principle applied by Warren's Court in criminal prosecutions to private civil litigation.

Chief Justice Burger has indicated the desirability of "lowering the profile" of the Supreme Court after the controversial Warren period. The face-lowering process may be well underway. Long-range predictions, however, are dangerous. After all, Earl Warren was a tough prosecutor for a long time before he became Chief Justice of the Supreme Court.

[17] Tate v. Short, 39 LW 4301, decided March 2, 1971.
[18] Boddie v. Conn., 39 LW 4291, March 2, 1971.

APPENDIX

JUSTICES OF THE SUPREME COURT, 1789–1971

Associate Justices

Term	Chief Justice								
1789	Jay	Rutledge, J.	Cushing	Wilson	Blair				
1790/91	Jay	Rutledge, J.	Cushing	Wilson	Blair	Iredell			
1792	Jay	Johnson, T.	Cushing	Wilson	Blair	Iredell			
1793/94	Jay	Paterson	Cushing	Wilson	Blair	Iredell			
1795	Rutledge, J.	Paterson	Cushing	Wilson	Blair	Iredell			
1796/97	Ellsworth	Paterson	Cushing	Wilson	Chase, S.	Iredell			
1798/99	Ellsworth	Paterson	Cushing	Washington	Chase, S.	Iredell			
1800	Ellsworth	Paterson	Cushing	Washington	Chase, S.	Moore			
1801/03	Marshall, J.	Paterson	Cushing	Washington	Chase, S.	Moore			
1804/05	Marshall, J.	Paterson	Cushing	Washington	Chase, S.	Johnson, W.			
1806	Marshall, J.	Livingston	Cushing	Washington	Chase, S.	Johnson, W.			
1807/10	Marshall, J.	Livingston	Cushing	Washington	Chase, S.	Johnson, W.	Todd		
1811/22	Marshall, J.	Livingston	Story	Washington	Duvall	Johnson, W.	Todd		
1823/25	Marshall, J.	Thompson	Story	Washington	Duvall	Johnson, W.	Todd		
1826/28	Marshall, J.	Thompson	Story	Washington	Duvall	Johnson, W.	Trimble		
1829	Marshall, J.	Thompson	Story	Washington	Duvall	Johnson, W.	McLean		
1830/34	Marshall, J.	Thompson	Story	Baldwin	Duvall	Johnson, W.	McLean		
1835	Marshall, J.	Thompson	Story	Baldwin	Duvall	Wayne	McLean		
1836	Taney	Thompson	Story	Baldwin	Barbour	Wayne	McLean		
1837/40	Taney	Thompson	Story	Baldwin	Barbour	Wayne	McLean	Catron	McKinley

Term	Chief Justice	Associate Justices								
1841/44	Taney	Thompson	Story	Baldwin	Daniel	Wayne	McLean	Catron	McKinley	
1845	Taney	Nelson	Woodbury		Daniel	Wayne	McLean	Catron	McKinley	
1846/50	Taney	Nelson	Woodbury	Grier	Daniel	Wayne	McLean	Catron	McKinley	
1851/52	Taney	Nelson	Curtis	Grier	Daniel	Wayne	McLean	Catron	McKinley	
1853/57	Taney	Nelson	Curtis	Grier	Daniel	Wayne	McLean	Catron	Campbell	
1858/60	Taney	Nelson	Clifford	Grier	Daniel	Wayne	McLean	Catron	Campbell	
1861	Taney	Nelson	Clifford	Grier		Wayne	McLean	Catron	Campbell	
1862	Taney	Nelson	Clifford	Grier	Miller	Wayne	Swayne	Catron	Davis	
1863	Taney	Nelson	Clifford	Grier	Miller	Wayne	Swayne	Catron	Davis	Field
1864/65	Chase, S.P.	Nelson	Clifford	Grier	Miller		Swayne	Catron	Davis	Field
1866/67	Chase, S.P.	Nelson	Clifford	Grier	Miller		Swayne		Davis	Field
1868/69	Chase, S.P.	Nelson	Clifford	Grier	Miller		Swayne		Davis	Field
1870/71	Chase, S.P.	Nelson	Clifford	Strong	Miller	Bradley	Swayne		Davis	Field
1872/73	Chase, S.P.	Hunt	Clifford	Strong	Miller	Bradley	Swayne		Davis	Field
1874/76	Waite	Hunt	Clifford	Strong	Miller	Bradley	Swayne		Davis	Field
1877/79	Waite	Hunt	Clifford	Strong	Miller	Bradley	Swayne		Harlan	Field
1880	Waite	Hunt	Clifford	Woods	Miller	Bradley	Swayne		Harlan	Field
1881	Waite	Hunt	Gray	Woods	Miller	Bradley	Matthews		Harlan	Field
1882/87	Waite	Blatchford	Gray	Woods	Miller	Bradley	Matthews		Harlan	Field
1888	Fuller	Blatchford	Gray	Lamar, L.	Miller	Bradley	Matthews		Harlan	Field

Term	Chief Justice	Associate Justices							
1889	Fuller	Blatchford	Gray	Lamar, L.	Miller	Bradley	Brewer	Harlan	Field
1890/91	Fuller	Blatchford	Gray	Lamar, L.	Brown	Bradley	Brewer	Harlan	Field
1892	Fuller	Blatchford	Gray	Lamar, L.	Brown	Shiras	Brewer	Harlan	Field
1893	Fuller	Blatchford	Gray	Jackson, H.	Brown	Shiras	Brewer	Harlan	Field
1894	Fuller	White	Gray	Jackson, H.	Brown	Shiras	Brewer	Harlan	Field
1895/97	Fuller	White	Gray	Peckham	Brown	Shiras	Brewer	Harlan	Field
1898/01	Fuller	White	Gray	Peckham	Brown	Shiras	Brewer	Harlan	McKenna
1902	Fuller	White	Holmes	Peckham	Brown	Shiras	Brewer	Harlan	McKenna
1903/05	Fuller	White	Holmes	Peckham	Brown	Day	Brewer	Harlan	McKenna
1906/08	Fuller	White	Holmes	Peckham	Moody	Day	Brewer	Harlan	McKenna
1909	Fuller	White	Holmes	Peckham	Moody	Day	Brewer	Harlan	McKenna
1910/11	White, E.	Van Devanter	Holmes	Lurton	Lamar, J.	Day	Hughes	Harlan	McKenna
1912/13	White, E.	Van Devanter	Holmes	Lurton	Lamar, J.	Day	Hughes	Pitney	McKenna
1914/15	White, E.	Van Devanter	Holmes	McReynolds	Lamar, J.	Day	Hughes	Pitney	McKenna
1916/20	White, E.	Van Devanter	Holmes	McReynolds	Brandeis	Day	Clarke	Pitney	McKenna
1921	Taft	Van Devanter	Holmes	McReynolds	Brandeis	Day	Clarke	Pitney	McKenna
1922	Taft	Van Devanter	Holmes	McReynolds	Brandeis	Butler	Sutherland	Pitney	McKenna
1923/24	Taft	Van Devanter	Holmes	McReynolds	Brandeis	Butler	Sutherland	Sanford	McKenna
1925/29	Taft	Van Devanter	Holmes	McReynolds	Brandeis	Butler	Sutherland	Sanford	Stone
1930/31	Hughes	Van Devanter	Holmes	McReynolds	Brandeis	Butler	Sutherland	Roberts	Stone

| | Chief | Associate Justices | | | | | | | |
Term	Justice								
1932/36	Hughes	Van Devanter	Cardozo	McReynolds	Brandeis	Butler	Sutherland	Roberts	Stone
1937	Hughes	Black	Cardozo	McReynolds	Brandeis	Butler	Sutherland	Roberts	Stone
1938	Hughes	Black	Cardozo	McReynolds	Brandeis	Butler	Reed	Roberts	Stone
1939	Hughes	Black	Frankfurter	McReynolds	Douglas	Butler	Reed	Roberts	Stone
1940	Hughes	Black	Frankfurter	McReynolds	Douglas	Murphy	Reed	Roberts	Stone
1941/42	Stone	Black	Frankfurter	Byrnes	Douglas	Murphy	Reed	Roberts	Jackson, R.
1943/44	Stone	Black	Frankfurter	Rutledge, W.	Douglas	Murphy	Reed	Roberts	Jackson, R.
1945	Stone	Black	Frankfurter	Rutledge, W.	Douglas	Murphy	Reed	Burton	Jackson, R.
1946/48	Vinson	Black	Frankfurter	Rutledge, W.	Douglas	Murphy	Reed	Burton	Jackson, R.
1949/52	Vinson	Black	Frankfurter	Minton	Douglas	Clark	Reed	Burton	Jackson, R.
1953/54	Warren	Black	Frankfurter	Minton	Douglas	Clark	Reed	Burton	Jackson, R.
1955	Warren	Black	Frankfurter	Minton	Douglas	Clark	Reed	Burton	Harlan
1956	Warren	Black	Frankfurter	Brennan	Douglas	Clark	Reed	Burton	Harlan
1957	Warren	Black	Frankfurter	Brennan	Douglas	Clark	Whittaker	Burton	Harlan
1958/61	Warren	Black	Frankfurter	Brennan	Douglas	Clark	Whittaker	Stewart	Harlan
1962/65	Warren	Black	Goldberg	Brennan	Douglas	Clark	White, B.	Stewart	Harlan
1965/67	Warren	Black	Fortas	Brennan	Douglas	Clark	White, B.	Stewart	Harlan
1967/69	Warren	Black	Fortas	Brennan	Douglas	Marshall, T.	White, B.	Stewart	Harlan
1969/70	Burger	Black		Brennan	Douglas	Marshall, T.	White, B.	Stewart	Harlan
1969/70	Burger	Black	Blackmun	Brennan	Douglas	Marshall, T.	White, B.	Stewart	Harlan

BIBLIOGRAPHY

Acheson, Patricia. *The Supreme Court: America's Judicial Heritage.* New York: Dodd, Mead & Co., 1961.

Barth, Alan. *The Heritage of Liberty.* Manchester, Mo.: Webster Division, McGraw-Hill Book Co., 1965.

Bowen, Catherine Drinker. *Yankee From Olympus: Justice Holmes and His Family.* Boston: Little, Brown & Co., 1944.

Clayton, James E. *The Making of Justice: The Supreme Court in Action.* New York: E. P. Dutton & Co., 1964.

Cooley, Thomas M. *A Treatise on the Constitutional Limitations.* 2d rev. ed. American History, Politics & Law Series. New York: Plenum Publishing Corp., 1969.

Corwin, Edward S. *Twilight of the Supreme Court.* Hamden, Conn.: Shoe String Press, 1970.

Garraty, John A., ed. *Quarrels That Have Shaped the Constitution.* New York: Harper & Row, 1964.

Haines, Charles G. *The Role of the Supreme Court in American Government and Politics.* 1944. Reprint. New York: Russell & Russell, 1960.

Jackson, Robert H. *The Supreme Court in the American System of Government.* Godkin Lecture Series, 1955. Cambridge: Harvard University Press, 1955.

Kelly, Alfred H., and Harbison, Winfred A. *The American Constitution: Its Origins and Development.* 4th rev. ed. New York: W. W. Norton & Co., 1970.

Kent, James. *Commentaries on American Law.* 4 vols. American History, Politics & Law Series. New York: Plenum Publishing Corp., 1969.

Lewis, Anthony. *Gideon's Trumpet.* New York: Random House, 1964.

Loth, David G. *Chief Justice: John Marshall and the Growth of the Republic.* Westport, Conn.: Greenwood Press, 1949.

McCloskey, Robert G. *The American Supreme Court.* Chicago: University of Chicago Press, 1960.

[253]

McLaughlin, Andrew C. *A Constitutional History of the United States.*
New York: Appleton-Century-Crofts, 1935.
Medina, Harold R. *Anatomy of Freedom.* New York: Holt, Rinehart &
Winston, 1959.
Mendelson, Wallace, ed. *Felix Frankfurter: A Tribute.* New York:
William Morrow & Co., 1964.
Perkins, Dexter. *Charles Evans Hughes and American Democratic
Statesmanship.* Boston: Little, Brown & Co., 1965.
Pfeffer, Leo. *This Honorable Court: A History of the United States
Supreme Court.* Boston: Beacon Press, 1965.
Prettyman, Barrett, Jr. *Death and the Supreme Court.* New York: Har-
court Brace Jovanovitch, 1968.
Pringle, Henry F. *The Life and Time of William Howard Taft: A
Biography.* 2 vols. 1938. Reprint. Hamden, Conn.: Shoe String
Press, 1965.
Schwartz, Bernard. *The Reigns of Power: A Constitutional History of
the United States.* New York: Hill & Wang, 1963.
Story, Joseph. *Commentaries on the Constitution of the United States.*
3 vols. New York: Plenum Publishing Corp., 1969.
Swisher, Carl B. *Growth of Constitutional Power in the United States.*
Chicago: University of Chicago Press, 1963.
————. *Historic Decisions of the Supreme Court.* 2d rev. ed. New York:
Van Nostrand Reinhold Co., 1969.
Tresolini, Rocco J. *Justice and the Supreme Court.* Philadelphia: J. B.
Lippincott Co., 1963.
Warren, Charles. *The Supreme Court in United States History.* 2 vols.
Boston: Little, Brown & Co., 1960.
Williams, Charlotte. *Hugo L. Black: A Study on Judicial Process.* Balti-
more: Johns Hopkins Press, 1950.

Index